Once a Rocker
Always a Rocker
A DIARY

Cowboy Mach Bell

Panther Rock Books

Marshfield Hills Massachusetts

Panther Rock Books

Once a Rocker Always a Rocker / Cowboy Mach Bell

FIRST EDITION

ISBN-13: 978-1-7334712-0-6 Paperback
ISBN-13: 978-1-7334712-1-3 E-book

For more about Cowboy Mach Bell
and the Joe Perry Project visit: **oncearocker.com**

To my lovely wife Julia

and to my rock'n'roll mentor Earthquake Morton

Let it rock

— MICK JAGGER

Once a Rocker Always a Rocker

A DIARY

CONTENTS

I
TAKE A WALK WITH ME SALLY

Tuesday February 23, 1982

Peggy's voice comes over the intercom.
"Call for Mark. Line three."
"Hello. Service Lab. Mark Bell speaking."
"Eyaaahh. You're hot brother."
"Earthquake? Wow. Great to hear your voice man. How're you doin'?"
"Great man. But you're gonna be doing even better when you hear this."
"Oh yeah? What's going on EQ?"
"Listen, Mach. I'm sitting here with Tim Collins.
Tim just signed Joe Perry to an exclusive management deal with Collins/Barrasso."
"Joe Perry? Really?"
"So listen, Joe needs a new singer. I mentioned your name to Tim and he told me to get you down here for an audition.
This Friday."
"…Jeez. I don't know about that, Earthquake."
"What are you talking about, Mach? This is the break you've been waiting for."
"Yeah, maybe. But I don't really do auditions. I mean I've never done one before...I mean…things have changed for me."
"Changed? How? What are you talking about?"
"I've been working here at the Music Box for the past few months. With my dad and my grandfather. Making steady money. Trying to be a normal person."
"You? A normal person? C'mon man, don't pass this up. This is a national act. You'll be touring and recording. Headlining everywhere. Think about it. After everything you and Thundertrain went through? You can't turn this down."

"Listen, Earthie…I really appreciate the offer and everything. But I don't know…I mean…The answer is no."
"I can't believe what you're saying, Mach."
"Sorry man."

I hang up the phone. Try out for Joe Perry? Why would I ever want to do that? Audition? Learn his songs, get my hopes sky high, pick out what to wear, show up in some rehearsal room and sing in front of Joe and his big shot friends? Reach out for that damn brass ring again and feel it, touch it, hold it…just before it gets yanked away. I can see it all now. Joe Perry turns around to light up a smoke - as I free fall back to reality and smash my face into the pavement and chip another tooth. Nothing to show for it, except maybe another dentist bill I can't pay. I've already got a big scrapbook full of refusal letters from every major record company. I can leaf through memory lane anytime I need to stir up the pain all over again.
I wander back to the racks of turntables, stereo receivers, tape decks and power amps. All waiting to be checked out, repaired and cleaned. I've been working full time here at the Music Box for almost a year. My first "real" job in almost a decade.

What the hell did I just do? Did I really say no? Lead singer of the Joe Perry Project? Jets, parties, hotel suites, limousines, open bars, models, stacks of money and rocking the world. Is that really what I just turned down? Have I gone totally insane? I'd kill to be rocking arenas every night, making records and raving up beside Joe Perry. Why the hell did I say no to Earthquake? I'm going to regret this day for the rest of my life.

Peggy's voice comes over the intercom.
"Call for Mark. Line three."
I grab the phone.
"Hello. Sevice Lab. Mark Bell."

"Forget it, Mach. We won't take no for an answer. This gig has
your name all over it."
"I don't know, Earthquake…"
"Listen man. Just learn these songs."
"well…okay…I guess."
"All right then. Let the Music Do the Talking, Discount Dogs,
Life at a Glance, I've Got the Rock'n'Rolls Again,
 No Substitute for Arrogance, Rockin' Train and
 Same Old Song and Dance."
"Got it. I'll do my best."
"Be at the Complex Annex in Cambridge at 1 p.m. this Friday."
"Okay, Earthquake. Will do."
"Tim says to bring a guitar too."
"Guitar?"
" Yeah. Charlie Farren played guitar."
"Okay. Got it."
"Eyaaahh. You're HOT brother."
"Sounds good, Earthie. And thanks for calling back."

I'm in a daze. I said yes.
And with that "yes" everything changes.
The hardened shell retracts to reveal the softie hiding inside.
The eternal smiley-faced optimist, the cheerleader, the
"hey gang let's put on a show" guy.
Let's face it. I was totally taken by surprise when my band
Thundertrain didn't become the biggest thing to hit the galaxy
since Uriah Heep. I'm still nursing the psychic wounds from that
big let down.

But man, if this Joe Perry Project gig pans out…

Here at the Music Box, just a few blocks from Wellesley
College, I'm perfectly situated for what I need to do next.
I dash up out of the basement lab, turn left and enter the record
department in the front part of the store. I pull both of the Joe
Perry Project albums off the rack. *Let the Music Do the
Talking* and *I've Got the Rock'n'Rolls Again.* Both on
Columbia Records. The first one, from 1980, has Ralph Morman
on lead vocal. The second, released last year, features Charlie
Farren as lead singer.
Albums in hand, I head to the area just outside the Sound Room.
The Sound Room is where my father, Bill Bell, holds court.
Demonstrating and selling top line audio gear, like Ampex tape
decks, Thorens turntables, McIntosh power amps and
Klipschorn loudspeakers to music listeners from all over the
world.
Outside the sliding glass door that leads to my father's audio
wonderland is Peggy's office and the TV department where
smaller consumer electronic stuff is on display. The Sony
Walkman is a miniature, battery operated stereo cassette tape
player with headphones attached. You can carry it around or
even stick it in your pocket. It sounds really good too.
I'll be borrowing this new Walkman model for a few days.
Grabbing a Maxell cassette off Peggy's desk I return to the lab.
After setting up a Dual turntable and a Nakamichi cassette deck
on an empty service bench, I begin dubbing the six audition
songs from the albums onto the tape cassette. The seventh song
is one of Joe's old Aerosmith hits that everyone knows.
No need to study that one.
Headphones on, I hit the play button.
Preparing myself to knock out Joe Perry and become his new
lead singer.

Wednesday February 24, 1982

This day is going to be tricky.

I'm in a car being driven by my best friend Ric Provost, he was the bass player of Thundertrain. In the back seat is my other best friend, Thundertrain drummer Bobby Edwards. Since the quintet known as Thundertrain broke up a couple years ago, the three of us have continued to write songs and play local shows together. Currently our power trio is called Mag 4. Today we're on our way to Longview Farm, a recording studio out in North Brookfield Mass. We're doing a follow up to our first single with close friend John Visnaskas as producer and Jesse Henderson as engineer.

I haven't breathed a word about my Joe Perry audition to anyone outside of my family. I usually share everything with Ric and Bobby but I'm nervous about how they'll take this news. I've been singing in bands with Ric for the past eight years and with Bobby for a whole decade, ever since we were both teenagers. I don't want to bum everyone out and spoil the recording session. We arrive at Longview. A brittle wind blows across the frosted pasture land. I haven't been out here since 1979 when Thundertrain was rattling Studio B, cutting demo tracks.

The first thing I need to do is check out the inside of the adjoining hay barn, something new, and very interesting has been installed there since I last visited.

A stage. I clamber up onto the wide platform and immediately feel the vibes.

This stage was built for Mick Jagger and the Rolling Stones. Six months ago they were all right here. In this barn. Secretly rehearsing together for five weeks during August and September. Preparing for the 1981 American Stones Tour.

After strutting back and forth across the boards for a while, I head inside the farmhouse and into the studio area where John and Jesse are setting-up for the session. Ric, Bobby and I have worked with Jesse before. Most notably back in the fall of 1976 when Henderson helmed the mixing board inside a mobile studio parked in front of the Rat at 528 Commonwealth Ave in

Boston's Kenmore Square. Those recordings of ten Boston bands, including Thundertrain, DMZ, the Real Kids and Willie Loco Alexander's Boom Boom Band were released in the spring of 1977 as a double album package called *Live at the Rat.*

For today's recording, Ric is playing a Fender Jazz bass through a Yamaha amp. Bobby is using the oversized Ludwig drum kit he played in Thundertrain. I've got a '58 Les Paul Junior guitar (owned by Ric) going through an Orange 4x12 cab powered by a funky old Kustom amp head.

The tune is called Winner Take All and a few hours later we get all the tracks we need. I lay down a decent vocal, possibly a keeper.

After tearing down our gear, I sit down in the studio lounge with Ric and Bobby. I finally tell them about my audition with the Joe Perry Project - coming up in 48 hours.

Bobby seems to recoil, he looks downward. Ric thinks it over for a nano-second before grabbing my shoulders.

"Congratulations Mark (he always calls me Mark). That's incredible. Perry's lucky to get you. You're gonna be great together."

"Yeah but Ric. It's just an audition.

Nobody said anything about me getting hired."

Now that my news has sunk in a bit, Bobby looks up and smiles at me.

"Don't worry Mach. He's gonna love you.

Wait until Joe jams with you."

"Well, I don't know about that. But thanks for the support guys. I really mean it."

Thursday February 25, 1982

I live in my parents' basement in Holliston Mass.
Last month I turned 29.
Up until last year I usually stayed in cheap motels and grimy
band bunkhouses whenever my band was out on the road, which
was often.
For a year or so we all shared a band house in Framingham. We
called it the Thundertrain Mansion. The mansion was located on
Old Connecticut Path across from the site of the Carousel Tent.
That canvas venue seated maybe 2,500 people. In the beginning
the tent featured stage musicals and traditional stars like Andy
Williams, Jerry Lewis and Joan Rivers. But by the late 60's they
began booking acts like Simon & Garfunkel, Frank Zappa, Iron
Butterfly and the Motown groups. I was 15 when I saw my first
concert at the Carousel in the summer of 1968 -
the Jimi Hendrix Experience. The following summer I was there
to see the new British band Led Zeppelin. The Carousel was
operated by promoter Frank Connelly. The man who brought
The Beatles to Boston. Frank would go on to manage Aerosmith
in their early days.
After we lost the Thundertrain Mansion I turned to couch
surfing. Thundertrain had improved my social life to the point
where couches were not very hard to come by. On the nights that
a couch failed to materialize I could usually dig up $2 and buy a
seat at one of Boston or Cambridge's 24-hour grindhouse
cinemas. The Harvard Square Cinema, the Kenmore Cinema and
the 733 (next to Paul's Mall) always had a double or occasional
triple feature running all night long.
If I could find a ride up to Lexington, Earthquake would let me
crash on the sofa downstairs in the Jelly Records headquarters.
So between all those options, not to mention the frequent all
night parties that always seem to find me, I've spent the last ten
years just bopping around with the clothes on my back and a
little flight bag with an extra shirt and a toothbrush.

Like Jim Morrison I don't wear underwear.

That all changed a few months ago when I decided to become a responsible, normal, tax paying citizen and work a 9 to 5 job. Lucky for me, my father co-owns a business along with my grandfather and they were nice enough to take a chance on me. So I moved back into my parents' basement in Holliston and my father gives me a lift into work at the Music Box every day. He's on the sales floor with my brother Andy, selling expensive hi-fi gear. Turntables, exotic cartridges with jeweled styli, tuners, graphic equalizers, tape decks and lots of speakers. Big beautiful loudspeakers. Meanwhile I'm downstairs in the Service Lab wearing a white lab coat. Taking in busted stuff, writing up slips, running the register and replacing needles in an endless stream of old el cheapo record players.

Today, while I'm changing the broken needles I'm also listening to this Joe Perry Project tape on the Walkman. Over and over again. Memorizing the song lyrics. At least the beginning and ending phrases, I'm used to fudging the middles. Counting the measures of the openings. Getting the arrangements straight. Concentrating on anyplace that the vocal is a lead in or a cue. After work I go back to my parents' house and head down to my corner of the cellar to continue my studies. The vocal styles of the two singers on these tracks are radically different from each other. And my voice bears no similarity to either. Not that it matters. I have absolutely no skills as a mimic. I never would have made it as a cover band singer. I can only do one voice, mine.

As far as the guitar. Tim asked me to bring one to the audition tomorrow so I will. Ric kindly lent me his '58 Les Paul Junior for the session. But frankly I've only jammed on guitar along with the audition tunes a few times. Just some rudimentary rhythm chords under the lead guitar sections.

I'm hoping that if Joe hires me he'll want me as high energy vocalist Mach Bell who plays occasional harp and shakes the maracas among other things. Not a singing rhythm guitar player.

Friday February 26, 1982

The audition is today at 1 p.m.

I listen to the tape a few more times. Pull on the black jeans I bought at Trash and Vaudeville in St. Mark's Place a couple years ago. Cowboy boots from Walker's, which add a couple inches, getting me up to about 5'9". My ex-girlfriend Debbie gave me this nice t-shirt from the Rainbow Bar & Grill. Manhattan trousers, Boston boots, Hollywood shirt. Wish my hair was a bit longer. I always had a huge mane in Thundertrain and I bet Joe Perry's hair will look great, he'll be looking cool as ever.

I've never met Mr. Perry. Never seen him out in the wild. The only times I've laid eyes on him are onstage with Aerosmith. I had a couple rare sightings of the other Aerosmith guitarist Brad Whitford and frontman Steven Tyler out in the Boston clubs but never Joe.

Time to head out to the Complex Annex in Cambridge.

I've been to the regular Cambridge Music Complex out on Alewife Brook Parkway plenty of times. That's where tons of Boston bands either rent a rehearsal room, book the soundstage, or just show up to hang. Unknown groups mix in with working bands like the Stompers, Private Lightning and Jon Butcher Axis. You'll run into the crew members, and sometimes even the stars, of mega bands like The Cars, Boston and the J.Geils Band.

This Annex is hidden a few blocks back from the regular Complex. I've never been back here. I didn't even know it existed. As I round the corner I see a couple Corvettes out in a parking lot. The Annex is a single story, white concrete building with a loading dock out front. It looks pretty much like all the other anonymous warehouse structures in this part of town. Except there's a roar coming from this structure.

As I near the open loading dock I can see a long hallway. At the end of the hall is a very solid looking door. From behind that door I can clearly hear an electric guitar. Riffing loudly, thundering, then tuning, then more seismic riffing.

I don't recognize these particular riffs but they all sound like Aerosmith. Gotta be Joe Perry.

Now an explosive burst of drums and cymbals begins, stops and starts up again. Now what? Do I hear a second electric guitar? Yes I do. That's weird. Oh, no. I thought I was the only person auditioning for this gig today.

As I reach the loading dock a familiar face bops out from around the corner.

"Hey man. Good to see you. Tim told me you were coming."

It's Danny Hargrove. The bass player from Rage. I run into him occasionally in the clubs, he's always friendly. Danny's a few years younger than me but he's been rocking forever. Back in the glitter rock days Danny had his clothes made by Eddie Kent, same as me.

"Danny? What's going on? What are you doing here?"

"Same as you. They brought me in yesterday. Singing and playing bass."

"Oh yeah? How'd it go?"

"Not too bad I guess. The Admiral asked me to come back."

Hargrove takes a long drag on his cigarette.

"Cool. What's that other guitar I hear?"

Danny points to the Corvettes.

"Brad Whitford"

"Whitford? No shit?"

"No shit. I guess his Whitford/St. Holmes thing is on hold for now. Brad wants to do some shows with Joe."

The sound of the two guitars and drums is getting more cohesive now. Building together on riffs that Perry seems to be creating on the spot.

I see the rehearsal room door swing open for just a moment.

The sound pressure released from inside sweeps down the hall like a tidal wave. One of the Project crew members emerges and he hustles towards us.

"Hey, Mach, I'm Jay. Thanks for coming down."
"Nice to meet you, Jay."
"I remember seeing you singing with Thundertrain down at the Rat. Incredible times man. Come on guys, I think the Admiral is all set to get started."
I hop up onto the loading dock and follow Jay and Danny up the hallway. Jay pushes open the door. Escaping sound waves nearly knock me flat on my back.
Inside. It's a lot to take in. There he is. Joe Perry. Standing ten feet away from me, looking like he just walked off the cover of Creem Magazine. Black silk shirt with sleeves rolled up just a turn or two, dark gray vest, silver Rolex dangling loosely from his skinny wrist, a necklace or three, leather belt, blue jeans ripped slightly at the bottom hem, to fit comfortably over the tops of a pair of soft leather boots - made in Italy for sure. The black hair is even more lustrous than I expected. Thick bangs cover his eyes. Riffing away on something that looks like a Strat but not quite. I don't think Joe even realizes that I've entered the room. Or maybe he just doesn't care.
Danny Hargrove makes a bee-line for the opposite end of the white-walled space and slings on a Les Paul bass. I notice that it's strung upside down. Plugging into a wall of Peavey bass cabs that reach the ceiling, Hargrove glides deftly into the ongoing jam, Hargrove looks and sounds right at home.
Just to the right of Danny is the other Aerosmith guitar legend, Brad Whitford. This is an unexpected treat. Brad hasn't changed much in the ten years since I first saw him perform at the Hopedale Town Hall. He's got sort of a Mick Taylor look and he's playing a sunburst Les Paul through a Marshall stack, just like he was back then. Can't beat that.

I see he's also got a custom made solid-body axe on a stand, I don't recognize the brand but it's red. Without missing a lick Brad offers me a small nod.

In the center of the room, which measures roughly thirty feet wide by twenty feet, is an immense and beautiful, custom made, double-bass drum kit. The front heads are both vividly painted in Ringling Bros. script "J.P.P. Ron Stewart".

Ron Stewart is absolutely hammering the mounted toms. As hard a hitter as I've seen. And I've seen Frosty. Then I notice that Stewart's entire kit is mic'd up, not just the kick. He's got large monitor speakers piled up behind the drums to further amplify his relentless attack.

The reason for the over amplification becomes obvious as I look behind Joe Perry and see the kustom-made Aerosmith amp heads and loudspeaker stacks that we've all seen him use onstage at so many Aerosmith shows. And on TV at California Jam. Joe is using the same amplification in this little room that he uses at Madison Square Garden or at the Cotton Bowl. That's not all. Way over to the far left, next to Danny Hargrove's bass rig, is yet another tower of speakers - that Perry can activate at will. Yikes.

Joe finally winds down his riffing long enough to acknowledge my presence. He extends his hand.

"Thanks for dropping by," he mumbles. Grasping Joe's hand, I realize that something isn't right with Perry. He's vibrating, no he's trembling. His color is off too. Underneath the sleek hair and the expensive rockstar garb he looks kind of ghoulish. Thin as a toothpick and more than a little green around the gills.

Crew member Jay has been setting up a mic on a straight stand with a couple of floor monitors. I'm facing the band, between the drum kit and Joe's set up. I tap my finger on the SM58 windscreen. Sounds like a thunderclap.

This is gonna be really loud.

"Did you listen to the songs?" asks Perry.

"Let's go man. Take your pick."

Joe launches into the opening riff of Life at a Glance.

A nice one off the first Project album. Written by Perry, it has everything I look for in a rocker.

Dynamite opening guitar riff, easy to remember lyrics, and a catchy call and response chorus that brings you full-circle, back to that driving guitar riff. We charge through the song and from where I stand it sounds pretty damn solid.

We kick into Discount Dogs, a Morman/Perry number and it feels as good as I'd hoped. It's so loud in here I'm not sure anyone can actually hear me. I know my body language and attack is coming through though. This business has a lot to do with how you stand and how you hold your instrument. I can see Joe glancing my way. He can tell I must have paid some dues somewhere along the line and know how this shit gets done.

Ain't No Substitute for Arrogance is a terrific Farren/Perry steamroller. My voice sounds nothing like Charlie's but that doesn't keep me from digging in. Even more than on the first two, the sound is jelling. Several of the crew members are hanging around the perimeter of the room. Nudging each other and smiling. I'm feeling confident now. Not just singing, I'm listening too. Especially to what Brad Whitford is adding to the mix. He's astonishing.

Same Old Song and Dance is next and holy shit, I've got Whitford and Perry on either side of me, chugging out their famous riffs. This is crazy. Before I know it, I'm in the thick of it, spitting out those gritty Steven Tyler lyrics. Are we having fun yet? The lead guitar breaks are phenomenal. When do we get this thing out on the road?

Rockin' Train by Morman/Perry has a funky vibe. Like something off Jeff Beck's Orange album. It's the tune where everybody gets to stretch out, leading up to a masterful drum solo from Ron Stewart.

Finally, the Project's biggest hit, Let the Music Do the Talking written by Joe Perry is a truly exciting song to perform.

Danny Hargrove joins me on the choruses and we blend. Joe quotes his own bottleneck-riff from Draw the Line during his extended guitar solo that leads to a climatic close. Things are moving along well, nobody wants to stop playing.

"What else do you know, Mach?" asks Brad.

"Stones. Jeff Beck."

"How 'bout Going Down?"

"You start man"

Whitford hits the driving intro line, Ronnie bashes in with an authoritative back beat and Hargrove and Perry plunge in head-first. Moving like an express train, we're really Going Down on this one. I growl whichever Don Nix lyrics I can remember and make up the ones I can't. This song is built for messing with and jamming. Everyone takes a swing or two. Perry is almost smiling and I can tell that Ron is rough & ready to move things forward with this gang.

Part of me wants to stay and keep rocking all afternoon, but my strategic side says better to quit while I'm ahead. Joe is a bit surprised when I quickly bid everyone farewell.

"Nice meeting you, Brad. Thanks, Ron. See ya, Danny. Thanks for inviting me over, Joe."

I shake the leader's shaky hand.

Wham bam thank you Sam. I'm out the door.

Jay and a couple of the crew chase me out.

"Way to go, Mach."

"Sounded great in there."

I wave back, yell "so long" and jump off the loading dock. As I land I can hear Ronnie launch into a drum fusillade that sounds like an ammo factory explosion.

"Not too bad." I smile to myself.

Saturday February 27, 1982

I'm back in Wellesley at the Music Box. Downstairs in the Service Lab.

Peggy's voice comes over the intercom.
"Call for Mark. Line three."

I pick up the phone. It's Tim Collins,
calling from the Collins/Barrasso office.
"Joe tells me everything went really well, Mach.
He says you sounded good."
"Oh yeah? That's cool."
"That's right. And Joe wants you back at the Annex this
Monday."
"That's great, Tim. So… I'm in the group?"
"Joe didn't say that, Mach. But he wants you to come back.
Rehearsal is at 1p.m."
"Okay, Tim. I'll be there."
I was hoping for a little more, but I'll take it. Joe probably just
wants to make sure I'm not a flake that blows off practice.
Anyway, everyday that I'm in there with the Project is one less
day for them to try out someone else. From what I picked up
yesterday Joe doesn't have a lot of time to waste.
I got a little carried away last night. Went to a party in Ashland
at some apartment. The place was jammed with local rock
musicians and girls who like that type of guy. Ric and Bobby
both got there before me. So everybody at the bash already
knew I'd been in Boston earlier, trying out for Joe Perry.
I arrived at the party to cheers, back-slapping and
congratulations. I mean, it was only an audition, but these guys
all seemed sure that I already had the job in the bag. I have to
admit the session went as smoothly as I'd hoped.
I also have to admit that I was enjoying the attention of my
fellow rockers and the admiration of the young ladies swooping
around me. Not too often that we local rock guys have anything
extraordinary to celebrate or get excited about. Just the fact that
I got a chance to sing with Joe Perry and Brad Whitford is
enough to put me in the upper percentile of coolness with my
friends.

So I didn't argue. I just let them all treat me like I was in the Project now. So I'm relieved that Collins called back and Joe Perry wants me to return. Hopefully one more time will do the trick.

At the end of my shift I go talk to Fred, the manager of the Service Lab. He knows about the audition. I tell him that I got a call back. Fred congratulates me. He's a guitarist/singer himself but more in the hillbilly country style. He understands that if things go my way, I won't be coming back to work again.

Sunday February 28, 1982

I call Julia and ask if I can stay at her place in Cambridge. Julia and I have been dating on and off ever since we met in 1978. It's okay with her, so I head into town. Her place is on Broadway just outside of Central Square. It's only a couple miles from the rehearsal Annex.

Monday March 1, 1982

Julia lets me use her car today. A Mazda GLC hatchback. First I drive her to work. Down Mass Ave across the Charles River and onto Newbury Street. I drop her off at SyncroSound recording studio which is owned by The Cars. Julia works for Eliot Roberts of Lookout Management. Eliot manages Dylan, Joni, Petty, Timothy Hutton, Neil Young, Devo, Ministry and The Cars among others. Julia coordinates the Lookout office in Boston out of SyncroSound. As I drive away, I spy Peter Wolf entering the studio.

I drive back to the slightly dilapidated apartment (Julia tells me the neighbors call it the Pink Palace because of the outside paint job). I clamp the Walkman on one more time. Reviewing the lyrics and arrangements.

At 1 p.m. I pull into the Annex lot and park Julia's GLC (stands for great little car) into an empty space next to Whitford's

Corvette and Perry's Porsche Turbo. I can already feel the sonic hurricane coming from the JPP rehearsal room.

Today Joe Perry is wearing a khaki green Boy Scouts of America shirt and it matches the color of his face perfectly. Joe is upright but he looks bad. Real bad. Shaking badly too. Brad Whitford and Danny Hargrove welcome me back with a nod and a wink. Ron Stewart is totally preoccupied, in the midst of a swirling drum solo/warm-up. It's damn loud in here.

Perry is messing around with his sound pedals. He keeps banging out this see-sawing, funky riff. Catchy as hell. Then he goes into this other one, a twangy, Stones-do-country sounding figure. Perry keeps going back and forth, working between these two hooky but very different guitar bits.

Finally, without a word, Joe blasts into Discount Dogs and the whole band is off and running. We run through the songs and then we run through them again. Sounds as good as last Friday. Better even.

"Lookie here folks. He's doin' it like the cowboys."

A familiar face just walked in the door of the rehearsal room.

"Doc? What are you doing here man?"

"Didn't anyone tell ya, Cowboy? I'm the road manager with this show."

Perry is looking at me quizzically.

I can tell he's thinking "cowboy?"

"That's great man. Jeez, I haven't seen you since the Drivers."

"Well, I think we're gonna be seeing a lot more of each other, Cowboy."

Along with bassist Earthquake Morton, drummer Doc McGrath made up the rhythm section of Boston's favorite party band, Duke and the Drivers. Signed to ABC/Dunhill in the mid-seventies, the band scored a smash single with What You've Got (Sure Looks Good to Me).

One time at a Thanksgiving Party held at the Webb (the house they shared in Lexington) Doc caught me trying to climb out the window.

"What the hell are you doing, Mach?"
"There's a long line for the bathroom. I'm gonna do cowboy beeps."
"Cowboy *what*?"
"Listen, Doc. When I was little I used to do beeps. When I did beeps outside behind a rock I called it cowboy beeps."
Doc started laughing his ass off.
"Hey look everybody. Beeps is doing it like the cowboys."
Ever since that day I've always been the Cowboy to Doc. And as of now it looks like I'm gonna be the Cowboy to Joe Perry and the Project too.

Tuesday March 2, 1982

Joe asked me to come back again today. At 1 p.m.
I have a surprise for him this time though. This will clinch my audition for sure. I get to the Annex and everyone is warming up loudly, like usual. And as usual, Joe keeps going back to that see-sawing, funky riff. But this time when he plays it, I grab the mic and begin to sing.
Took a boat to China / Took a jet to Rome
Lost, found, turned around / Rocked my ass back home.
Perry glances up - he almost makes eye contact with me for the first time ever. He keeps playing.
I might love the ladies / You know I love the life
Up, down, all around / I wanna do it twice
"Here comes the chorus, Joe" He pauses while I sing
Once a Rocker, Always a Rocker / Can you hear the beat?
Perry plunges back in, adding a swinging rhythm under the chorus melody
Once a Rocker, Always a Rocker / Now you're gonna feel the heat.
Verse, chorus = voila.
I rip into the second verse as the rest of the band joins in.

Hargrove sings a high vocal line on the chorus. Whitford adds
stinger guitar notes at the end of each refrain. Ronnie keeps a
heavy, straight-ahead beat going underneath, leaving the
funkiness to Joe Perry who drops in a short, slippery guitar
break. The whole thing clocks in at just under three minutes.
Perry/Bell have written their first song.
Joe is so ill, I mean his hands are twitching. His speech is
incoherent. I want him to say "Okay, Cowboy. That's it. You're
hired. Welcome to the Project." But I'm not even sure he's able
to process the fact that we just composed a new tune, a catchy
song that revolves around an excellent new Perry guitar hook.
I really hope Joe can pull himself back together.

March 3, 1982

I call my brother Andy to wish him a happy birthday.
He turns 24 today.
Joe handed me some homework last night. We're gonna work on
Toys in the Attic today as well as Helter Skelter. The Beatles
tune I know pretty well. I've sung it before in a band or two.
I go over to Cheapo Records in Central Square and pick up the
Aerosmith record for a buck.
I followed Aerosmith in the beginning. They played locally and
were a huge influence on me back then. They literally changed
my life and I held them in the highest regard.
But after they got signed to a record deal, I began to envy their
success. With the phenomenal rise of Dream On and the
excitement surrounding their second album, my jealousy grew.
In 1973 I began playing in bars. First with Biggy Ratt, then with
Thundertrain. Mostly playing our own original songs. The
constant requests for me to sing Aerosmith hits really got to me.
I grew to resent Aerosmith and their tremendous popularity. Of
course by then their music was inescapable, constantly blaring
out of radios and jukeboxes everywhere I went. So I was very

aware of Toys in the Attic, but last night was the first time I ever went out and bought an Aerosmith record.

I drive Julia's car to rehearsal at the Annex at 1 p.m.
We run through the six audition songs plus Going Down and the new one, Once a Rocker. Apparently Joe and Brad used to play Helter Skelter with Aerosmith. We launch into that one and it sounds pretty decent. A bit rough on the vocal cords but I'm used to doing shouters. Now it's time for Toys in the Attic. I have to admit it's totally surreal standing here between Brad Whitford and Joe Perry as they barrel into their high energy hit. Danny Hargrove and Ronnie Stewart have no problem at all pumping-out the familiar rhythm underneath. I bet Danny performed this tune a thousand times with his band Rage.
So it's basically Aerosmith redux until the singing starts.
Whoa hold on. That doesn't sound like Steven Tyler. Who's messing with my high? Damn it, it's me, the Cowboy. What am I doing here? Trying to sing the theme song of 70's American youth? How the heck am I supposed to sing it anyway? Should I attempt to ape the Tyler style (and fail miserably)? Should I do it my own way, in my own voice and just sound - wrong?
Lucky for me everything is so damn loud in here nobody can really hear what I'm doing - or what I'm trying to figure out how to do.
I think this is going to be a problem.
But the boss seems happy enough. At the end of rehearsal he hands me something and speaks to me for like the second time since we met.
"There might be something in here, Cowboy."
As I leave the room I run into the road manager Doc.
"Hey, Cowboy. Sounds pretty good in there."
"Thanks. Hey, Doc. Am I in this group or what?"
"Did Joe ask you to come back?"
"Yeah. But he didn't say I'm hired."
"Don't worry about it, Cowboy. Just keep coming back."

Thursday March 4, 1982

Last night I pored through the little blue notebook Perry handed
me at rehearsal.
Everything is written in Joe's caveman hand writing:
Phone numbers, addresses.
Song titles: Take a Number, Lick and a Promise, Chit Chat, Just
for the Record, Let the Music Do the Talking, Life Time Record,
Off the Record, Off Your Rocker, Warm as a $2 Pistol, Your
Channel Doesn't Come in on My Set, I'm Sick Because I'm
Idol, I'd Kill For a Kiss, It's All Done with Mirrors, Creatures of
Habit.
His original lyrics for Bright Light Fright, Life at a Glance,
Ready On the Firing Line, Conflict of Interest.
Joe's four-page synopsis for a movie that involves a battle of the
bands and a romantic triangle between a football player, a
cheerleader and a young rock guitarist.
Lyrics for a paranoid song titled I'm Alone Again.
Crude drawings of a volcano and a spaceship.
Notes about trying out different drum rhythms and bass lines.
Some are based on Chuck Berry tunes.
A note to cover Don't Be Cruel and Heartbreak Hotel.
The words "The Joe Perry Project" drawn out repeatedly onto
little bass drumheads using different scripts and re-positioning
of each word.

Finally I find what I'm looking for. Lyrics to an untitled song.
I love the way they look,
I love the way they feel

No rehearsal today, but I have a meeting with Tim Collins at
1:30 p.m. Hopefully I'll be hearing lots of good news. Joe's
probably putting me on salary. How much?
Maybe a nice bonus up front?

I'll give Julia back her great little car and buy a nice Corvette of my own. Hmmm, I wonder what color?

Black would be cool or maybe blue. What about a Corvette in British racing green?

I drive the little Mazda over to 280 Lincoln St. in Allston.

A Boston neighborhood right next to Cambridge. I enter a two story, modern looking glass and brick office building that faces out towards the Mass Turnpike aka Interstate 90. I head upstairs to the Collins/Barrasso Management office. There's a waiting room with a receptionist desk.

"Hi. I'm Mach Bell. Tim asked me to come over."

"Yes of course, Mr. Bell. Please have a seat. I'll let him know you're here."

I sit down. Billboard and Cashbox magazines are on the coffee table. There are a few gold records up on the wall. Still the One by Orleans, Sunshine by Jonathan Edwards. Both are managed by Collins/Barrasso. Not hard rockers like us. I see a big, framed record promotion poster of Joe Perry leaning up against the wall, waiting to be hung up I guess.

The door to Collins office swings open and out steps Tim. He's a young guy. My age, maybe a year younger. He has a neat haircut, a button down shirt, glasses and a friendly face. We shake hands and he beckons me inside.

"Good to see you, Mach. It's been awhile."

"Yeah, Tim. Since Thundertrain I guess."

"How are those Thundertrain boys doing?"

"They're good. Cool Gene got married. I've been playing with his brother Ric and Bobby in Mag 4."

"And what about Steven?"

"Steven Silva? He's doing great. Playing lead guitar every night with a cover band and finally making some good money."

"He's a good player. So…how are you liking working with Joe Perry?"

"It's pretty amazing, Tim. Thanks for thinking of me."

"Greg brought up your name and I immediately thought you'd be a good fit."

"Earthquake has always looked out for me. So, am I in the Project or what?"

"You're in. Joe says he's very happy with you."

"Did he tell you we wrote a song together this week?"

"Yes he did. Very impressive. We're going into the studio at the end of the month so keep on writing."

"Studio?"

"Right. The Project will rehearse for three more weeks and then you'll be cutting a demo. We'll be getting Joe a new record deal."

"No more Columbia?"

"We're done with them. I'll be shopping the tape to all the labels while the band is out on the road. Joe is thinking of maybe doing the next album with a bunch of different singers. Some of his famous friends, you know, big names."

"Big names?"

"Don't worry, Mach, you'll still get to sing on a couple tracks."

That totally takes the wind out of my sails. Right now I'm struggling, trying to figure out how to perform all these Ralph and Charlie and Steven Tyler vocals. If the next JPP record is a whole bunch of other guys' voices for me to try to copy…
I think I feel an identity crisis coming on.

"We're looking at excellent touring possibilities. I'm working on getting us some opening slots with Black Sabbath right now."

"That would be cool."

"Joe wants to play. A lot. That's why he's with us. Steve Barrasso and I aren't just managers you know, we're booking agents too."

"Yeah. I remember all those Duke and the Drivers dates you put together."

"This is going to be bigger. A lot bigger."

"Sounds really cool. So, um, Tim…what about money?"

"What about it?"

"Well…I mean…I'm at rehearsal everyday. I had to quit my job and move to Cambridge."

"I never told you to quit your job, Mach."

"No. You didn't. But it's not easy to schedule work around a daily 1 p.m. rehearsal that lasts all afternoon. I'm not knocking rehearsal. I mean, I'm gonna need it if I'm gonna be the frontman for this band."

"Nobody said anything about you being a "frontman." You're the singer."

"Okay, Tim. Singer…but money…"

"Listen, Mach, you'll get paid each time the band works."

"Paid by the gig?"

"That's right."

"All right. I guess. But how do I eat until then?"

"Tell you what. I'll front you one hundred dollars per week until you start to work."

"A hundred?"

"That's the best we can do. Stop here by the office tomorrow. My secretary will have a check for you. Anything else?"

" Ummm…no. I guess not."

"Don't worry, Mach - Joe and the Project are going places."

"Okay, thanks Tim."

Well I guess I can forget about the Corvette for now.

Friday March 5, 1982

Dropped Julia off at SyncroSound in Boston.

Drove back to Cheapo Records and picked up Aerosmith *Rocks* for a buck.

Then back to the pink palace to study Back in the Saddle.

Next I swing by 280 Lincoln and pick up my $100 check.
I'm driving through Porter Square on the way to rehearsal when
I hear the shocking news on WBCN.
Pulling into the Annex parking lot everything is eerily quiet. The
Corvettes are both in the lot but the Annex is silent.
Entering the rehearsal room I see members of the road crew
milling around with long faces. Danny is dragging on a cigarette
in the corner. Ronnie keeps to himself, messing with the lugs on
a snare drum.
Brad and Joe are huddled close together. Obviously bumming.
The death of John Belushi hits us all hard, but Brad and Joe
hardest for sure. They were John's personal friends, I don't
know how close, but friends. The news reports coming in from
Hollywood are sketchy. Everyone suspects drugs, hard drugs,
were involved in Belushi's way-too-early check-out.
Joe starts mumbling about his late friend Bon Scott. The AC/DC
frontman and Perry were extremely close. AC/DC were a
regular opening act on Aerosmith tours and Bon died just two
years ago, after a short life of very hard living. Perry is
definitely dealing with his own issues at this moment. I don't
know enough about drugs or addiction to gauge whether Perry is
suffering from having way too much or way too little stuff in his
system, but something is way off, it's obvious that he's very ill.
This morning's deadly news from a bungalow behind the
Chateau Marmont hotel must be extra hard for him to hear.

We finally get back to the business at hand. Everyone powers
up, tunes and gets their sound. Perry is messing around on his
guitar and I don't have to wait very long before he eases into
that twangy, down home, countrified guitar riff that he's been
working on all week. I begin to sing:
"I love the way they look / I love the way they feel
C'mon babe, I'm not made outta steel
Over the phone I can act real cool
But face to face I lose control

You drive me crazy, make me wanna scream
Black Velvet Pants cause an instant scene
I love the way they look / the way they feel, yeah."

That gets us back to the top - that twangy guitar hook.
Then we slide into the second verse with the whole Project
jamming along.
This tune is writing itself as we go. I point to the sky and the
band modulates up for the middle eight:
"Well your Black Velvet Pants are all I need
To make life worth living and easy to lead
Black Velvet Pants I'm infected for sure
I'm in your hip pocket just waiting for more yeah…"

Joe ladles up a bourbon-drenched lead guitar break that resolves
back into that sweet twangy guitar hook, a quick repeat of the
first verse and a rollicking finish:

"I love the way they look / I love the way they feel"

"Damn, Cowboy. That's a good one."
"Thanks, Joe…You wrote it."
"What d'ya mean?"
"I mean you wrote those lyrics. The little blue book,
remember?"
"Those words were in there?"
"Yup. Every single one. Just lying there.
It's called Black Velvet Pants by the way."

I saw Joe Perry smile for the first time today.
I was hoping it would boost his confidence and his health when
we co-wrote Once a Rocker the other day. But today he (pretty
much) wrote Black Velvet Pants all by himself. Go Joe go.

The rest of the rehearsal is intense. Joe takes a swing at his South Station Blues. A great tune from the current lp. His vocals are thin right now but it's a damn good song. We run through Toys in the Attic and then tackle Back in the Saddle.

Perry surprises me on this one. He pulls out a Fender VI. I never saw one before. It's a big six-string bass. The sound of Brad Whitford wailing on his red custom axe, coupled with the thunder Joe is producing out of this Fender thing is astonishing. No wonder the Back in the Saddle riffs sound so damn heavy. Note to self: Gotta find a place for the Fender VI in one of the new tunes we'll be writing.

We finish up with a couple more Charlie songs from the last record. The title song, I've Got the Rock'n'Rolls Again, has lots of stops and starts. A bit tricky to get the hang of but the lyrics are cool and it's up my alley. I'm figuring East Coast, West Coast will be a breeze. I'm familiar with the song from radio where it gets a lot of play. On the record it's just a solid, fast-paced rocker that opens up with a single snare drum hit. What I didn't anticipate, is the drum introduction that Ron Stewart adds when the Project plays the song in concert. As usual with Ron, it's a carefully constructed intro. It builds in intensity before mounted-tom accents signal the opening line: *In the East Coast, In the West Coast.*

To my great embarrassment I just can't feel the timing of the final tom tom hits - the beats that lead straight into the all-important first line. This leaves me either singing the line too late or too early. Either way I'm left sounding incredibly lame, drunk, or like a total amateur who can't count. Of course Dan, Joe and Brad all understand Ron's timing perfectly, exposing me as the musical dunce.

We go over the opening several times. I'm studying Stewart's lead-in with all my might, but I just can't feel his timing. It's like jazz or something.

Very embarrassing. At least I scored some points with
Black Velvet Pants.

Saturday/Sunday, March 6/7, 1982

No rehearsal today or tomorrow.
Joe told me to learn Sweet Emotion over the weekend.

Monday March 8, 1982

I pick up Hargrove near his place in Porter Square on the way to
rehearsal.
Like me, Danny doesn't own his own wheels. It's good to have
him to talk with. We're both pretty much in the dark about what
exactly transpired in the Project previous to our arrival. Up until
a few months ago Joe Perry was being managed by Don Law,
the biggest concert promoter in New England, if not the world.
Recording for the top label CBS. Touring with bands like Rush,
Journey and Heart. Then, all of a sudden, singer/guitarist/writer
Charlie Farren leaves the band and takes bassist/singer/writer
David Hull with him. CBS/Columbia drops the Project and Don
Law hands over management to Collins/Barrasso. Weird.
Rehearsal goes well. Except I still can't hit the opening of East
Coast, West Coast, which pretty much wrecks the entire song for
me. I wish we could just play it like they recorded it. If only
Ronnie would take pity on me and change his lead-up beats to a
4/4 time signature, but that ain't gonna happen. To my ears he's
playing a blown-up version of Joe Morello's Take Five drum
solo before segueing straight into a rocker in Chuck Berry time.

For now, Hargrove is helping me out by shadowing the opening
vocal line. Danny hits it with ease every time while I half-mime
the words. What's wrong with me?

Tuesday March 9, 1982

No rehearsal today. Joe told me to learn Bright Light Fright. Joe
wrote the lyrics to that Aerosmith song and it's great. Very punk
rock with a galloping tempo.

Other than that, I lie around and watch The Price is Right. I'm
messing with this Video Cassette Recorder that Julia leases from
a local company called Redifusion. This machine can tape stuff
right off the airways. Movies, commercials, anything. You can
even set it in advance to record a show while you're sleeping or
not around. Amazing technology but really expensive. VCRs
cost around a thousand bucks a piece but Julia is only paying
about $39 a month to rent this one.

Wednesday March 10, 1982

The Joe Perry Project rehearse today at 1 p.m.

Did I mention that our band is loud? Real loud? I'm no stranger
to high volume rock'n'roll. When I went to see the Jeff Beck
Group at the Boston Tea Party I stood right in front. I did the
same with Led Zeppelin, Hendrix, Steppenwolf, The Nice,
T. Rex, Crazy World of Arthur Brown, no problem. Turn it up.
Not to mention I spent over five years with Thundertrain, an
Ampeg and Marshall amp-stacked band renowned for our
spectacular loudness, we lost plenty of work due to our
excessive volume.

But the fearsome sound-waves generated by the JPP, especially
in this small rehearsal room, are a whole new frontier for me.
I'm talking gut-churning volume. Lucky I don't eat much, and
never before singing. I will never stoop to wearing ear plugs but
I have been sneaking some toilet paper wads into my ears these
past few sessions. I surrender.

After rehearsal, I take the T out of Boston and meet up with
Bobby and Ric. Together we drive out to Longview Farm.
Before getting down to work on the Mag 4 mix, the engineer
Jesse and our producer John V ask me how things are going with
Joe Perry. I boast to everyone that the music is coming along
really well, which it is. Everyone is pretty excited to hear that
Brad Whitford is part of the band.
On the subject of our leader, I lie.
I tell them Joe is doing great, when he actually looks to be one
foot in the grave. I also say nothing about the fact that money is
in short supply. I keep my story upbeat, focusing on the
Corvettes, the huge stacks of expensive gear and Joe's super
cool leather pants. Like a magician who never reveals the secrets
behind his illusions. It's only natural for me to go into full
cheerleader mode when it comes to my band.
Winner Take All and Do the Mag end up sounding magnificent.

Thursday, March 11, 1982

Back to the Cambridge Annex at 1 p.m.
The crew is buzzing that our first gig is coming up in two
weeks.
Joe and Brad are working on a new riff. It moves like a really
big snake. Reminds me of the first Jeff Beck Group at their most
bombastic. Pretty complex too, I'm not sure how or where a
vocal would fit into it.
We work on Bright Light Fright which is fun because Joe and I
share the mic doing a tandem lead vocal. Perry leads the band
through First One's For Free. I think this song is from a
previous incarnation of the JPP but was never recorded. Joe
sings the lead vocal all alone, I just shake my maracas. So, along
with Once a Rocker and Black Velvet Pants that gives us three
original songs for our upcoming demo session.
After dinner Julia takes me to the Paradise to see a band that Ric
Ocasek recorded at SyncroSound.

Her friends are called Romeo Void. They're from San Francisco.
Their record, Never Say Never, was released last month and is
doing really well. They perform the kind of emotional synth-pop
that radio loves to play these days. Not my favorite brand of
music, but the guys in the band are all very nice people and the
singer Debora Iyall is fantastic.

Friday March 12, 1982

I stop by 280 Lincoln and pick up my $100.
Rehearsal is at 1 p.m.
Jay is our soundman and today is his birthday.
Steve Ricardo is a deejay out in Framingham. He asks me to do
a taped phone interview for his radio show. After dinner I go
into town to see singer Gary Shane. Lots of people in the bar
buy me drinks, which is good since I'm broke.

Saturday March 13, 1982

Rehearsal at 1 p.m.
Joe and Brad are still playing that monster-snake riff.
Afterwards, I go out to Holliston for some of my mother's great
home cooking.

Sunday March 14, 1982

There's a jam at Joey's Depot. I show up at the Holliston
watering hole and people buy me beers. Everyone seems
friendlier since I joined the Joe Perry Project. I'm pleased to
see my friend, and former bandmate, Michael Hendricks.
Later I get to listen to my taped interview being aired over
WDJM. Not too bad.

Monday March 15, 1982

Collins and Barrasso are coming over to see the band tomorrow
for the first time. So Danny and I dig into today's workout even
more than usual. I'm still putting this damn toilet paper in my
ears. Lucky my hair is long enough to hide my shame.
Tonight is the unveiling of the "new" Rat.
Owner Jim Harold closed his little hell hole for a few days and
promises a big transformation. He even sent out invites for the
grand re-opening this evening.
Doorman Mitch greets us at the entrance with a big smile and a
hug. We head down the long staircase. Hey, the place really does
look better. First and foremost, the stinky, sticky, cigarette-burnt
floor has been totally re-carpeted. Fresh smelling red carpet,
very Hollywood. I like it. The room is still the same, they didn't
move the two main bars or anything, but the walls have a fresh
coat of black paint and I think some of the light fixtures are new
too. The famously gross men's room is still pretty gross but the
urinals and the exposed toilet are all working tonight.
Great party.

Tuesday March 16, 1982

The JPP crew has torn down all the gear and trucked it from the
Annex over to the regular Complex where everyone else
rehearses. Tim has rented the soundstage for two days. It's a full
size concert stage with seating for a couple dozen people.
At 1 p.m. I arrive to see the amp-line and drums all set up the
way they'll be arrayed when we begin touring in a couple
weeks.
One thing is really odd though. I'm looking for my mic stand.
Why isn't it stage center where the lead singer is supposed to
work? I see a mic in center stage but it's Joe Perry's. His stand is
easy to pick out, it's the one with the built-in foot pedals fanning
out at the base.

The pedals are attached by a cable to a tall rack of guitar signal processors, back by the amp stacks.

I finally locate my mic stand.

It's way off to the right side of the stage.

I'm supposed to stand back there in the corner and sing?

Our managers Tim and Steve arrive. After quick hellos we get down to business and begin knocking out the set. We might be even louder in here than we were at the Annex. I go stand in my corner, singing with toilet paper plugging my ears.

After about 10 songs the managers stand up, approach the stage, congratulate Joe and then off they go.

We continue on with our set while the crew works. Ed, who is Joe's guitar tech, is stringing up the Rich Bich with 10 fresh Ernie Balls. Our lighting guy Woody, stage manager Cort and soundman Jay are busy sorting cables and loading road cases. Doc oversees the scene.

After the set I head to the men's room to get rid of this stupid toilet paper. I reach into my left ear but instead of coming out, the paper gets pushed inward. It's stuck in there deep. Way deep. I can't get a grip on it. Damn.

Wednesday March 17, 1982

Welcome to Cambridge Hospital. Julia called in late to work so she could come with me.

The emergency room doctor walks towards me with some large, scary looking tweezers and forcefully extricates the wad of paper from my noggin. Unfortunately he also removes a slug of ear wax that I've been cultivating for the past fifteen years of hard rocking. A chunk about the size of a shotgun shell. That hunk of wax has been my sole protection from the decibel bombardment I subject myself to on a daily basis.

So, with a virgin left ear I return to the soundstage at 1 p.m. I go back to my position in the corner of the stage and we dive into the set.

Here I am. Standing way back here.
Feeling like the tambourine player of the Partridge Family.

Thursday March 18, 1982

The Project crew is busy today trucking all the gear out of the
Complex soundstage and back to our room at the Annex.
No rehearsal.
Julia brings me to the Boston Garden tonight to see her band
The Cars headline. These guys are the hottest thing out of
Boston right now. They released their fourth album
"Shake It Up" four months ago and it's doing great for them.
Producer Roy Thomas Baker gets the same lush background
vocals for The Cars that he does for Queen.
The radio friendly sound.
Of course Julia has full access to the entire Cars backstage. The
band, crew, tour manager and the Don Law production crew all
know her by name and joke around with her. I'm a stranger to
all this arena-rock stuff. I just keep my mouth shut and try to act
like I belong.
Ric Ocasek picked me up hitchhiking down on Commonwealth
Ave one day, six years ago. He swung to the curb and beckoned
me in. Ric looked funny, scrunched inside his VW bug.
Driving along, he quizzed me about how he might get his band,
then called Cap'n Swing, onto the Live at the Rat record we
were cutting. Thundertrain had recently played at an agent
showcase in Medway with Cap'n Swing. I didn't have the heart
to tell nice guy Ric that his band name stunk and that they were
too weird looking to be part of the Rat scene.
About a year later Ocasek's group, now called The Cars, opened
for Thundertrain at a hockey arena up in Berlin NH. They didn't
look funny anymore and the new name was actually kind of
cool. A few weeks later The Cars released their debut album and
shot to the top of the pops right out of the box.
Let the Good Times Roll indeed.

All the Cars guys, Ric, David and Elliot in particular, have always been very nice to me. I've known David ever since he played drums with DMZ, a young Rat band who I'd occasionally join onstage for a song or two back in 1976.

Friday March 19, 1982

Swing by the office to pick up my weekly $100 and then it's off to the Annex for the 1 p.m. rehearsal. I don't know when Joe Perry and Brad Whitford arrive at the Annex every day but both of them are always grinding-away along with drummer Stewart by the time Danny and I show up.
I enter the room to the roar of the giant snake riff. The one Brad and Joe have been refining for the past few days. Even though it has a rock beat, there is something peculiar about this piece. It's not just a short cool riff like Once a Rocker or Black Velvet Pants. The whole song is a riff, a riff that coils, climbs, descends, strikes and re-coils repeatedly.
We're back in our regular room again.
I don't have to sing in the corner here.

Sat/Sun March 20/21, 1982

I sure would like to get one more new original song for the demo we'll be recording this week. Lying on the couch at the pink palace. Searching for inspiration. I begin to thumb through "Leonard Maltin's 1981 Movie Guide" which is a thick dictionary of just about every Hollywood film released since 1929 with a short review attached.
Poring through the film titles, my peepers land on *When Worlds Collide*. I remember that movie. A pretty decent sci-fi from 1951. The title kinda sums up the sound of Whitford and Perry's guitars as they clash and duke it out, riding the snake riff that's been haunting me. Worlds colliding.
Okay so I have a title. Now what?

I wander through the movie guide and see *Other Side of Midnight*. Not my kind of film, a sudser from a few years back. Maybe I can put a twist on it?

"On the wrong side of midnight / On the wrong side of town
Scream of the sirens is the only sound
Your Daddy doesn't like it, Mama she cried
On the wrong side of love / When Worlds Collide"

Now I'm rolling, I quickly write out two more verses in the same rhythmic cadence.
Is there a melody? Not sure. Is there a chorus? Not sure.
A hook? Yes.
The hook is the snake riff.
Just like the hook of Once a Rocker is Joe's see-saw funk riff.
The hook of Black Velvet Pants is Joe's country-honk riff.
That's how I see it anyway.
I mean, some people might tell you that the hook of Smoke on the Water is when the singer wails Smoke on the Water. Others might say the hook of I Can't Get No Satisfaction is when the singer moans I Can't Get No Satisfaction.
I'm not buying that.
As far as I'm concerned the hook of Smoke on the Water is the guitar riff.
The hook of I Can't Get No Satisfaction is the guitar riff.
Same with Iron Man, Cat Scratch Fever, Heart Full of Soul, Purple Haze, Back in Black, Psychotic Reaction and Dirty Water. Let's not forget Draw the Line, Train Kept A-Rollin' and Walk this Way.

Monday March 22, 1982

While warming up at the Annex today, it wasn't long before Joe and Brad began grinding-out the marauding snake riff.

Only this time I begin to rap over it:

"The girls are pretty / But they don't know a thing
On the wrong side of love / For a dime store ring
You're missing all the action / If you stay inside
Streets start burnin' / When Worlds Collide"

That last line cues Ronnie and the others to segue into the
answer riff, a swirling, dangerous sounding thing that leads back
into my next verse. Once again the tune is taking shape and sort
of arranging itself now that the players have a vocal maypole to
wrap the riffs around.
When Worlds Collide is a different type of tune.
Very atmospheric, cinematic even.
It lacks a traditional sung chorus or bridge. In this piece those
parts are played, not sung.
Whatever it is, everyone seems happy with it.
Then we run down the whole set.
Our first concert is coming up this weekend.

Tuesday March 23, 1982

Last rehearsal. From here on it's gonna be hotels and motels,
makeup and ice cream, touring the world. Today we concentrate
on the songs we plan to record tomorrow. Brad tells us a bit
about the recording studio that he recommended to Joe and Tim.
We'll be recording about 30 miles west of here, out in Carlisle.
A place called Blue Jay.
One of the few Boston area studios that Thundertrain never
visited. Whitford says Blue Jay has a room and equipment that
rivals the stuff that NYC and L.A. have to offer.
After we finish rehearsal the crew begins to pack.
Doc tells the band to meet here tomorrow at 1:30 p.m.

Wednesday March 24, 1982

I pick up Danny and we head out to the Annex in Cambridge.
Pulling into the lot we see a brown van. Doc is at the wheel. The
JPP crew already left hours ago with a rented Ryder truck full of
gear. Danny and I climb into the van. Doc greets us.
"Jonathan Edwards just finished touring in this vehicle, so be
careful. There might still be some granola underneath your seat
cushions."
Corvettes roar into the lot. Ron Stewart and Brad Whitford hop
into the two bench seats behind the one Hargrove and I are
sharing. The Porsche arrives and Joe Perry jumps into the
shotgun seat next to Doc.
The road manager flashes a shit-eating grin.
"All right boys. Fasten your seatbelts and leave the driving to
us." A moment later we're out on Route 2 heading west.
Joe pops a cassette in the tape deck. Some good hard rocking
stuff begins to play but I don't recognize it. We all sit silently,
gazing at the passing leafless New England scenery, quietly
listening to the tape. Something is familiar about this. But what?
I finally realize that it's the Whitford/St. Holmes album. A great
sounding record. Brad made it a year ago, right after he quit
Aerosmith. The vocalist is from Ted Nugent's band and they cut
it somewhere down south I think. I'm curious.
"So what happened? I mean this sounds really good."
Whitford gazes distantly out the window. Smiling slightly.
"That's a good question."
Joe Perry is silent. Brad speaks in riddles.

Almost an hour later Doc announces,
"Gentlemen, you have arrived."
Arrived? Really? This is it?
We pull into a wooded lot. I see a doorway but it's not

attached to anything. Just a shack backed up against a hillside. It looks like the hut I built behind my parents' house when I was eleven. Are you serious? That little thing is a recording studio? Entering through the door, I realize that Blue Jay is built into and beneath the hillside. It's all underground.

We enter the Batcave.

It's a spacious cave and a nice one too. There's a tidy hangout space with couches and a fridge and gold records on the walls. Then you go down a hallway to the control room. A long mixing desk with at least 24 channels. A couple of those big-ass Ampex machines running 2-inch reels. All kinds of controls, processors and plate reverb. A variety of monitor speakers. The room is nicely decorated too, not a tech rat-nest like some of the joints I've recorded at. Lots of wood inlay in herringbone patterns, modern couches and new carpeting.

The control room's glass windows look out into the studio area, also very handsome, with the same detailed woodwork, raised areas, a vocal booth, some reflective surfaces and movable, padded partitions. Hundreds of cables are neatly hung next to a locker full of expensive looking mics with German names.

Ron Stewart's kit is already set up next to a piano. The crew are working on Danny's bass rig and Brad's Marshall stacks.

I always hear stories about how Jimmy Page recorded some of his hugest sounding riffs through a Fender Deluxe Reverb or Rick Nielsen recorded a hit through a Pignose. That ain't gonna be happening here. Joe Perry brought his full amp-line with him and it's stacked high to the ceiling.

Not much for the Cowboy to do today but watch and learn.

After the equipment is sorted out for hums, squeaks and rumbles everything gets mic'd up. It takes a while. Direct mics for the guitar amps, ambient mics for the room sound, all kinds of mics on all Ron's drums. Then each band member has to go in on his own and jam away at full volume, while the engineer sets all the peak levels and makes sure things don't overload.

Harmonic distortion is great but overloads will wreck the track.
Then there's more tweaking, getting proper mic placement on
each speaker cone, maybe changing out a few mics. Tuning in
just the right tones.
By the time that's all done it's almost midnight.
Time to go home. Haven't recorded a peep yet.

Thursday March 25, 1982

Did I mention that Joe is looking better?
Not a lot better, but a definite improvement from when we first
met almost a month ago. His color has turned from green to
vampire and he's not shaking visibly anymore. I rarely see his
eyes, they're always covered by those thick bangs but when I
do, they still look pretty vacant. His speech is hard for me to
understand, but I've only heard Joe speak a few sentences since
I've joined this club.
It's usually just Let the Music do the Talking on this lot.
At 3 p.m. Doc dumps us out of the Dodge van at Blue Jay and
we get right to work. We start cutting the beds for five songs
today. The drums, bass and both Brad and Joe on the guitar
backing tracks. We record Going Down (a cover song),
First One's For Free and Black Velvet Pants (both by Joe) plus
When Worlds Collide and Once a Rocker (both by Joe and me).

After the last track is completed I go back into the control room
where I notice that the tape box has No Time For Women
written on it.
"What's this?" I ask the engineer.
"What's what? No Time for Women? It's the song you guys just
recorded."
"No it isn't. That was Once a Rocker."
"Hey, sorry man, I asked Joe for the title and he told me
No Time for Women, so that's what I wrote on the label."

Friday March 26, 1982

It's 3 p.m. and I'm back in Carlisle, at Blue Jay.

I'm a little nervous this afternoon because today is the first time Joe Perry is gonna hear what I actually sound like. I mean, I've been singing nearly every day with him for the past month but I think I already mentioned the volume thing. I can't hear myself so I doubt anyone else can either.

So, I'm in the vocal booth with a big $2000 Neumann mic aimed at my face. I've got the cans clamped to my ears. We start off with When Worlds Collide. This one is more of a rap. Not a very melodic song. Pretty easy to warm up on.

Joe Perry likes to record *not* the way Aerosmith did it. That is, Joe and Aerosmith (from what I've heard) would sometimes record a whole album with all the band parts, including finished lead guitar solos, before the singer had even finished writing the lyrics, let alone sung anything.

In the Project, Joe wants the singer to record his parts over the bed tracks and then - after that's all in the can - Joe will add his lead guitar stuff at the end.

Makes sense to me.

I see enthusiastic thumbs-up for my first vocal performance of the day. So we move right along. I only do three, maybe four, takes on each of the other three songs.

In the control room they keep each vocal take on a discrete track. That way, during mix down they have extra takes to choose from if I hit a brown note. Or they can blend a couple of my vocal tracks together for the popular "doubling" effect heard on lots of rock records.

I step out of the Batcave for some fresh air while Perry records his lead vocal for First One's For Free.

With all the vox in the can, Joe straps on his Tele-Rat and begins adding lead guitar to the five tracks. Joe has a lot of experience in record production, he likes to stay inside the control room while adding his overdubs.

He confers with the engineer as he plays. A long guitar cable coils out through the control room door, wandering back to the mountain of amps and cabs in Joe's section of the studio.

Most of the music is straight ahead. Joe knocks out response riffs to the call riffs Brad cut yesterday on Going Down. Black Velvet Pants and Once a Rocker (No Time for Women) come together in no time. Joe augments what I've just done vocally with some tasty counterpoint and support lines. First One's For Free flows freely. Joe saves the big fireworks for When Worlds Collide. Pulling out the stops with frantic soloing, bizarrely beautiful signal processing - and even a backwards tape effect. Trippy and chilling.

It's late, my mind is blown, I think we might have something here. Have to wait til tomorrow to make sure.

March 27, 1982

"You sound great, Mach"

That's Elyssa Perry speaking.

I'm sitting behind Joe's wife. A young woman I have never seen outside the pages of Rock Scene and Creem magazines. She's sitting close to Joe's side on the bench seat just in front of mine. Doc is at the wheel of the van, whisking us up to New Hampshire for the 5 p.m. soundcheck. The demo tape we just completed about 14 hours ago is blasting out of the tape deck.

"Nice going, Cowboy"

That's Joe Perry speaking.

Hargrove slaps my shoulder. Damn. This tape sounds really powerful. We look at each other with mile-wide grins. We did it. It's a killer demo and now we're cruising to our first concert.

Michael Striar presents
The Joe Perry Project

We pull up in front of the Capitol Theatre in Concord NH.
Hargrove and I stare at the big marquee hanging out over the
sidewalk. Doc wheels the van down an alley, back to the stage
door where I'm surprised to see a big bunch of kids already
waiting for us. There's an excited rush towards the van. Joe
Perry slides open the side-door of the vehicle and is met with a
flurry of high-fives, thrusted pens, autograph books, guitars to
sign and various JPP and Aerosmith albums. When the fans
realize Brad Whitford is also in the van - they cry out as though
they just struck gold. People are leaping and yelling and pushing
against the Dodge as Hargrove and I try to make our way
towards the stage door. Joe is greeting every kid he can while
Elyssa tugs on him and guides him toward the venue. Doc
pushes through the mob, waving his arms and promising all the
kids a great show tonight. We all mush our way inside as the
stage door slams with a clank. Are we having fun yet?
Inside, I find a beautiful 1,300 seat theater dating back to
vaudeville and the golden age of the movies. The stage is deep
and wide. Woody is up in the rafters adjusting the lighting. Ed is
lining-up Joe's axes on a rack adjacent to Perry's rolling tower
of processors. Jay is doing mic checks while stage manager Cort
second-guesses every other detail. Seeing the monumental JPP
amp-line and drum kit all set up on a real stage for the first time
has me all revved up.
Ronnie's custom built Eames drums are displayed atop a high
riser. Brad's Marshall stacks gleam in the stage lights. No doubt,
this stage set up is an imposing but very promising sight for any
rocker entering the premises.
The soundcheck is lengthy. I didn't get to do these things very
often in Thundertrain.

Brad and Joe both take considerable time blasting out passages of songs while conferring with the house sound guy and the monitor mixer.

Side-stage fills are rejiggered, floor monitors re-angled. When it's my turn, I run into my corner, sing a verse, give the sound guys a thumbs-up and dance off the stage. Joe shoots me a weird glance.

I want to make it in this band. I knew I had to show up on time for all the rehearsals. I did, and I was always prepared.

I knew that I could solidify my position if I could write some new songs with Joe. Done. My current challenge is to try and get on the good side of the boss's wife. The van ride up was a good start. Elyssa seems to approve of my performance on the demo. As showtime approaches I get a chance to chat with her. She isn't very hard to talk to. Pretty soon I find out that we both share an interest in a particular genre of movies.

Horror and sci-fi.

The backstage dressing room is nice. Clean and with a good place to lounge around. There are platters of cheese and crackers, fresh fruit, tasty rolls and deli meats. Cold beer, some sodas and bottles of vodka, bourbon and rum, complete with an ice bucket and mixers. Hargrove and I are ogling this free layout. We turn and stare at each other, wide-eyed and grinning like devils.

Steve Barrasso and Tim Collins enter. Promoter Michael Striar rushes through to shake hands. Elyssa is whispering in Joe's ear. Local girls, all dolled up, are allowed to come in briefly, to meet Brad, Joe and Ronnie.

The opening act, The Dream, are on stage as the theater fills up. I've never seen these guys before, a new band. They look really young. Like teenagers. Joe is 31 already and I'll turn 30 next year. We must be the oldest rock band on earth.

There are already a ton of kids in the auditorium with long lines still waiting to get in. I envy the lead singer of The Dream a bit, because he gets to entertain this growing crowd from center stage, not the side corner. Center is where a rock singer should be. They finish their energetic set to a good ovation. This crowd is ready to get down and get with it. As The Dream exits the stage I briefly congratulate the singer, he tells me his name is Gary Cherone.

Our dressing room empties out as we prepare to go on. Hargrove is in jeans, boots and a blue coat. Whitford and Stewart wear jeans and t-shirts. Admiral Perry is wearing black leather pants and a black scarf, the dangling Rolex and a tobacco-colored coat, sleeves rolled up to the elbows. I'm wearing my good luck black jeans and a blue denim jacket. The heels of my cowboy boots are extra high. I'm only one Smoot tall (5'7") but with heels I'm practically as tall as Joe and the others.
Wagner's Ride of the Valkyries theme rises up in the auditorium. This prerecorded opening music is met by cries of "Joe fukken Perry." Stomping and screaming ensues and suddenly Doc kicks open our dressing room door, flashlight in hand and hustles us out. I follow Danny as Doc quickly herds us down some stairs and through a pitch black corridor. Stage manager Cort is at the back of the line, guiding his flashlight along the floor, making sure everyone makes it out safely. I hit the darkened stage and can see hundreds of kids pushing up against it, getting as close as possible.
The roar picks up as the audience begins to see the silhouettes of the Project members taking our places. They erupt as Joe Perry, last in the line, makes his entrance, striding out across the blacked-out stage.
The Admiral plugs into his bank of amps and knocks out some roaring, squealing tones from his Strat. These are met with an ovation. As the Ride of the Valkyries reaches a crescendo, Perry stomps a switch on his pedal-board that creates this huge oscillating tone that sounds a lot like the deadly flock of

helicopters in the famous *Apocalypse Now* scene. The crowd is going berserk at this point. The opening theme tape reaches a massive climax, with the trumpet fanfare from the William Tell Overture.

Over the last sustained trumpet call, Ronnie Stewart counts us in and BANG - the stage lights blast up full-ON as the new Joe Perry Project launches into Toys in the Attic.

The audience is further astounded when they see not only Joe Perry playing their favorite song but, could it be? Yes it is. Brad Whitford is standing in the spotlight right next to Perry. Rocking out on Toys together. These two guitar giants haven't shared a stage since Perry quit Aerosmith three years ago.

I'm stuck way over here in deep right field, but I'm quickly adjusting to it. Why not? In fact I'm loving it. Kids are hanging over the lip of the stage on my end, pointing up at my face, singing along with me, smiling, reaching out, trying to touch my boot as I glide forward. I'm singing the refrain and suddenly I feel pressure on my shoulder. It's Joe. He's leaning against me hard, we're both singing into my mic, harmonizing together, and rocking our asses off. Like buddies. Reelin' and a rockin'.

I think the set went like this:

Toys in the Attic
Life at a Glance
Discount Dogs
Ain't No Substitute for Arrogance
Back in the Saddle
Mist is Rising
Heartbreak Hotel
No Time For Women (Once a Rocker)
Black Velvet Pants
Going Down
When Worlds Collide
Rockin' Train (w/ Ron's drum solo)
Soldier of Fortune

East Coast, West Coast
I Got the Rock'n'Rolls Again
Let The Music Do the Talking
Encore: Train Kept A-Rollin'

Sunday March 28, 1982

When I wake up I re-enter the dream.
I'm Joe Perry's lead singer.
A month ago I was replacing broken needles in crappy kiddie
record players. Now I'm in a band with Brad Whitford and Joe
Perry. Recording songs that Joe and I co-wrote a few days ago.
Last night we played a sold-out theater, packed with screaming
teenagers.
Most rock musicians only dream of doing stuff like this. My
waking world has become a dream. I'm on a high and I don't
want it to end. All I want to do is get back in that Dodge van and
race-off to the next adventure. Hanging out and making music
with Joe and his Project. Raising hell together.
I'm back here at the pink palace. Nobody to raise hell with.
No screaming teens to be found. It's very quiet here.

Monday March 29, 1982

Danny Hargrove comes by the pink palace. Like me, he's trying
to grasp everything that's changed for us in these last few
weeks. We talk about Joe and Brad, the rehearsals, the soundstage, our new managers, the recording session. Most of all we
try to re-live the high of Saturday night's gig.
But it's impossible. We're both hooked on the Project.
Already hopelessly addicted. We need more.

Tuesday March 30, 1982

Danny Hargrove, Julia and I all go to the Channel.

It's a concert nightclub that opened in Boston a couple years ago. The place can hold over a thousand and and it has multiple bars, a huge stage and really good sound.

The starring attraction tonight is a reunion of Duke and the Drivers. That's right.

With my mentor Earthquake on bass and the Project's own road manager, Doc, on drums. All the guys in the Drivers use stage names. Doc is known as Dr. Feelgood Funk D.D.A. (doctor of drug abuse).

The place is packed and the Drivers play all our favorites: Rock'n'Roll High, Check Your Bucket, Ain't Nothin' A Young Girl Can Do For Me and of course the hit What You've Got (Sure Looks Good To Me). Doc looks like he's breathing a little heavy as he bashes out the last few numbers - but he manages to survive the show.

Wednesday March 31, 1982

Danny and I are sitting side by side in the Dodge van. Ron Stewart is in the way-back with his headphones secured, whacking-away on a practice pad. Doc is at the wheel. We motor down to one of the suburbs of Boston and pull up in front of a multi-level glass house. Very modernistic.

Out pops Brad Whitford. He flings a small suitcase into the back of the van and hops onto the empty bench seat behind Danny and me. Doc wheels north, back towards Boston. About a half hour later we arrive in the best part of Newton, near Boston College. We zip up an incline and take a bend. At the top of a steep driveway we pull up in front of this villa-type mansion. One of those Tudor places, like I saw while riding the city bus through Beverly Hills last year. I see a Bentley and the black Porsche Turbo. Looks fast.

We all just sit. I'm not sure what to say. Doc does most of the talking. He's a funny guy, but sometimes in a cynical way.

Eventually the Admiral emerges out the big front door. He has a
little leather bag in one hand and the garbage slung over his
shoulder. Funny sight, watching Joe Perry amble towards a
trash can at the edge of the driveway. With a flick of the wrist he
flings the garbage bag into the can before jumping into the
shotgun seat next to Doc.
"All right, boys and girls, time to go make some money,"
exclaims Doc as he speeds out of the Perry estate.
A few hours later Doc announces:
"Hotels, motels, gentlemen."
We're parked out in front of the Quality Inn in Albany NY.
A couple minutes later Doc returns from the check-in desk with
our room keys.
"Go upstairs and relax boys. We have a 5 p.m. sound check.
Be ready to roll at 4:45."
We're all sharing rooms. Brad and Joe are rooming together.
I'm with Ron Stewart.
I throw my bag in the corner. Ron pulls a chair out from the
wall, arranges his practice pad on the table, slaps the head-
phones back on and in an instant he's paradiddling again.
I'm not sure what he plays along with but I don't think it's
AC/DC. More like King Crimson or Yes, or maybe the latest
fusion album from Beck.
J.B. Scotts is a venue right in the middle of Albany. A big
concert club, like the Channel in Boston, that books established
national touring acts and new bands signed to big labels trying
to break into the market. I always heard about this club when I
was with Thundertrain. We'd be playing five-nighters (for bad
money) at Dudley Do Right's, next door in Troy NY. People
would come up to me to ask "why aren't you guys playing at
J.B. Scotts? That's where the *good* bands play."
I always took it as a back-handed remark.
Anyway, I've finally made it to J.B.s, and not as a warm-up
band on an off night with no crowd. The Project is headlining
here tonight and from what I hear, the tickets are selling-out fast.

Sound check goes smoothly. A few kids were at the stage door to meet us, but not like the other day. I'm set up at the far end of the stage as usual. At least I'm standing next to Joe, so I can share a bit of the star's spotlight.

We go out for dinner together after the soundcheck and then Doc brings us back to the hotel.

"Okay guys, get some rest. I'll ring you at 11 p.m."

11 p.m? Wow, we must be going on pretty late.

So, we leave the Quality Inn at quarter past 11 and arrive at J.B. Scott's at 11:30. The place is mobbed. A thousand easy. Most of these kids have been in here partying for hours now, everyone is smashed.

Backstage isn't as grand as the Capitol Theatre, but there is cold beer and a few bottles of bourbon and vodka. We ready ourselves for battle and a few minutes later I can hear Ride of the Valkyries blasting out of the huge PA system.

We perform pretty much the same set as Saturday, except we add in Buzz Buzz, a great David Hull song, and the Aerosmith classic Same Old Song and Dance. I'm loosening-up and feeling more confident tonight. I talk to the audience more, and do some introductions during Rockin' Train.

Following the set our dressing room fills up with well wishers, drug dealers, groupies and other Joe Perry superfans.

Then I see Joanie. The cute girl who baked a lasagna and toted it through a snowstorm down to the unheated band house where Thundertrain used to stay whenever we played Dudley's. Joanie is in the TT Hall of Fame for that act of kindness. That was in '76 and little Joanie is a lot more grown up now. I'm happy to see her. A guy pushes up to me and introduces himself.

"Great set man, I'm Bill Rezey."

Wow. I know that name. Rezey is the booking agent who controls this whole region. Thundertrain dreamed of working with him but Rezey was too busy booking the big money club acts, like Talas with Billy Sheehan.

"C'mon with me, we're goin' to a party."

I follow Bill out the stage door. There's a big recreation vehicle parked right next to our little brown van.

"C'mon in, Mach, I'll show you around."

Inside the big Winnebago I see some sultry looking chicks slouching on the luxe furniture. There's a big bar set up. A cool looking guy is sitting, smiling - wait - I think I know that guy.

"This is Mach, he's Joe Perry's new singer. Pour him a shot girls. Mach, this is David Silver from Modern Records."

"It's a pleasure to meet you, Mach."

I shake David's hand. Trying to figure out - and then it comes to me -David was host of "What's Happening, Mr. Silver?" the trippiest show ever to make it onto television. It ran on the PBS stations in the sixties in Boston and a bunch of other cities. I never missed an episode.

One of my favorite Mr. Silver shows was when David began the program, speaking in his very proper British accent, by asking the viewers to fetch an extra portable TV and set it up just to the left of the one they were currently watching.

He gave everyone a couple minutes to do that. Then Mr. Silver told us to tune the left TV to channel 44 and the right TV to channel 2. Both frequencies were operated by PBS in Boston.

A moment later, a man on the TV to the left was paddling ping pong balls over to a lady on the other set. Back and forth between the TV sets the ball begins flying. The sound of the ball hitting the paddles was in stereo too. Then a guy on the right hand set begins blowing smoke rings across the room to the left hand TV, which causes a girl who wanders into the left hand set to start coughing.

The gags continued for the whole half hour. Ernie Kovacs would have loved it.

So I have a great time meeting this very cool cat David Silver. He's a little taken aback that I not only know who he is, but that I can also recall so many of his programs from 14 years ago, very vividly.

While Bill, David and I are drinking and talking, the girls have begun doing some kind of wiggly dance, and the vehicle we're in has been rolling. We end up making it to a little rock bar in time for last call.

Thursday April 1, 1982

Doc has us all up and out of the hotel by 11 a.m. We hit a truck stop diner. I order cherry pancakes. I drizzle my tall stack of flap jacks with red colored syrup.

From behind his dry toast and eggs Joe glares at my pile.

"Cowboy. How can you eat that crap?"

I admit that it does look pretty disgusting.

Hours later we arrive in Hazlet NJ, where Doc books us into rooms at the Sheraton.

I'm with Ron again. Ron seems to be a nice guy. I used to see him whenever I went to E.U. Wurlitzer on Newbury Street, just a couple blocks up from SyncroSound. Wurly's is the main rock equipment store in New England. You have to travel to Sam Ash or Manny's on 48th St. in NYC to find a similar level of great instruments and gear.

Ron ran the drum department at E.U. Wurlitzer for years. It's in the back. Anytime Bobby Edwards needed new sticks we'd be there. Bobby would be handed a bushel of 5Bs, which he would diligently sight-down, one by one, and roll back and forth on the counter. Checking for balance and warping.

Out of forty sticks, Bobby might choose six. Ron Stewart was performing back then too. Usually with ITMB (the Incredible Two Man Band). Plus he was married to Sue, the music store's bookkeeper.

But then the Joe Perry Project happened. Ron left the store, and I guess the marriage ended too, because now he's married to a young, pretty gal named Renee. I think Ron met Renee while the Project was touring down in Texas.

Ron seems to be a good guy, even though he's barely said two words to me since I joined the Project. Last night he woke me from my deep slumber. He was kicking out a vigorous double bass drum pattern in his sleep. Ron lives to drum.

We drive down the Garden State Parkway a few miles to the Fountain Casino. Holy smokes, look at the size of this place. A huge airplane hangar of a nightclub. With a massive marquee out on the highway, like a Las Vegas casino. Walking through the immense space I see posters for Twisted Sister and Trigger. Two big club acts that I ran into back in Thundertrain days.

We caught Twisted Sister in 1974 down at the Electric Elephant in Newport RI. Sister were playing polished David Bowie and Mott covers while dressed in glitter, make-up and expensive looking platform boots.

Thundertrain was taking over at the same club the next week and planning on doing a lot of those same cover songs. We were a brand new band at the time and nowhere near as slick and professional as these Twisted Sister guys.

Then, a couple years later, we met up with Trigger at an agent showcase in Rowley MA. We were messing around backstage, as usual, while the Trigger men sat around a table playing poker. High stakes too.

The Trigger mob were dressed to kill, and throwing around big wads of cash. When they hit the stage they were no BS.

No sense of humor was detected. These Jersey guys made us feel like total hicks in comparison.

So it all makes sense now. We're 18 miles north of Asbury Park NJ and right across the river from NYC. This must be that big money New Jersey cover band territory I've always heard about. Actually, if Thundertrain had ever managed to get booked into the Fountain Casino, I would have been very nervous about playing to a mostly empty room. I mean, you could put hundreds in this cavern and it would still look sparse.

Thankfully, the Joe Perry Project pulls another big, enthusiastic crowd tonight. The Good Rats are the opener and they're an excellent group. Not a sell-out tonight, but a respectable showing for sure. Once again, the place has already been open for hours by the time we hit the stage at midnight.

Everyone is wasted.

Midway through our set, I get to take a break, while Joe sings Mist is Rising and Heartbreak Hotel. During Mist, I watch as Woody floods the stage floor with fog and employs some of his eerie lighting effects.

Friday April 2, 1982

Doc books us into the Sheraton Hotel in New Rochelle NY. The town where Rob and Laura Petrie lived on the Dick Van Dyke Show. The town next door is called Mt. Vernon, it's right between Yonkers and the Bronx. That's where the Project is playing tonight, at a club called Left Bank.

I guess they call it Left Bank because the building was previously a real bank. I have a word with Joe during soundcheck.

"Joe, that new song we co-wrote,
it's actually called Once a Rocker."

"Are you sure, Cowboy? I heard you say No Time For Women."

"No, Joe. There's a line in the second verse that goes
Got no time for movies / Got no time for rent… but I never say no time for women."

"Okay, Cowboy. If you say so."

So now it's Once a Rocker on the set list. The Admiral's been letting me write the set lists for the past few shows. Outside of the opening and closing numbers Perry doesn't really care what order he plays them. It makes more of a difference voice-wise for me. I like to pace the show so that I don't go totally hoarse before the night is done. After I write the song list, I show it to Joe for approval and then Doc gives it to a crew member who has good handwriting to make copies for all of us.

This venue is a medium-sized stone building and the bank vault is still here, right next to the stage. With the room being a lot

smaller than the past two gigs - and this being Friday - the
crowd is really packed tight to the walls tonight.
Loud as hell in here, that's for sure. We put on a good show and
Joe Perry is looking better everyday. Getting him off the estate
and out playing for his people is good medicine apparently.
After the fans leave, Danny and I poke around the corners of the
building just in case any bundles of money got left behind when
the bank closed down.

Saturday April 3, 1982

Step right up, we're at "New Jersey's Rock'n'Roll Big Top,"
The Circus in Bergenfield NJ. I'm back in the dressing room
marveling at the lewd, crude drawings, poems and messages
scrawled over every square inch of the room. Here's a nice one:

Dear Joe Perry,
Welcome to The Circus.
What the hell is wrong with you Joe?
You quit Aerosmith to play here?
Have fun kicking yourself in the ass.

That's not very nice. I set my bag down to block it.
I don't think Joe would give a shit if he saw it. He doesn't seem
to care what people think or say. But it bothers me a lot.
Thundertrain used to play Manhattan frequently back in the
seventies. The Fleshtones opened for us at Max's Kansas City,
and another time at Max's we opened for Alex Chilton. We did
some shows with the Bonnie Parker Band at Gildersleeves.
But our usual gig was down in the Bowery, at CBGB's.
We played that room at least seven or eight times, usually
teamed up with the Dead Boys. Those clubs were basically
dives, but they drew lots of high-profile people. One of the first
times Thundertrain played CBGB's, a front table was inhabited
by Laraine Newman, Jane Curtin and Gilda Radner.

It was typical to see heads of major record labels and Danny
Fields from *16 Magazine* out in the crowd.

Various Tuff Darts, Blondies, and Ramones would be hanging
around the backstage area.

The Circus on the other hand is an everyday working class
rock'n'roll bar. No Saturday Night Live stars or record company
presidents are anywhere to be seen. The stage isn't very high
and pipes run across the ceiling. The place isn't very big. The
decor is horrible. The dressing room stinks. The word CIRCUS
is spelled out in goofy multi-colored letters that are glued to the
70's era phony wood paneling that spans the back of the stage.
This is the kind of dump where the best rock'n'roll is bound to
happen. It's the first place we've played that resembles the kind
of roadhouse/nuthouse venues that Danny and I are so used to.
Joe Perry and Brad Whitford playing in a hole like this? On a
Saturday night? Just across the river from NYC? Five bucks to
get in and cheap drinks too? What are you waiting for?

You know it's gonna be a great night.

Of course the place is jammed out to the sidewalks.

Sunday April 4, 1982

I'm back at the pink palace. The shouts of the girls and boys still
ringing in my ears.

Monday April 5, 1982

Danny comes over. We play the five song demo tape over and
over again.

Tuesday April 6, 1982

It felt like spring when we did those NJ and NY dates last
weekend. Today the Northeast is getting hit with a major

blizzard. 60 mph winds, Logan Airport closed down, 50 car pile up on the Mass Pike, over a foot of snow.

Wednesday April 7, 1982

Shoveling out.

Thursday April 8, 1982

I can't wait for tomorrow. We're playing in Massachusetts for the first time. My friends and fans can come see me singing with the Project.
The only songs I really feel 100% comfortable on are When Worlds Collide, Once a Rocker and Black Velvet Pants. They're original and they've been recorded with my voice, so there is no earlier version to compare them to.
Everything else sounds a little weird when I sing it. I've made up my mind, for now anyway, to just use my own voice on everything. Fact is, when I think I'm maybe doing a decent job mimicking Steven Tyler, or the other guys who recorded these songs on the albums, I'm only lying to myself.
I end up sounding not quite like me and a long shot from sounding like them.

Friday April 9, 1982

We are on the way to the gig when I first hear about it.
Mark Parenteau, the afternoon deejay at WBCN, has pulled some strings. I think somebody else cancelled at the last minute, so suddenly tonight's JPP show is going to be recorded for a radio broadcast. That's cool, I guess.
A little early though, I mean this is only the sixth show that Danny Hargrove and I have done with the band. I still haven't even figured out the intro to East Coast, West Coast.

We arrive in Hull, a beach town twenty miles south of Boston. A skinny peninsula, famed for Paragon Park with its big, scary wooden roller coaster and the endless, sandy Nantasket beach. Plopped right between the beach and the amusement park is a grand old ballroom called Uncle Sam's.

Well, today its called Uncle Sam's, but back when I was a teen with a transistor radio jammed inside my ear, it was called The Surf. The big east coast AM radio station WBZ would park their Sundeck Studio out in the parking lot alongside The Surf all summer long. Spinning hits by The Young Rascals, Little Stevie Wonder, Sonny and Cher, the Vogues, the Rolling Stones, Bobby Hebb and the Standells. 'BZ would run hourly surf reports, talk to chicks passing by in bikinis and run kookie contests. Deejays with names like Juicy Brucie Bradley would hype the bands who were playing The Surf that night. Groups like the Rockin' Ramrods, Moulty and the Barbarians, The Lost, The Pilgrims, Barry and the Remains and yes, even The Yardbirds.

" But Mark, are we really ready for WBCN to broadcast our concert all over the Boston area? I've only played five times with this band so far."

Parenteau walks over and leans into me, hard.

"Forget the Boston area, Mach. This is for "*Captured Live.*"
It's gonna be broadcast all over the world - by satellite.
They've already done one with Triumph, Marshall Tucker, Donny Iris…Chevrolet sponsors it on the RKO Network.
It's huge."

I see a sound truck parked out back, and a crew of engineers are already wiring up the stage. Mark does a pre-show interview with Perry. A producer with a clipboard tells me that the show, as broadcast, will be edited down to one hour and the interview will get spliced into the finished program. Even though it's hardly a beach day, a rowdy crowd fills up the venue quickly.

After the concert, Julia and I go out for a late dinner with Steven
Silva and his girlfriend Heidi.

Steven seems impressed with what he just witnessed. Funny
hearing my former lead guitarist say anything positive about a
performance that involves me. By the end of Thundertrain we
were at each others throats most of the time. In the end, Steven
even advocated for my removal from the band.

Saturday April 10, 1982

E.M. Loews is right in the middle of Worcester. Only a forty-
five minute drive from my town Holliston and even closer to
Hopedale where Joe Perry grew up. It's near to Natick and
Framingham too. Towns that loomed large in the early days of
Aerosmith and all the days of Thundertrain.

A former movie theater on Main Street, E.M. Loews has a
capacity of 2,660 and tonight the Joe Perry Project will sell it
out. My parents are here, along with my two brothers. My sister
Cathy is away, with the US Air Force. Many of my friends and
former bandmates have made their way out to Worcester for the
event. Of course Ric and Bobby are here.

It's a very important night for me.

I think everyone wants to be acknowledged for what they do
somewhere along the line. Earning a degree, or winning a
trophy, or receiving some kind of tangible affirmation for one's
work. For most of us guys who grew up playing in local rock
bands, acknowledgement is pretty hard to come by and it's
usually fleeting, if and when it comes. Somebody rushes by and
drunkenly yells "Hey man, great set," and for that moment it
feels good - but then it goes away again.

As I see it, the "major label record deal" that so many of us
chased, was mostly about vindication. To be accepted by a
music-business community we longed to be a part of. More
about pride than about getting rich. I have long dreamt of a night

like this, headlining to a packed house, under beautiful lighting, with a great production crew, on a massive stage, in a huge theater, in the heart of the city, where my friends and relatives can all come and see what I do. In the dream something like this might have happened after Thundertrain finally clinched the "big record deal." But tonight even surpasses that dream.
To be up here in front of thousands, singing alongside the best loved, hard rock guitar team to ever come out of America.

Sunday April 11, 1982

This is all starting to go to my head.
But what else can I do?
Last night I played the biggest gig of my life.
The day before that, our concert got recorded for an international radio broadcast.
Six and a half weeks ago - I never would have believed it.

Monday April 12, 1982

I go out to Wellesley and visit the guys at the Music Box. My father shows me this great new blaster from Panasonic. It has the basic boombox features, a tape deck, built-in condenser mics and an FM/AM radio tuner. It has nice stereo LED meters and very useful RCA stereo ins and outs on the side panel.
The unit is very compact, about the size of a large Italian grinder and it has really powerful, full range speakers, with large magnets and heavy duty voice coils. This little thing has an amazing sound. Sold. It'll be great on the road.

Tuesday April 13, 1982

I've been here at the pink palace long enough that the bill collectors have tracked me down. I owe. Not really that much but more than I can afford to pay back. A few hundred to a dentist. Five hundred bucks to a Master Card account I blew-out four years ago.

Wednesday April 14, 1982

I go down to Kenmore Square where my friend Blowfish is waiting at the upstairs bar at the Rat. His real name is Paul and he's a comedian and a rock writer. He called me yesterday, asking if I'd do an interview about my new gig. The story is for Boston Rock magazine, which is published and distributed by Newbury Comics. I share a few tales, we drink a beer, and I'm on my way.
Blowfish is a really funny guy.

Thursday April 15, 1982

Back on the road. Doc is driving us west on I90, the road we call the Mass Pike.
I ask Brad Whitford about the *Sgt. Pepper* movie.
I saw the flick when it came out a couple years ago. I'm really curious. I don't know many people who have been in a big Hollywood film. And this was a movie produced by Robert Stigwood, starring Steve Martin, the BeeGees, George Burns, Alice Cooper and Donald Pleasance among many others. Peter Frampton played the hero. Of course Aerosmith were cast as the bad guys, the Future Villain Band.
"Didn't take very long." Says Brad nonchalantly.
"They brought us out to a soundstage on some backlot and filmed everything in a few hours."
I know from watching the movie that Aerosmith performed up on an elevated stage, miming to a pre-recorded track of Come Together, while Tyler takes advantage of the female lead, Strawberry Fields.
"What about the Future Villain Band outfits you guys are wearing?"

"Some ladies from wardrobe measured us a few times and they knocked out the suits. The production even measured our guitars and made wooden prop doubles of them in the shop."

I was hoping to hear a lot more details and stories about hanging out on the set but no. That's all I get.

And when it comes to Aerosmith stories, forget about it. Brad shares only a few tidbits about the venues they played, as we pass from city to town.

Admiral Perry has absolutely nothing to add. He just jams another tape into the van's cassette player. His current favorite, Never Mind the Bollocks, Here's the Sex Pistols.

After checking into the Ramada Inn at 679 South Rd in Poughkeepsie we head over to The Chance.

Just in time for 5 p.m. soundcheck.

This time our van is met by another eager throng of JPP enthusiasts. Such a cool way to enter a new (to me) town. Joe, Ron and Brad sign photos and records that the fans brought along. These kids are super cool and polite. They even act like they're excited to meet Danny and me.

The Chance is a former vaudeville house. 900 seats.

I don't think The Stones ever played here, but everyone else has. Maybe the Stones too. A really nice theater with a really nice crowd. We rock.

Friday April 16, 1982

Driving between eastern New York and the lower New England states doesn't usually take much more than a few hours.

These are smaller states with lots of cities and towns packed tightly together. Tonight we're playing in the quaint little village of Pawcatuck CT.

It's a little confusing to me, because not very many miles north, is the town of Pawtucket RI, a town that most of us New Englanders are very familiar with.

It's where the PawSox baseball team plays.

Pawcatuck, Pawtucket, the Native American names are easy to confuse.

It's my first time in Pawcatuck, a seaside village contained within Stonington CT, and not far from Westerly RI.

Tonight the Joe Perry Project with special guest Brad Whitford, play the Rosalini Showcase. It's an intimate and apparently recently built venue. Kind of fancy looking, I doubt many punk or hard rock acts have ever played this hall before. But a decent sized, noisy crowd shows up to see the Project.

We rock, it's kinda weird, we roll on.

Saturday April 17, 1982

Did I tell you Joe likes guns? Brad too. Sometimes on these rides they both like to read this survivalist magazine called Soldier of Fortune. My dad used to let me take target practice down at the Holliston town dump when I was about 7 or 8.

His old .22 rifle was really beat up.

After JFK got shot, my father tossed the little rifle overboard on one of his sailing trips out of West Falmouth. I've never touched a gun since.

Whitford has brought along a new toy for our ride today. He hands a military looking rifle up to Joe in his shotgun seat.

I don't know anything about firearms but that thing looks like some kind of machine gun to me.

"Don't worry, Mach. It's just a replica." Brad assures me.

It freaks me out how real the thing looks. It's as big as an actual weapon, it's made of steel and looks pretty hefty.

We're playing at New Hampshire College in Manchester. The concert is being held in a good sized hall. A crowd of students have come out for the show. My good friend John V from Pure & Easy Records is here, along with a few of his friends, to check out this new band I'm singing in.

Openers Private Lightning are onstage.

These local guys are doing well for themselves, with a debut
record out on A&M Records. The group is led by a brother-sister
duo and she plays electric violin, which gives them a different,
difficult to categorize sound.

Everything is going great until…

Somebody backstage, I'm guessing Admiral Perry, thought it
would be fun to add a little extra drama to our stage entrance
here at the College.

Joe's faithful guitar-tech Ed is a veteran of the United States
Marine Corp. Eddie seems like a pretty sweet guy to me but he
does have a rough side. Ed growls a lot, and he occasionally
spouts off about wanting to spread "hate and discontent."

Being a vet, Ed is often dressed in camouflage trousers or some
sort of fatigues.

Anyway, once our spine-chilling Ride of the Valkyries starts
spilling out of the huge pile of onstage PA cabs, Ed has
apparently been instructed to go out onstage toting Brad's
replica firearm.

I'm totally in the dark about this plan. Unexpectedly, I suddenly
see our roadie, in his camouflaged pants and cap, march across
the front edge of the stage, displaying Brad's military-style gun
(replica) over his shoulder.

Following orders, he marches all the way across the stage, does
an about-face, and marches back to where he came from,
disappearing behind the side curtains.

The audience of buzzed college kids are watching this scene
unfold with consternation, some nervousness and confusion.
"What's with the gun? Who is that guy? What's going on?
Should we do something?"

No time to think about it. Doc leads us out into our places and
the Project is off to the races. Rocking innocently.

Doc must be drinking the same Kool-Aid as Joe tonight, because
after the concert is over, as we leave the campus in the brown
Dodge van, Doc suddenly breaks bad.

Seeing a campus guardhouse, with a lowered wooden-gate out front, Doc guns the engine, burns rubber, and rams our vehicle straight through the gate. Sending shards of broken lumber flying into the night. Hargrove stares at me wide-eyed.
I stare back at him. Are we all gonna die tonight?

Sunday April 18, 1982

We lived. But our manager Tim is ripping mad and very disappointed about what went down last night. He'll be having words with Doc and the Admiral for sure.
Our stage manager Cort didn't dig it either.
He resigns from the crew.

Monday April 19, 1982

Whoopee. I got a tax refund.
Because of my (old) job at the Music Box, I paid taxes for the first time in ten years. A check for $416. I'm rich.

Tuesday April 20, 1982

Heading out to Holliston to enjoy Spring.

Wednesday April 21, 1982

Now that I'm rich, I stop by the Holliston Savings Bank and open up an account.
I haven't had one of these in ten years either.
Then I take the train back into the city. I stop by the Paradise to see a local new-wave act called the Modes. Then I roll down Commonwealth Ave to the Rat, where the Real Kids and the Dawgs are raving.

Thursday April 22, 1982

JPP was supposed to play Clark University in Worcester MA
tonight but we got cancelled.

Friday April 23, 1982

We meet up at the Cambridge Complex at 9:30 a.m., hop in the
brown van and take off for Long Island NY. Several hours later
we arrive at the Tides Motel where we drop off our bags. Then
it's on to the Northstage Theater in Glen Cove.
As usual, my mic is set up way over in the right hand corner of
the stage. It's not like I have to just stand there all night.
I'm free to move forward, up to the edge of the stage and I
occasionally roam over to where Joe is set up in center stage.
After soundcheck we all go out for dinner.
Before I know it, it's 11:15 p.m. and we're whisked back to the
Northstage. The place is doing big business this Friday night.
The largest crowd I've seen since E.M. Loews.
My cousin Michael lives up the road in Bayport. He's here with
his wife. It's great to see him again and I'm proud that he can
hear me sing with Joe Perry in front of a big crowd. Joe is
wearing a Boy Scout shirt and extremely tight, caramel colored
leather trousers. Cool. I'm still doing the black jeans and denim
jacket. It's not like I have a closet full of stuff to pick from. Brad
is in jeans with a sleeveless t-shirt, as is drumming-machine
Ron. Side-stage I run into Maxanne Sartori. She works for a
record company nowadays, but she used to be the afternoon deejay at WBCN. She was the first person to play Aerosmith on
Boston radio. Maxanne also premiered Thundertrain's biggest
hit, Hot for Teacher! back in the bicentennial summer of 1976.
Tonight we play our best show so far.

Saturday April 24, 1982

Travel day back to Boston.

Sunday April 25, 1982

The clocks sprung forward today, late risers get extra sunlight.

Monday April 26, 1982

It's Tim Collins birthday.
Tim and Steve Barrasso are busy booking a big Coast to Coast
trip for the new Joe Perry Project. I'm dying to start a real tour.

Tuesday April 27, 1982

On the road we're each given a $15 per diem for food but it's
ours to spend as we please. So, if we're out for a week (or more)
the per diem adds up to $105 per wk. There is usually some sort
of hospitality platter in our dressing room every night. Crackers,
chips, cheese, cold cuts, veggies and dip. Free soda, beer and
alcohol too. Sometimes we're invited to the crew meal, a catered
dinner provided to all the workers after the soundcheck by the
promoter. Of course our air conditioned rooms are paid for and
they often have free HBO. So it's not just the traveling, rocking,
partying and meeting new people that I crave. Life on the road
will be more economical and more luxurious than hanging
around the pink palace all day, and the local clubs all night, on
my own skinny dime.

Wednesday April 28, 1982

I awake to screaming. Not just one voice or two.
It's a whole huge gang of screamers. It must be recess time
again. The palace is directly across Broadway from the

Longfellow Elementary School.
This is one of the days Julia took her car in to work, so I slept
late. Around lunchtime the school bell rings, and hundreds of
kids swarm out into the fenced playground.
Screaming their lungs out.
It's our drummer Ron Stewart's birthday. Not sure how old he is
today, maybe a year or two younger than me.

Thursday April 29, 1982

No laundry room at the palace. Cowboy is laundry boy. I hike
up Broadway to the corner laundromat with a sack of dirty
clothes slung over my shoulder and a fistful of quarters.

Friday April 30, 1982

Running deep into the heart of New York state today. Once we
hit Schenectady, Doc heads south on Route 88, all the way down
to State University New York (SUNY) in Oneonta. We book into
the Oneonta Holiday Inn, in the hills of the northern
Appalachian Mountain chain. No gun replicas this time. We're
on our not-best, but at least halfway-decent, behavior.
Danny and I have a lot of pent-up energy, having not played
since the previous Friday down in Long Island.
We don't know a soul here. That's okay with me. While I enjoy
performing in front of friends and family, being out here in the
wilderness totally loosens me up.
It allows me to present myself in ways I wouldn't feel
comfortable doing in front of my friends and relatives.
I've never forgotten my mother's disapproval of a report she
was reading in the local Framingham News back in 1973 after
Aerosmith did a show with Reddy Teddy at Caesar's Monticello
out on Route 9.
The reviewer wrote that "lead singer Tyler leapt across the stage
as he gripped his genitals."

Mother turned to me and scolded "Mark Bell, I better never hear that you've been leaping across any stages while gripping your genitals."

Saturday May 1. 1982

Doc checks us out of the Holiday Inn. After breakfast we begin a long ride down to Bristol RI. The Dodge van has three bench seats, plus a big area in back for our luggage and the occasional guitar case. So we can take turns laying out on a bench and grabbing a nap if we want.

We finally make it to Roger Williams College and search out the gymnasium. There's a tour bus parked outside. Inside the gym we find an impressive stage has been built and a massive sound system has been erected above it. Students are milling around, watching the crews set up the gear for the sound checks.

I run into my comrade James Montgomery who is on the bill tonight. James is an amazing frontman who started out in Detroit. Montgomery's been top-dog of the New England blues scene ever since he relocated here in the early 70's. James writes and sings and he plays a really mean harp. He knows (or knew) all the famed Chicago and Mississippi bluesmen personally.

A big throng of fans are circled around an imposing figure standing by the stage. It's Clarence Clemons, Bruce Springsteen's Big Man. The E Street Band is on a break, so Clarence is currently touring with his own group, the Red Bank Rockers. James Montgomery will open the show tonight. Followed by the Project, and then the headliners, Clarence and his band.

I helped run sound at a very early James Montgomery Blues Band / Sidewinders (Billy Squier's band) show at Wellesley College back in 1972.

A couple years later, the Montgomery Band landed a major deal with Capricorn Records (the Allman Brothers label) and Thundertrain's first really big concert, in early 1975, was

opening for James in New Bedford, at the Capital Theater.
By late 1976 Thundertrain (we were getting popular by then)
were still opening for James at Lakeview Ballroom in Mendon.
I used to think to myself " I'll know I'm finally making some
headway around here the day James Montgomery goes on stage
before me." If but for a moment, that day has finally come.

Montgomery opens up the show with his big city blues and
raunchy harmonica. JPP supplies the flashy hard-rock blast.
Then the Big Man finishes off the night, with soulful R&B and
high-riding saxophone.
The bill reminds me of the kind of mixed-bag shows we used to
enjoy in the late sixties and very early seventies, at rooms like
the Boston Tea Party. An evening might open with Louisiana
Man Doug Kershaw and his fiddle, or Tracy Nelson and Mother
Earth. Next, the MC5 or Cat Mother and the All Night News-
boys would come on and rock for awhile. The night could end
with Sha Na Na or Jethro Tull or the Velvet Underground.
The nightly line-ups were all over the place back then.
These days it's usually a bill of three metal bands or three
country bands or three jug bands.
They don't mix it up so much anymore.

Sunday May 2, 1982

I'm back in Cambridge and Blowfish calls me. Boston Rock
wants to publish the interview we did in their upcoming issue.
Do I have a picture of the Project they can run?
We've only played a dozen concerts, I doubt anyone ever
thought to take a photo of us.

Monday May 3, 1982

Rex Smith is the co-host of "Solid Gold" a nationally syndicated
pop music show. Each week the program spotlights a half-dozen

artists who have a hit on the charts. It's not nearly as rocking as Midnight Special or Don Kirshner's Rock Concert used to be. If you're really lucky, maybe John Cougar Mellencamp or Joe Cocker are on, but more likely it's gonna be Sheena Easton and Haircut One Hundred.

Rex wants Brad Whitford to fly out to Hollywood right away and work with him on some sort of record, or new band he's putting together. Apparently there's money involved, so Brad has no choice but to accept the offer.

Whitford tells us he might return someday but for now our show this Friday will be Brad's swan song with the Project.

Tuesday May 4, 1982

A gentleman named Michael Nolette from the Framingham area calls me. He says he's a photographer, and he has some good shots of us at E.M. Loews from a couple weeks ago.
I arrange to meet him at his place.

Wednesday May 5, 1982

Hanging around Julia's apartment. Even though the outside of the building is beat-up, she has done a really nice job painting and decorating the inside. Julia used to work for interior designers in London before she moved here in 1978.

Her father is American, her mother is British, and Julia was born in Toronto where her father was working for Time magazine. She was raised in London. They lived in Alexander Square, not far from the Kings Road. Julia attended Queen's Gate in South Kensington. During netball practice on the athletic grounds, teenager Julia would listen to The Yardbirds, as they rehearsed in the nearby field house.

Queen's Gate boasted lots of famous names like Camilla Parker Bowles and Vanessa Redgrave - but the name I'm most

interested in (beside Julia's) was her classmate Twinkle. Twink
was a pink-leather clad, bubble-car driving pop star who sang on
bills with the Rolling Stones and with loads of other British
Invasion stars during 1965-66. At age 16, Twinkle had a UK Top
5 hit with "Terry" one of those my-boyfriend-got-killed-in-a-
car-wreck numbers that were trending back then.
Guitarist on the track was Jimmy Page.
Julia moved to the States around the same time Thundertrain
was signing a management deal with Allan Kaufman. AK was
managing and doing sound for Cap'n Swing, who later
became The Cars. AK roomed with Elliot Easton back then.
With the success of The Cars, Allan decided to open a music
management company, signing soul man Bill Bellamy, Revere
Beach rock trio Sass and my high-energy band Thundertrain.
Years earlier, my mentor Earthquake Morton had been a roommate of Julia's brother, William. So when Julia arrived from
London she called on the only person she knew here,
Earthquake. At the Webb, Earthie's home in Lexington, Julia
was given a tour of the Jelly Records office. On the wall hung a
poster for the Thundertrain album *Teenage Suicide.*
That was the first time Julia ever saw my face, on a poster,
posing with menace along with the other Thundertrain guys,
hawking our debut record.
Julia found work briefly with none other than Tim Collins.
She also took an unexpected job at AKtive Management where
Earthquake was working at the time. When the regular secretary
called-in sick once too often, Earthquake called on his friend
Julia to takeover the position.
Just a few hours after Julia started her new job, I arrived at the
AKtive office. I was taken aback to find a British beauty
working at the reception desk of my manager's office. I turned
on my heel and rushed back down the elevator to a flower stand
on the corner of Milk and Congress. I only had $3 on me, but it
was enough to buy her a humble bouquet.

Our national tour begins next week, but it sounds like the first two dates in Philadelphia and Harrisburg PA have already been cancelled.

Thursday May 6, 1982

I go out to meet Michael Nolette. His photos are fantastic. Nolette shows me several black & white prints. Some are blown up really large, over a foot across. It's the first time I've seen what the Project looks like with me in it. I'm impressed by the quality of these photos. My father is a good photographer, he always had a darkroom in our house, so I know what to look for. I wish I could whip out some cash and pay Michael what these are worth. I wish I could tell him that Tim Collins will be happy to buy these excellent shots. Truth is, I'm flat broke, and who knows what manager Tim might do or say.
I explain to Michael that I'm in a bind financially at the moment. I also tell him about the article in Boston Rock. He kindly gives me a few small b&w prints to take home with me. I promise Michael that I'll try hard to ensure he gets a credit if his photo is published.

Friday May 7, 1982

We meet at the Cambridge Complex at 3:30 p.m. Into the van we pile and Doc whisks us up to Hampton Beach NH. This is another resort town and in a month or two it will be crawling with tourists, bikers, little kids and barely-clad sunbathers. The Hampton Beach Casino is an impressive hall with multiple bars and long tables that each seat sixty or so. The Casino looks down to the boardwalk and out to the Atlantic Ocean. Surrounding it are arcades, souvenir shops and fast food stands. My brother Andy is here to see the show again. So is Kathy, a girl I once dated. I was able to secure her a photographer pass. Kathy used to work at the A.Wherehouse with original

Aerosmith rhythm guitarist, Ray Tabano, filling orders for Aerosmith and Ted Nugent posters, t-shirts and other merchandise.
Jon Butcher Axis was going to open for us tonight but had to cancel. So ace guitarist Johnny A. is doing the honors.
There's been non-stop promotion for this concert, with big ads in the Boston Phoenix, the Real Paper and lots of radio spots.
The Casino is shaking by the time we go on. As the show progresses, I'm watching Brad Whitford from my corner of the stage. That guy is like Gibraltar. I'm trying to imagine what we'll sound like without him in the line up.

Saturday May 8, 1982

The show went well last night.
Sad to say good-bye to Brad though.
I'm starting to understand a big difference between Danny and me, and the rest of this band. I'm not talking about talent or experience, or the fact that those others, including Ronnie, have recorded multiple albums for the biggest label and toured arenas, stadiums and festivals for years.
No, the difference I'm starting to comprehend, is that those guys are all a lot further along in life. They have commitments, responsibilities and debt to deal with.
Ron has been married a couple times, plus he's got a place and a car. Brad has that big glass house out in the country, a wife and all his rock star possessions. Same with Joe Perry - and his mansion looks even bigger than Brad's.
Admiral Perry has an expensive wife and expensive cars, plus he has his first child to provide for.
Hargrove and I are having the time of our lives, laughing it up and enjoying our good fortune. We own nothing. Have zero money, zero credit. No kids, or wives, or cars, or apartments. Not even a dog, or a fish bowl to worry about.
Neither of us has a clue about what it means to pay taxes, have a mortgage, alimony, car payments, a wife or a kid. Hargrove's

only expense is cigarettes - which recently went up 20 cents, to 85 cents a pack. We sure as hell don't know what it must feel like to have generated millions - through concerts, recordings, films, merchandising and publishing - and have it all fade away, just a few years later.

I can't blame Brad Whitford for seeking a green pasture.

Sunday May 9, 1982

From what I gather, we'll be playing a lot more of these big concert clubs and medium-sized theaters with an occasional huge show thrown in.

It's a change from what the Joe Perry Project was doing previously. With Don Law at the helm, the band would be added to a big Nazareth, ZZ Top or Journey arena tour as the opening act. Collins/Barrasso have a whole different strategy for Perry. While arena shows are prestigious, being the opener isn't always so great. You go on early while the crowd is still arriving. And openers don't usually make much money. Go into a concert club that can hold a thousand or more kids as a headliner, and charge around $8 a head, and maybe even do two shows in one day. There's potential to enjoy a much better payday than by opening at the big arena across town.

Plus, you get to call the shots and play longer. With a name as famous as Joe Perry and with the Admiral's loyal fan base, ticket sales don't hinge nearly as much on airplay or even having a current record deal.

Monday May 10, 1982

The office issues us a three week itinerary of shows that begin on the East Coast, head West through Texas and then move up through the Mid-West. That's just the beginning, there'll be a West Coast swing added once the tour gets rolling.

Tuesday May 11, 1982

I'm down at the Rat again. Bidding farewell to all my buddies
and fans. "I'll be gone for two months, maybe longer." Most of
of these kids have been coming to see me play since '76 when
we recorded "Live at the Rat" down here. Everyone is happy for
my success with the Project.
Guys are buying me drinks and girls are sobbing with joy. I
finally leave - and head up to Bunratty's in Allston and go
through the whole routine all over again. What a showoff.

Wednesday May 12, 1982

I pack up my stuff. Three pairs of pants, a few socks, half a
dozen chopped-up t-shirts. A few leather belts and a toothbrush.
I'm already wearing my cowboy boots and my denim jacket.
Grab my new blaster and I'm out the door.
We meet at 5:30 p.m. at the Cambridge Complex.
The Dodge van is roomier now with only four of us.
Ron is in the way-back listening with his headphones and
smacking his drum pad. Joe is riding shotgun. Danny and I are
on the first bench seat, right behind Joe and Doc.
The bench seat behind us is empty.
The first big tour begins.

Thursday May 13, 1982

We drive through the night, ending up in Catonsville, a suburb
of Baltimore MD.
After a good rest we leave the hotel and make the 5 p.m.
soundcheck. No stage-door crowd to meet us.
Before we begin the check, Joe goes out to confer with
soundman Jay and Doc. I stay back in the dressing room,
listening to James Brown on my new Panasonic deck.
When I'm called to the stage, I'm surprised, relieved and

euphoric.

The set-up has been slightly rearranged. Joe Perry's mic stand
has been moved a bit to the side - over in front of his amplifiers.
My mic stand has been moved out of the back corner -
and placed center stage.

We soundcheck a few songs and it's a whole new ballgame,
being bullseye between Joe and Danny, and having Ron's drum
kit right behind me, kicking me in the ass.

Tempering my excitement is the fact that the Project sounds a lot
different without Whitford in the line up. Perry is figuring it out
on the fly, re-phrasing and thickening-up his guitar tones,
making things flow, while keeping everything powerful.

Ronnie and Hargrove are pouring on the musical secret-sauce, to
smooth out the gaps. I'm shaking my tambourine and maracas
for all they're worth.

We finish the soundcheck and decide to move the unstoppable
Train Kept A-Rollin' into the lead off position.

Several hundred show up to hear us play in Maryland.

It's not our best show, and it's not only because of the change in
the line up. Something's up with Joe.

Friday May 14, 1982

The Admiral is slumped in the front seat of the Dodge van. He
hasn't spoken since last night. We're heading into Washington
DC. Danny and I are rubber necking, we spy the Pentagon
building in the distance.

Doc hears an ad and cranks up the radio.

"Tonight. This Friday. At the Wax Museum.
Don't miss - The Joe Perry Project."
Let the Music Do the Talking segues into Sweet Emotion.
"Joe Perry, former lead guitarist of Aerosmith.
Tonight. At the Wax Museum."
The bed track cuts to the riff from Same Old Song and Dance.

"Show begins at 9. The Wax Museum at 4th and East Street.
Indoor parking for over 1000 cars."
The bed goes back to Let the Music Do the Talking.
*"Don't miss Aerosmith's Joe Perry - and the Joe Perry Project.
Tonight Only. At the Wax Museum."*

I've been hearing radio ads just like it everywhere we go. It's a
great way to roll into a new town, I just wish that Aerosmith
didn't have to be such a big part of the promotions.
Joe Perry is relapsing. Right before my eyes. Looking more and
more like he did the first time we met. Like I said before, I have
no idea whether Perry has too much, or not enough stuff in his
system, or maybe he's just exhausted. Whatever it is, he's
shaking again. The color is draining out of him.
The Wax Museum is a cool-looking place, like a little theater.
Unfortunately our soundcheck doesn't sound good. I'm finally
center stage now but I'm nervous that Joe is going to topple
backwards into his speaker cabs. That's how wobbly he looks.
Showtime comes and we push our way through the set.
Opening with Train Kept A-Rollin' which feels somewhat
sturdy. Things are slowly falling apart through Life at a Glance
and Arrogance. I can't put my finger on it. The loss of
Whitford's sonics surely exposes more of the shortcomings in
my vocals. But there's more to it.
It's like Joe is a millisecond off from the rest of the band.
Halfway through Once a Rocker, I'm dancing back to Joe's side
of the stage, getting into the music, when I feel something warm
near my ear. It's wet.
The fans are screaming and pushing up against the stage. They
try to reach up and touch Joe. Halfway through Buzz Buzz I feel
glop moving down my cheek. Reaching up to my face and into
my hair, my fingers feel something sticky.
My hair is all stuck together. What the hell?
I free my hand from the mess and continue singing. A couple
songs later, Joe is soloing on Heartbreak Hotel, this is my

chance to race back to the dressing room and find a mirror.
Dammit. What a mess. Somebody whipped a mouthful of wet
bubble gum into my hair. A massive wad. A few packs at least.
Thanks a lot Washington DC. Now I have pink gum-hair matted
and melted over the whole side of my face and it's only getting
worse. Looks like hell - feels disgusting.
Joe is finishing up his Elvis tune. I have no choice but to go
back out, in the center spotlight, and finish the show.

Saturday May 15, 1982

Last night I got back to the motel covered in sticky sweat.
Really pissed-off that some stranger would do that to me. I find
some scissors and begin hacking off my hair. The bubble gum is
stuck all the way up into my scalp. Chunk after chunk of
blonde/bubblegum plops to the floor. I bitched about it last night
to the guys after the show, but they all have problems of their
own. I don't think things are good on the home-front for Ron or
Joe. This tour has to succeed in order for them to survive.
We're driving further down through Maryland to tonight's
concert on the shore, in Ocean City.
My hair's a wreck and my confidence is blown.
I know I don't sound anything like Steven, Ralph or Charlie. I
know I can't follow Ron's opening cue for East Coast, West
Coast. But did you really have to throw that crap at me? At least
I was trying to look like I fit in. That is, until I just had to chop
all the hair off one-side of my head.
Nobody in this van wants to hear me moan over my lost locks.
They all remember how the kids in Philadelphia used Aerosmith
for target practice. And those were broken glass bottles and
firecrackers the "fans" were hurling, not just chewing gum.
When we finally hit the stage at the Back of the Rack the
Admiral is yellow/green and his eyes are slammed-shut. His
skinny frame is buckling. Ronnie is bound and determined to
make this tour happen. Joe or no Joe. Ron pours all his heart into

his drumming. The Joe Perry Project is almost falling apart at the seams, but Stewart keeps us on track through sheer brute force. His Rockin' Train drum-solo brings down the house.

Sunday May 16, 1982

The Joe Perry Project tour pushes further south into Virginia. I'm resting on one of the benches trying to grow my hair out. Ronnie is in the way-back with his headphones on. He's tapping along to Freeway Jam on his practice pad. "Max Condi. Max Condi." Danny Hargrove is begging Doc to turn-up the air conditioner. Joe is slumped low in his seat. Twitching like a bug. Something is seriously wrong but nobody dares to question him. I sure don't. The van's cassette machine is blasting AC/DC Back in Black as we enter the city of Richmond. The gig tonight is at a nightclub called The Much More. I'm not sure how much more of this Admiral Perry can take. He's going down.

Monday May 17, 1982

Cruising south into North Carolina. The concert last night wasn't very good, unless you were hoping to see just how messed-up Joe is since he quit Aerosmith. The truth is, just a week ago, the Admiral was looking and playing just fine. Nobody would believe that though. Not seeing him today. Tonight the Joe Perry Project is booked in Jacksonville, right next to Camp Lejeune Marine Corps base. Danny and I are on the bench seat, right behind Doc and Joe. Ronnie is in the way-back torturing his drum pad. For Those About to Rock is blaring on the van's cassette deck. Doc calls out: "Look to your left gentlemen. Let's Keep America Beautiful."

Over in the highway mcdian we see a group of orange-suited guys. Bent over at the waist, picking through the weeds for bits of trash. Rifle-toting guards are stationed fore and aft. As we get closer we see the shackles on the workers' ankles.

Dang, it's a real chain gang.

Down the road apiece, we see another gang working under the blazing sun.

That's when, out of the corner of my eye, I see Joe Perry rise up out of his seat. But not in a normal way.

Rising like something from *The Exorcist*.

His body goes rigid, straight as a rod. His head, almost touching the ceiling of the van, turns eerily towards Doc. The Admiral's eyes are open - but his pupils are rolling back. The veins in his face and neck are bulging. He's frozen. No - now he's going into spasms. What the hell is going on?

Doc yanks on the steering wheel and the van swerves, cutting off traffic, bouncing onto the shoulder of the highway as Joe jerks violently in his seat.

I feel something behind me.

It's Ronnie Stewart, swooping forward, diving over the two bench seats that separate him from Perry.

The Dodge rumbles and shakes to a halt, plowing into the gravel as Ron lands on the front console and jams his wallet into Perry's open mouth. "Bite down." barks Ron.

Joe is totally out of control, having a seizure.

Doc leaps out, runs, and grabs some towels and water from the back of the van.

He applies a wet compress to Joe's throbbing forehead.

"Take it easy boss. Everything's gonna be alright," assures the road manager.

Hargrove and I are petrified.

The Admiral's muscles finally relax and he manages to fall back into his seat. He hasn't swallowed his tongue - due to Ron's fast thinking. After seeing Stewart's quick response, I have to think to myself "has Ronnie been through this with Joe before?"

Doc gets us back on the road and somewhere near Greenville we
stop at a roadside medical place.

Not a hospital, just one of those little clinic places.

The band kicks around in the dusty parking lot while Joe gets
checked out. After an hour they let him go.

Apparently the medics ran the normal checks and found nothing
obviously wrong. Did the Admiral fess up and tell the staff his
full history of narcotic and alcohol use? Or give them a list of
the substances that he is currently still consuming or
suddenly not consuming? You be the judge.

Joe seems steadier though. I mean, he still looks really bad but
maybe he can make it through the concert tonight.

What choice do we have?

We're at the venue, the Chateau Madrid. Not really much of a
chateau, back in Holliston we'd call it a big tin shack. Even
though it's a Monday, the place is packed rock-solid with, you
guessed it, the United States Marines.

The ceiling is low and it's really hot in here. Woody has the
lights set up like a ring of fire surrounding the compact stage.

Ride of the Valkyries gets a gung-ho ovation. Servicemen and
women go wild when Perry marches out on stage and unleashes
his *Apocalypse Now* helicopter attack.

We plow into Train Kept A-Rollin' and the U.S. Marines are on
our side. We buzz through Buzz Buzz and Once a Rocker and as
the Admiral begins the fourth song of the night…

…Hell breaks loose.

Joe Perry suddenly freezes solid. He crashes down - flat on his
back in the spotlight. His Travis Bean guitar falls on top of him.
He's hard as a rock, then he's suddenly flopping around, blood
vessels popping-out of his gray-hued skin. Same horror show as
earlier today, except now he's lit-up on center stage with scads
of military people staring in disbelief and concern.

Ronnie Stewart leaps off his drum throne, vaults over the
massive drum kit, lands beside the Admiral, and once again

administers the wallet. Woody cuts the stage lights.
The Chateau Madrid is a total blackout.
Servicemen and women are stomping and shouting out Joe's
name. It's a confused scene to say the least.
By the time the house lights come up, our soundman Jay has
hustled Danny, Ron and me off the battleground, and back into
the dressing room.
Our sly road manager, Doc, is already yelling at the confused
club manager. Accusing him. Telling him it's all his fault that
Joe Perry nearly got electrocuted by the nightclub's faulty
wiring. Doc threatens the guy and makes him pay our guarantee,
while assuring him that we'll swing back around to do a
make-up date. Cash in hand, Doc hails a cab. He and our
still-reeling leader hightail it out of there.
Upset and crestfallen, I stuff my belongings back into my gig
bag. The crowd is streaming out of the Chateau Madrid,
wondering what the heck just went down. Before Jay hustles me
out to the van, I notice something. Down behind a chair in the
dressing room. Left behind, on the
floor in a dark corner. Joe's beautiful
ivory colored leather jacket. I fold it
carefully and put it in my bag.

Hero Ron Stewart. He sprang into
action when the Admiral lost it down
in North Carolina.

Danny, Brad, Joe, Mach and Ron on drums.
Worcester MA 4/10/83   Michael R. Nolette Photograph

Long Island NY 4/23/82 Brad, Ron, Joe and Mach

II
ADRIANNA

Tuesday May 18, 1982

I'm asleep in a motel in Jacksonville.
At this very moment, Doc and Joe Perry are jetting out of North
Carolina bound for Logan Airport in Boston.
Woody and Ed have already packed up the Ryder truck with all
our gear. Trucking back home.
Jay finally comes around and rouses the rest of us. Late check
out and we're in no hurry now. Tomorrow's gig at the Agora in
Cleveland has been canceled. We sullenly toss our bags into the
back of the van. I can see that Ron is pissed. Mr. Stewart isn't a
partier. He doesn't drink or get high. He's serious about the
music and he needed this tour to go well - and get done.
It's gonna be a long ride home.

Wednesday May 19, 1982

Rolling up through New Jersey and on up into New England.
I finally reach the pink palace at 11 p.m.
Julia is surprised to see me.
"Didn't you guys just leave to do a two month tour?"

Thursday May 20, 1982

We were supposed to be in Toledo Ohio right now.
The new issue of Boston Rock came out today.
"Mach Bell Joins Joe Perry" reads the headline.
"I've been with Joe Perry for 66 days, Mach relates,
and he's had on 66 different pairs of leather pants.
To get up for a gig, Joe spends twenty minutes listening to
The Sex Pistols' Never Mind the Bollocks very loud."
The Blowfish article includes a nice shot of the Admiral and me.
The photo credit reads Michael R. Nolette.

Friday May 21, 1982

The office calls. Tim tells me that Joe is feeling a little better but
some changes have to be made.
"Be patient." Tim also mentions the Boston Rock article.
"Joe really liked the things you said. Great interview, Cowboy."

Saturday May 22, 1982

The bill collectors keep calling me here. The Project was
supposed to be in San Antonio right now.

Sunday May 23, 1982

Charlie Farren and David Hull have started up a band called The
Enemy. They're headlining all over the place, including some
venues we (used to) play like Uncle Sam's and the Hampton
Beach Casino. I wonder what Ronnie is thinking.
I'm pretty sure Stewart could've joined his former bandmates
when they split from the Project. He would have been part of
their functioning, presumably money-making band.

Monday May 24, 1982

I'm laying low in Cambridge. One good thing about the
Admiral's awful collapse is that it happened in Jacksonville NC,
which is basically Pluto, as far as people up here are concerned.
Nobody ever brings a camera to a club gig. Obviously no film
crews were there. The JPP tour certainly wasn't being covered
by Rolling Stone, Joe Perry is off the radar as far as the music
press is concerned. I'm sure there is zero record of what
happened way down there in North Carolina. That's why most
of my friends still think I'm out in the Mid-West right now.
Kicking butt, on tour with the Project.
I have an earlier itinerary, sent out by the office, that had the JPP
opening for Black Sabbath on that same 5/17 date at Madison
Square Garden.

If Joe had gone into spasms and collapsed in NYC in front of a sellout crowd at the Garden we'd be way worse off.

Tuesday May 25, 1982

Danny comes over. We walk to nearby Inman Square where a little bric-a-brac shop sells bottles of awful tasting wine with expired dates for 99 cents each.
We attempt to drink our blues away.

Wednesday May 26, 1982

We were supposed to be in Detroit tonight.
As for Joe's recent sickness, the rumor going around is that Elyssa wasn't happy about Joe going out on the long road trip without her. In order to get her way, Elyssa went into Joe's bag just before he left town and removed a bottle of medication or drug he was taking. She knew that Joe's health would suffer immediately without the stuff. Then Joe would have to fly her and the meds to wherever he was.
Just a rumor - but no crazier than a lot of the other wacky Elyssa stories I've heard over the years.

Thursday May 27, 1982

Had to go to the Holliston Savings Bank, where I just opened an account a few weeks ago, to withdraw $300.
I'm no longer rich.

Friday May 28, 1982

I go out to the office today and meet with Tim Collins.
I nervously tell him about the bill collectors who are harassing me and causing me a lot of anxiety. Tim listens carefully.
He admits to me that his office has been getting calls from people Thundertrain still owes money to as well.

Ray Thomas, who repaired our blown speakers every month and
Frank Borsa, a kindly booking agent who fronted us money to
purchase some PA equipment.

Now that I'm singing with superstar Joe Perry, everyone
assumes I'm riding the gravy train and lighting my Cuban cigars
with hundred dollar bills.

Tim pulls out a calculator and figures the total of my personal
debt, plus my old band's debt, at somewhere around two grand.
I'm embarrassed to have tallied up such a number but Collins
practically waves it off.

"Listen, Mach, just leave the phone numbers of the collectors
with my secretary. I'll work out a deal with them. You won't be
getting any more calls. Just keep your mind on the music."

Saturday May 29, 1982

I feel a huge weight off my shoulders after talking to Tim
yesterday. What an understanding guy.
I should have gone to him with my problem sooner.

Sunday May 30, 1982

I venture out of the apartment today and head up to
Tyngsborough. There's an outdoor rock festival and the
headliner is the David Johansen Group.
David, the band, and his drummer Frankie LaRocka, are all
great as usual. Wish it was me playing up on that stage.
Joe Perry Project were slated for Greenville PA tonight.

Monday May 31, 1982

Tim calls and asks me to be at the office at 8 p.m.
Somebody wants to see me.
I arrive. It's the Admiral. He steps my way and gives me a hug.
Perry looks a hell of a lot better than he did the last time I saw
him two weeks ago.
Lying flat on his back and struggling for breath.
Tim asks us both to take a seat.

"Joe's making a lot of progress, but there's more work to do."
Joe glances my way as Tim continues.
"Tomorrow morning, we're going to be checking Joe into the
Lodge." I'm not sure what that means.
"He'll be able to get some real rest. It's not easy at home. The
staff over there is great." I nod my head.
"Where is the Lodge?"
"Oh, not far, it's right over in Westwood."

Tuesday June 1, 1982

So I guess Joe is getting checked into that place right now.
I wonder how long he has to stay there?

Wednesday June 2, 1982

Morning is here and the pink palace phone is ringing.
"Hi Mach, how are you?"
I'm trying to recognize the voice…
"Great…uh…what about you?"
"So, I was wondering if you'd like to come with me, and visit
Joe today?" Oh. It's Elyssa.
"Yeah, okay…I mean…is it okay for Joe to have visitors?"
"I'm his wife. Of course it's all right. But do you think you
could pick me up?" Oh that's right, Elyssa doesn't drive.
 "Ummm, yeah. Sure, I guess."
"Thanks, Mach. Around twelve-thirty?"
"Okay Elyssa, see ya."

Ninety minutes later I'm out in front of the Admiral's villa in
Julia's little white GLC. Joe's black Bentley is still parked where
I saw it last. Don't see the Porsche. I walk up to the carved
wooden door and bang the brass knocker a couple times.
Fidgeting around, waiting, feels like I'm on a damn date or
something.

Elyssa flusters out the door. Talking a mile a minute, flailing her little wrists and tiny hands around. She's saying something nasty about Tim Collins but now she's complaining about the maid or the baby-sitter, I'm not sure which.

She seems to have a beef with everyone. In some strange way I find her ranting rather amusing. We make our way down the walk and I open the car door for her. Little Elyssa is about the size of a violin, she weightlessly plops into the front passenger seat as her non-stop yammering and empty threats against everyone, and everything, continue.

I zig down towards Route 9 West, and zag onto 128 South, which brings us to Route 109 West. Elyssa is terribly upset about everybody, and since Joe hasn't been around for a day, I guess she has to unload all her neuroses on me.

She's a funny little bird.

I tool down a country road through Westwood, I doubt Elyssa has a clue or care about which way I'm driving.

We enter a wooded area. It's peaceful and I see cabin-like structures scattered around. I park the car and open the door for Mrs. Perry. She's on better behavior now. Nobody wants to be detected as a nutcase in a place like this. We walk towards a bigger looking building.

Elyssa is alluring, wearing leather boots, fitted jeans and a silk blouse wrapped tightly around her tiny waist. Expensive handbag, gold bracelets jangling on both wrists. She's a very fragile and high-strung looking poppet. She and Joe must be the two most vulnerable looking earthlings I've ever met.

But while Joe is instantly lovable, I'm not exactly sure about Mrs. Perry. We walk inside to a reception area where Elyssa suddenly dials-up her charm.

"Appointment? No. But we've come all this way. Oh, please - can't I please see my husband just for a minute or two? It would mean everything to me. Oh, thank you, thank you so much."

We're escorted down a nature trail through a grove of pines to a long, low building. We wait in the front room and a minute later, our guide emerges with the Admiral in tow.

Joe seems a little taken aback to see Elyssa here already.

He gives her a little hug and rolls his eyes at me. Joe is dressed
more like a civilian than I've ever seen him before.
Regular blue jeans and a white Fruit of the Loom t-shirt. And
he's barefoot. Joe shoots me another look that says "Don't say it,
Cowboy, I already know that Elyssa conned you into this."
We only stay for about fifteen minutes. Joe is definitely looking
better and speaking the clearest I've heard. His eyes are
focused. I'm hopeful that the Project can get back to rocking
really soon.

Thursday June 3, 1982

Tim calls me at home. He heard about the visit Elyssa and I paid
to Joe yesterday. Collins doesn't go so far as telling me it was
wrong, he simply advises me,
"Watch out for Elyssa."

Friday June 4, 1982

Once again, Elyssa calls me at the pink palace.
In a cute voice she begs me to drive her out to the Lodge again.
"Please, Mach. You're the only person I can trust."
She's a hard girl to turn down.
 I'm starting to get an idea of how difficult it must be for the
Admiral to say no to her.

Saturday June 5 - Friday June 11, 1982

This week seemed to take a month. Every few days, Elyssa
convinces me to drive her back out to Westwood again. She's
starting to calm down a bit and during our rides we've begun to
get into some good conversations.
It's obvious from observing her that Elyssa is battling a lot of
the same bad habits as her husband. But they're both wicked
smart people, with good senses of humor, and a wealth of
remarkable shared experience.
Elyssa is much easier to engage in conversation than Joe.

It takes a pry bar to get a word out of the Admiral, but you'd
probably have to beat Elyssa over the head with a pry bar to get
her to shut up.
Finally, on Friday I get a call from Tim at the office.
"Can I ask you a favor, Mach?
They're releasing Joe tomorrow morning. The Admiral said he'd
like it if you would pick him up."

Saturday June 12, 1982

It's 8 a.m. and I'm waiting out in front of Joe's cabin in
Westwood. Not a minute later, Perry comes bounding out,
holding a little gym bag.
"All set, Joe?"
"Yeah, Cowboy. I graduated."
"Cool man. We all knew you could do it."
We stride up the nature path towards the parking lot.
I reach into the back seat.
"Here Joe, I got you something."
"No way. Where'd you find this?"
"Lying in the corner. Down in North Carolina."
Joe slips into his leather jacket, we hop into Julia's GLC
and race away from the Lodge.

Sunday June 13, 1982

Joe was relieved to get sprung and go home yesterday.
I don't blame him, I bet he missed his son a lot.
Elyssa isn't as bad as I'd heard. I kinda like her.

Monday June 14, 1982

"So what's going on with Steven Silva?"
"Steven? I'm not sure Tim.
Last I heard he was working in a cover band."
"Well what do you think about him joining the Project?"
"Steven?"
"I've been kicking it around with Joe.

He's used to having a second guitar.
Charlie played guitar you know."
"That's true."
"So you don't have a problem working with Steven?"
"No. Of course not. I guess it wouldn't hurt to ask him."

Tuesday June 15, 1982

Joe and Tim tell me that the office is busy booking dates.
They're even looking at an offer to bring us down to South
America for a couple of shows.

Wednesday June 16, 1982

Steven Silva is going to audition with us this Saturday.
I admit I'm a little worried about it.
I've developed a very close friendship with Danny Hargrove and
I'm starting to feel one beginning with the Admiral.
Steven can be a tough guy to be friends with.
In some ways he's a bit like Ronnie. Steven is private. He
spends a lot of time working out his guitar parts and reading
literature. He's not a mega party animal like Hargrove and me.
Steven's not a druggie like Joe. Silva likes to write songs but he
doesn't write well with others. I don't see him collaborating on
tunes the way the Project did so magically back in March.
I'm also not sure that Steven, who's been pulling down weekly
money with his popular cover band, is going to be overjoyed
about the lack of dough around here.
Not wanting to spoil the illusion of my overnight success, I have
kept it a total secret that paydays are a hit or miss situation on
this Pirate Ship.
Danny and I haven't seen a nickel since the tour went off the
rails a month ago.

Thursday June 17, 1982

Joe Perry calls me at the pink palace. He wants me to come out
to his house at 1 p.m. tomorrow.

Tonight my father, Bill Bell, meets me in Boston at a seafood restaurant. His summer vacation begins tomorrow and as usual he'll be sailing the Kialoa over to Provincetown, and then out to Monhegan Island, and finally up to Downeast Maine where my parents have their summer place on the coast.

We enjoy conversation, laughs and a delicious dinner together.

Friday June 18, 1982

I get to Joe's mansion in Newton at 1 p.m.

The Admiral greets me at the door and this time he invites me inside. This place is like a set for a movie about a rock star.

I wander down the imposing entrance hall, at the far end I see a suit of shining armor, standing at attention.

The adjoining drawing room has a massive stone fireplace. Persian rugs, antique tables and ornate lamps abound. The room is two stories high. On the second level, a carved wooden balcony wraps around most of the space.

A lot to look at. I peek out the windows to the back garden area, glance around at all the upholstered furniture, and then up to the regal mantelpiece, where I'm surprised to see these cool, colorful large-scale models of my favorite Toho film stars, Godzilla, Rodan and Mothra.

"From when I toured Japan," offers Joe.

"They gave us so much stuff over there. I have swords and robes and electronics - you wouldn't believe all the stuff."

Elyssa enters the room holding her child, she smiles and welcomes me. I'm unhappy to see that she doesn't look as good as last week. Washed-out, generally unhealthy-looking.

"You guys want some apple juice?"

"Sure" replies Joe.

Elyssa disappears.

Joe turns to me and says,

"When I started the Project, she told me I should hire
 Robert Plant to sing."

"Plant? Really?...he's pretty good." I calmly reply.

Joe and I look at each other and shrug our shoulders.

"I have this idea," murmurs Joe as he gets up.

I follow the Admiral out past a grand staircase. Beside it, I see a bench strewn with cables, mics, guitar picks and foot pedals.
In the middle of the mess is a portable multi-track tape recorder, one of those 4-track cassette models.
I follow Joe down a passage to a kind of glass room.
I guess you'd call it a conservatory.
"So this is all I got, Cowboy."
"Okay…"
"Take a walk with me Sally."
I gaze downward. Thinking for a moment.
"Take a walk with me Sally?"
"Yeah. It means something. I heard it in a dream."
I pull out my pad and jot down "Take a Walk with Me Sally."
Elyssa enters with apple juice in expensive looking little round bottles. Apple leaves are embossed in the glass.
Tastes pretty good.

Saturday June 19, 1982

Tim Collins has booked the rehearsal room for us again at the Annex. For the next two weeks the Project will prep for concert dates the office already has lined-up for us, with more offers coming in daily. Thankfully, Joe's meltdown in North Carolina got swept under the rug. Nobody in the business knows about it. How could people know? Unless someone bought a full page newspaper ad to blab about it.
Today at 1 p.m. my colleague Steven Silva is already tuning-up as I arrive at our Annex rehearsal room.
I greet Steven, moderately, I don't want to jinx him.
It's great seeing the JPP crew all back together again for the first time in over a month.
Once everybody gets their sound figured out, we blast off. Steven has obviously done his homework.
He's playing well as we groove through the set.
Even more apparent is the way Perry is performing today.
Not like I've heard him before in this group.
There is strength, force and focus.

This is how I imagine Joe Perry sounded when he founded his Project. The Admiral didn't need a second guitar when he started this band.

Sunday June 20, 1982

Steven phones me. We talk for a while and I assure him that his guitar playing couldn't have sounded better yesterday.

Monday June 21, 1982

Tim and Joe Perry have business and the band gets the day off.

Tuesday June 22, 1982

Today is Julia Day.
But first, I go to rehearsal at 1 p.m.
Steven got a call-back and we review the whole set.
I'm watching, listening to Joe play - and sensing something big is happening. After rehearsal, I meet Julia in Boston and we celebrate her birthday.

Wednesday June 23, 1982

We're back at the Annex. Just the four of us this time.
Joe has regained his health and his clarity. His guitar playing is on edge. The mist has risen. We torpedo through the song list with new muscle and energy. Then I sing my latest lyric, titled by Joe's dream, and loosely inspired by events of the past few months.

Telephone is ringing / Someone's pounding on the door
Gimme half a chance / To get up off the floor
Grab my Stratocaster and I put it in my case
Headin' out the back / when I meet her face-to-face
Take a walk with me Sally
And tell me girl, What's on your mind?

The band backs up my urgent vocal with a traditional 1, 4, 5 progression in a Little Richard, Chuck Berry-style.
The song Walk With Me Sally is born in an instant.

Thursday June 24, 1982

Joe wants to sing. I'm always up for singing.
Perry invites me back to his villa today at 1 p.m. for some singing. He has his mini recording studio set up, and we both work on blending our vocals.
I'm not sure if anything got recorded but we both have a really good time. Singing together is always a good thing.

Friday June 25, 1982

We're at the Annex again but Ron Stewart gets the day off.
Joe, Danny Hargrove and I are concentrating on more singing today. We work on the vocal parts of Rockin' Train, Arrogance, Life at a Glance, Let the Music Do the Talking and everything else we know.
I really appreciate this. We're finally hearing each other. I'm singing more like I did on the studio demo where I didn't have to compete against the din.
This work is gonna pay off for sure.

Saturday/Sunday June 26/27, 1982

The way the Project is sounding, and rebounding, I figure this might be the last wide-open summer weekend we'll get for awhile. Julia and I slip away for a 48 hour vacation.

Monday June 28, 1982

Back to rocking at the Cambridge Annex.
The crew is buzzing about returning to work this weekend.
I think our drummer's marriage is on the rocks.

Tuesday June 29, 1982

Tim calls and asks me to bring my birth certificate to the office. They need to get a passport for me.
We're back at the Annex rehearsing - when long-lost Brad Whitford comes strolling in. Back from the West Coast but only for a second. We're glad to see him and he hangs around for awhile. Brad is happy to see and hear the Admiral back on top.

Wednesday June 30, 1982

The office secretary calls me at the palace.
"Tim wants to know if you have a list of your fans' addresses."
"What?"
"He wants to know if you have a list of everyone who likes you, with all their names and addresses." That's a crazy request, but Mr. Collins is in luck, because I actually do have such a list, scrawled out over many matchbook, setlist and notebook pages. Nearly a thousand Thundertrain and Mag 4 fans, complete with their names and addresses.
"Great, Mach. Can you bring all that information to the office please?"

Thursday July 1, 1982

The Joe Perry Project rehearses our set at the Cambridge Complex Annex today at 1 p.m.
We've moved Toys in the Attic back into the opening position.
Joe has convinced me to try singing The Wanderer -
The old Dion and the Belmonts hit.
It's the one about a guy who roams from town to town and never settles down. He's got one girl on his left and another one on his right and he has still another girl that he'll be with tonight. When asked which one he likes the best, our hero reveals the name of yet another girl, tattooed boldly across his chest.
It's a funny, rocking song and our version isn't bad. For some reason Joe must think I'm some kind of a playboy.

Friday July 2, 1982

One more good rehearsal before we rock'n'roll for the masses.
Mercifully, East Coast, West Coast is out of the rotation for now.
That song would be a killer - if not for my problem
understanding Ron's drum opening. Wish we could just play it
like they did on the Project record. Oh well.

Saturday July 3, 1982

My long wait is almost over.
We're finally going back to work tomorrow.
I'm daydreaming. Recalling a day in early 1971.
I was eighteen. Hanging around a little guitar store that had
recently opened behind the Holliston pharmacy.
Music'n'Things. A nice guy named Danny ran it. A teenager
from Sweden, named Pia, worked behind the counter. I was
hanging around, flirting with the counter girl, when I noticed
this weird looking poster.
It was taped to the back of the shop's front door.
This Monday at Lakeview Ballroom
The Joneses'
Aerosmith
$2
It was the worst looking poster I ever saw. Drawn with a colored
pencil, or maybe a crayon. The penmanship was poor. Still, I
was excited to see that The Joneses' would be playing up Route
16 in Mendon that Monday. And I had $2.
Never heard of that opening band though.
What does it say? Aerosmith? I bet they aren't as good as my
band, Joe Flash.
We should've got that gig. Approaching the ballroom on
Monday night, I could see the converted school bus, the one The
Joneses' always traveled in. The D'Angelo brothers were the
stars of the band and their dad, a former Worcester postal
worker, drove their bus.

Over by the stage door, I spied an MGB roadster (British racing green) parked beside a beat-up delivery truck. Painted on the side of the panel truck was an R. Crumb-type character.

A bald guy, doing the keep-on-truckin' pose. But he was truckin' the wrong way, facing backwards instead of forward. That's the opening band? Must be hippies.

Along with my sister Cathy, and a couple of her girlfriends, we line-up with a bunch of other local teens, eager to pay our two bucks and get inside.

Entering the ballroom, I see a pretty good crowd assembled. The room is low and long, shaped kind of like a bowling alley. There are folding tables with chairs arranged along both sides of the wooden dance floor.

My sister and her friends push their way up to the front for a good seat. As I near the wide stage, I'm transfixed by the weird assortment of gear that has been jig-sawed together, creating a wall that stretches across the entire stage.

Behind the ragged-wall I can see the tops of The Joneses' matching Marshall stacks. But there is nothing matching about this opening act Aerosmith's mish-mash. A Fender bandmaster is heaved on top of a Sound City cab - next to an Ampeg amp beside a Dual Showman cabinet - that rests on a Marshall amp beside a Sunn speaker box. In between all this well-worn gear is a nice five-piece drum set, I think it's a Ludwig, sitting on a slightly raised platform. As I'm taking all this in, I can't help but notice a very odd looking guy, wearing short-shorts, strolling briskly up the center aisle, past the crowd and towards the side stage doorway. His face is...different.

Never saw a guy who looked like that before.

What's up with his lips?

The room fills up and somebody behind me starts whacking an empty ashtray on his table. Rhythmically. Others join in. Feet begin stomping in time to the ashtray beat. What's going on?

Is this bedlam being orchestrated by someone?

Everyone seems pretty anxious to see this unknown band.

Whoosh. Here it comes. A drummer appears and immediately begins playing a funk beat as a tall blonde bass player enters, plugs in, and lays down a Live at the Apollo-type groove. Is that a Mosrite bass? A guitar player with long, straight brown hair and a beaded choker around his neck begins chirping a loud but soulful rhythm on his Gibson ES.

Then, over to the right, this fukken rock star character appears. His head is lowered and his face is obscured by a thick mane of shiny black locks, I think I see a streak of color in there too. He's got a white peasant shirt tucked into black jeans with a row of silver studs running up the length of the outer seams. He plugs a gold top Les Paul guitar into that crazy jigsaw amp-line. Planting his feet, and arching back, he releases a tornado of ferocious licks interspersed with thick, meaty power chords. He raises his head for a moment to glower at the rest of the band. The sound tightens-up as that strange lad, the one I saw earlier, catapults out to center stage.

Now he's sporting a three button hand-me-down jacket and banging on a cowbell. The short-shorts are gone - but those big lips are still stuck to his face.

Hopping onto the drum riser, I see he's got regulation tight trousers with flat-bottomed shoes. A silk scarf is draped around his neck. He spins 'round, throttles the mic stand, and squeals something about "popcorn" into his SM58.

The audience is up and grooving along with the intense jam. Suddenly it stops - turns on a dime - and bashes into the heavy opening chords of Led Zep's Good Times, Bad Times.

Heavy and in the pocket. Just before the vocal should begin - they segue again - into the opening riff of Route 66.

Do these guys only play instrumentals?

No. The singer's voice is amazing. He's taking Route 66 to cities it's never been to before.

I'm gob-smacked, they play it better than the Stones.

Speaking of the Stones, next we get a couple of Stones covers, Honky Tonk Women and Live with Me. Both are remarkable. Then they pound-out a fantastic rendition of Peter Green's Rattlesnake Shake. I'm in awe, because I love going to see Peter and his Fleetwood Mac at the Tea Party, but I have to admit, these local guys play it just as well - and even heavier. Not to mention these guys, especially Mr. Lips and Rock Star over there, with his gold top Les Paul - have sex appeal and showmanship that far exceeds Mr. Green and Co.

The bomb is dropped when Rock Star scratches out the most basic rock riff on earth - but turns it on its head - exploding into this original tune they call "Somebody."

My jaw is hanging wide-open, this original song stands up to those Fleetwood Mac and Rolling Stones classics they just finished playing. Damn, it's even better.

"Somebody" is instantly memorable. I'm singing along in my head, watching this front-guy absolutely rip up the stage.

Rock Star sneers, leans back and launches into a guitar break which is immediately unforgettable. Now the two of them are leaning into each other, Lips is harmonizing with Rock Star's lead guitar melody. The crowd is mesmerized. I'm sold on this new band Aerosmith.

Incredibly, it only gets better the more they play. The lead guitarist remains stone-faced and serious, while the singer swaggers and loons around like a circus chimp. Lips toots on a wooden flute that hangs from his belt, he shakes his butt at the giggling girls.

Aerosmith has a second original song for us.

This one is called Mama Kin.

Hearing that powerful riff for the first time - I can't wait to try playing it on my Firebird. Cathy and her friends nearly faint when Lips sings *"I won't be choosy / you can send me a floozy."*

One of the greatest rock performances I've ever seen. Following a roaring Train Kept A-Rollin' the band makes a quick exit - while the Lakeview crowd goes absolutely nuts. I'm reeling from what I just saw. I've seen some big acts but I never related to them like I just did to this band. Led Zeppelin, Foghat, Fleetwood Mac - those guys are all from somewhere far away. I could never be anything like them.

But these guys, at least some of them, must be local. And they're just as good as Savoy Brown or the The Faces. Better even. A door swings opens up inside my brain. I'm seeing a whole new level of what might actually be possible for a local boy. Later, as we drive back down Route 16 to Holliston, we're all buzzing about Aerosmith. Cathy sums it up

"They're the best British band to ever come out of Mendon."

Sunday July 4, 1982

"Good to see you again cousin."
"I'm not your cousin."
"Calm down hommes."
"I am calm. And I'm still not your cousin."

Doc and Danny Hargrove are back to their usual schtick.
Joe rides shotgun and Ron is in the way-back hammering on his
drum pad, his headphones protect him from the comedy routines
that go on up front. The brown Dodge van is rolling north, up
Route 95. Headed toward Topsham, a medium-sized town on the
coast of Maine, north of Portland.
Tom Kalil is the promoter of this outdoor festival. He's been
keeping busy, the David Johansen show I attended the other day
was Tom's as well. We reach the festival grounds and Doc drives
the van slowly through throngs of kids. I can see the stage area,
built against a hillside. There's a tour bus parked beside the
stage and a few other vans parked between the stage and a
facilities building.
The headliner today is Joan Jett and the Blackhearts.
I haven't seen Joan since Thundertrain opened for her underage
band, The Runaways, down at the Rat. That was a memorable
night, with a star-studded audience. In the crowd was Iggy Pop,
who had just played over in Harvard Square earlier that evening.
Iggy brought along his producer/keyboard player David Bowie
to check out our show.
Following the spectacle, we all drank White Russians and ate
Chinese take-out food up in Jim Harold's upstairs office.
During the party, I was seated right between Runaway Jackie
Fox and a very reserved, but smiling, David Bowie. Bowie was
dressed-down that evening, sporting a simple flannel shirt.
That was five years ago. Meanwhile, Joan Jett continues to do
really well for herself. I Love Rock'n'Roll, a cover song she
recorded with the Blackhearts, went to number one on Billboard
and remained there during the time I was auditioning and rehearsing with Joe Perry. Jett topped the charts for seven weeks.

I have to admit, I was thinking about I Love Rock'n'Roll while I
was penning the lyrics to our Once a Rocker.

I 'm not familiar with today's opening band. Some guys from
Long Island. The Stray Cats.
Apparently the festival crowd isn't familiar with these Stray
Cats either. There are only three of them. A skinny singer/guitar
player with cuffed jeans and hair piled-up in a pompadour.
Looks like something from twenty-five years ago.
The skinny drummer plays standing up. He's got a snare drum
and a crash cymbal. That's about it. The skinny bassman is
rocking one of those doghouse double-basses, like they use in
the symphony orchestra.
Not much chance these three weirdos will be any good.
"We want Joe fukken Perry" brays a drunk in the front row as he
flings his empty beer can at the Stray Cat singer.
The Cats waste no time and dive right into their act. I'm trying
to make sense of it. The guitarist is actually pretty good. He's
playing this big jazz-box style axe.
More beer cans are whizzing up at the stage while the trio
launch into something called Stray Cat Strut. It's not so horrible.
But the crowd begs to differ.
"Here's another one off our brand new album," pleads the singer
as he dodges a plastic bottle.
"Get off the stage. *Now*." bellows a fan.
The skinny trio decide to cut their set short after a final upbeat
number called Rock This Town. That last song inspires the
rowdy crowd to spray beer and more debris all over the stage.
Cans and bottles rain down as the unknown, unwanted Stray
Cats beat a hasty retreat. Poor skinny guys.
We're up next. Have mercy.

Joe Perry is met with sustained cheers as he takes over the stage.
Slamming into Toys in the Attic, I feel like I'm floating on air.
The Project is firing on twelve-cylinders and the Admiral is
charging to the front of the stage with authority. The audience is
calling up to him, and he's shouting back at them - before

rocketing back to the amp-line, riffing solidly all the way. Perry is totally in the drivers seat, leading his Project into battle. Danny, Joe and I have new control and cohesiveness in our vocal parts too, I'm suddenly feeling a lot more secure on the mic. In the six weeks since we last appeared in public I've even managed to grow a little bit of my hair back.

We segue from Once a Rocker, straight into Walk This Way. Joe's famous opening guitar riff is greeted deliriously by the festival crowd. This is my first time performing the tune in public with Joe. Of all the Aerosmith songs we cover, this one is the most up-my-alley vocally. It's a fun one to perform and the audience response is off the charts. We also premiere our brand new rocker Walk with Me Sally. The first time you hear it you figure it must be a forgotten track from a Jerry Lee Lewis or Gene Vincent record. That's because the 1, 4, 5 chord progression is utilized on so many rock standards, like Hound Dog, Tutti Frutti and Johnny B. Goode. But this one is all ours. We extend the mid-section instrumental break with solos from Danny and Ron as well as the Admiral.

Following an encore of Train Kept A-Rollin' we roll out of the Topsham Fairgounds in glory.

Monday July 5, 1982

Phone call:
"Hi, Cowboy. I hear the show went pretty well yesterday."
"It was great, Tim. Joe was amazing."
"He's getting better. Definitely. But he still has a long way to go."
"But, Tim, Joe was in total control of the crowd yesterday."
"Look, Mach. I'm going to need your help. I know how you feel about Elyssa. You two seem to get along but if she calls you again - just hang up the phone."
"Hang up? Okay…I mean…why? What's going on with her?"
"Joe's moving out of the house."
"His mansion? Where's he going?"
"I'm still working on that. Joe is under a lot of pressure right now. He has legal issues and money problems but most of all,

his marriage to Elyssa is sinking him. The drugs, the drinking…
a lot of it has to do with Elyssa."
"What about the band?"
"Don't worry about the Project, Mach. Steve and I are putting
together shows right now. Keeping Joe out on the road is vital.
It's the safest place for him to be right now."
"What about his kid?"
"Look, Cowboy, there's nothing easy about this situation. Joe's
been trying to get out of there for a long time. Joe's mom is on
board with his move. I even think Elyssa's parents understand.
Everybody knows about the crazy things that go on over there.
Elyssa isn't good for Joe. So if she calls, just don't talk to her."
"Okay, Tim. I get it. Tell the Admiral I'm in his corner."

Tuesday July 6, 1982

I drop my birth certificate off at the office. They're getting me a
passport. We work on The Wanderer some more at the Annex
today. Funny song.
This will probably be our last rehearsal for a while.

Wednesday July 7, 1982

We go back to work tomorrow. I'm lying around the pink
palace. President Reagan is blabbing about something on the
TV. I can't hear him because the sound is turned down. Human
League is playing on the radio - Don't You Want Me Baby?

Thursday July 8, 1982

The Admiral is left-handed and so am I. Danny's left-handed
too, and so is Ron. Everyone is this group is a southpaw.
A few of us have to meet at the office this morning at 10 a.m. to
go and get our passport photos taken.
I'm pretty excited about tonight. I'm playing with the Project for
the first time in Boston. We're at The Channel, the big concert
club overlooking Fort Point Channel. Johnny A's Hidden Secret
opens the show. Tickets are $7.50.

Tonight is the craziest dressing-room scene I've ever been in.
So many local friends, fans, groupies, former bandmates,
ex-girlfriends… hell, it seems like everyone in Boston knows at
least one of us. This is show number 20 for Hargrove and me.
I sure am glad we waited until Joe regained his health before we
played a home game.

Friday July 9, 1982

We're back in the Dodge van.
Doc only has $40 left in the Halliburton, so he still owes me $5
for this weekend's per diem. It's great to touch money again.
The other day I added up my total earnings from the Project so
far - $1,670.
We roll through Providence RI on I95 South. Not too far down
the road we enter the town of Warwick. Doc follows colorful
signs leading us to Rocky Point Amusement Park. I played an
amusement park gig in NY state with Thundertrain a few years
ago. Rocking an outdoor stage on a summer night in the midst of
carnival lights, a sea of children, teens and families.
A favorite memory of mine.
Doc hustles us from the Dodge and towards a small cement
structure adjoining a brightly lit stage. I see some kids pointing
right at my face and yelling with excitement.
Wow. Someone recognized me?
Am I getting famous now?
The fans cluster around the windows of our little building.
Three kids are staring at me.
"That's him. It's Brad Whitford."

Security allows two men to enter our dressing room with some
lights and a videotape camera. Big pieces of equipment.
One sets up the camera while the other asks Joe for an
interview, to be broadcast on a music show that plays on a local
TV channel down here in Rhode Island.
I watch for awhile. It's a fairly lengthy interview and I learn a
few things. Interesting to hear Joe talk about music.

Actually it's interesting to just hear him talk, something he doesn't do around me very often.

Joe's diction has improved a lot from when I first met him.

A band called Cracked Actor is warming up the sellout crowd.

Package deal, you get to see the rock show and ride all the rides (except the roller coaster) for $6.95.

I guess you pay extra for the coaster rides. We go on at 9 p.m. and Rocky Point is jammed. We play a colorful set. I really dig gazing at the tilt-a-whirl, gondola, haunted house, Ferris wheel, Orbitron and zipper rides all spinning-round while I entertain this happy, very young crowd on a perfect July evening.

Saturday July 10, 1982

Continuing south on I95 into Connecticut. Looking for a local town that I admit I've never heard of, called Madison.

For each engagement the office issues a "gig sheet" to the road manager and to any of us who would like a copy.

The sheet lists important info, like the name and phone number of the promoter, the sound company, the other acts and the hotel/motel and venue addresses. Each sheet also includes the all-important driving directions.

Rock venues, even the famous ones, aren't always easy to find. Because of the noise level, rowdiness, illicit drug use and the occasional peeing on the neighbor's property that often accompanies these establishments, you won't always find them in the well-lit, nicely-kept, better part of the metropolis.

No. Rock'n'roll roadhouses tend to be located behind the industrial park on the long, dark road out of town - or across from the city dump.

Doc is a clever guy. As he zeroes in on these showrooms, he keeps the map book opened up across his lap, the gig sheet in his left hand and the mic for the CB radio (it's mounted up on the dash) in his right hand. I guess he steers with his knees.

Anyway, Madison turns out to be a one-horse town.

Just east of New Haven.

Doc pulls off into the dusty parking lot.

"Lookie here cousin. This is it. Icabod's."

"I see it. But I'm still not your cousin," growls Hargrove.
We bring the rock to Icabod's and a decent-sized crowd comes
out to party with us. I'm sure it was somebody's birthday. Two
other people might have been on their first date tonight, they
might even get married someday. It was probably another kid's
first concert - a night never to be forgotten.
I try to remember all that stuff when I do these shows.
It's always an important night - for at least one person in the
audience. But honestly, for most of these wing-nuts, it's just
another excuse to get wasted, try to get laid, or both.
Good show, but tough to top the high I had at the amusement
park last night and the excitement of my first Boston show with
the JPP the night before that.

Sunday July 11, 1982

Tat, rat, tat, rat, tat tat tat…
That's what we hear all the way back to Boston.
Three hours of Ronnie, beating on his practice pad.
Headphones glued to his head.

Monday July 12, 1982

I don't know where the Admiral is staying these days.
He's homeless. I hope he's doing okay.

Tuesday July 13, 1982

I have a meeting with Tim today at the office at 10 a.m.
He outlines everything that's going to happen a week from now.
It's a lot to take in.
I tell him that I have nothing to wear and he hands me a C note.

Wednesday July 14, 1982

I go clothes shopping at Oona's, and at the thrift shop outside
Central Square.

Thursday July 15, 1982

Reading a Billboard and a Variety that I grabbed at the Out of
Town newsstand in Harvard Square. I love to read about who's
in and out in film and music industry front offices. As a kid,
back when I started my album collection, I was always studying
the production credits, the studio names, and any other
small-type that I could find. At the movies I'm the guy who sits
through all the end credits.
Killing time on a long van ride, I will often bring up something I
just read about in Cashbox. Maybe some new idea or style I see
trending on the foreign charts.
The Admiral is never impressed with my trade talk. He slowly
turns in his seat and gives me the Sicilian death eye.
"Cowboy. To be cool - is to be quiet."
We're back at the Route 9 Holiday Inn in Poughkeepsie NY.
I've played here before with Joe. The Chance. Once again the
squadron of superfans are waiting outside to welcome us as we
arrive for soundcheck. The show is exciting - but I don't think
we packed the room as tightly as we did a couple months ago
with Brad in the band.

Friday July 16, 1982

We hit Long Island for a return show at Northstage.
Like last night, it feels like we're back here a little soon.
No choice. We have to go where the offers are.
I'm already totally spoiled. I would have died to play a fantastic
gig like this when I was in Thundertrain.

Since Brad left for California, I've been rooming with the
Admiral. It's late. We're both really buzzed. I'm switching the
TV channels. *In Like Flint* is playing on a local station.
James Coburn is on the screen chasing a bunch of spy-girls, and
that's when the Admiral says:
"Coburn. I like him."
"Me too." I agree.

"I met him." mutters Joe.

"No shit? How'd that happen?"

"I dunno, I was somewhere with Aerosmith. We were at this place in the desert and someone said that James Coburn lived right up the road. It was around midnight. I really like Coburn and I wanted to go find him, and meet him."

"Uh, oh. So what happened?"

"So, I just went out and looked for his house and when I found it, I started banging on the front door."

"In the middle of the night?"

"Yeah, I guess. I was a little messed up. Anyway, I kept on banging and finally James Coburn opened the door. He was just standing there. In his pajamas."

"No shit? So what happened then?"

"Nothing. I just said Hi, I'm Joe, and I really liked you in *The Great Escape*."

"What'd James Coburn do?"

"He just looked at me for a while. Then he said "Thanks very much Joe." And then he went back to bed."

Saturday July 17, 1982

We bring our charged-up new Joe Perry Project back to Albany. Yup, we're at J.B. Scott's.

Our set seems to be getting longer every night. Not because we're adding songs.

No. It's just that we'll be playing any regular tune off the set list, let's say Buzz Buzz. We get to the end of the song and hit the final ringing chord. Being band leader, the Admiral will often add a flourish of notes as the final chord fades away.

But our drummer Ron is taking this as an invitation to a musical duel. Stewart seizes on Joe's final note and replies with sympathetic rolls across his mounted-toms, adding double-kick drums, building to a furious crescendo.

Ron finally comes to rest with a The End cymbal crash.

Obviously Joe Perry has to top that.

With a massive feedback-wave, igniting a swarm of skyward-spiraling notes.
But beneath Joe's firework sonics, Ronnie has launched a slowly building, surf-like cymbal-wash which finally erupts into multiple crashes and multiple rim shots.
No way Perry won't answer back on his guitar.
The kids in front don't mind the musical gunfight at all.
Fists pump and shouts ring out.
Meanwhile, Danny and I loiter on the sidelines.
I'm flirting with the girls in front while Hargrove counts his change for cigarettes.

Sunday July 18, 1982

My little sister Cathy is on a short leave from the USAF.
She flies into Boston and continues up to Bar Harbor where she is greeted by my parents.
Our road manager Doc is flying to South America today.
He went ahead of us to make sure our gear arrives safely and gets through Customs.

Monday July 19, 1982

Jay, Woody and Ed pick me up in front of the palace at 9 a.m.
Hargrove is already onboard, sitting on the front bench of the Dodge van. I join him and the five of us cruise over to Logan International Airport.

We meet up with Admiral Perry and Tim at the curb.
We all board an Eastern shuttle, departing Boston at 11:45 a.m.
Arriving minutes later at La Guardia NY at 12:20 p.m.
We meet up briefly with the booking agent, Mark from Detroit, and the Canadian rock band Wrabit. All of us are driven from La Guardia to JFK Airport where we await our next flight.
I'm more than a little excited about meeting all these people and being part of all this airport activity. I have no problem convincing my friend Hargrove to join me in the terminal

cocktail lounge. I propose a toast to our unexpected and ongoing success. After a few hours of repeated toasts and slurred speeches, Doc locates us. He drags Danny and me out of the bar. He guides us to the gate for Viasa flight #801.

Last ones on, and with stupid grins on our faces. We topple into our seats and prepare for the four-and-a-half hour journey to the Maiquetia Airport. It's 4 p.m.

Once airborne, the flight attendants roll by with carts laden with free liquor and treats. Feeling like the king of rock, I indulge in everything they'll give me.

A few hours into the trip, I suddenly don't feel so good.

As we make our descent, I close my eyes. Tummy whirling. I don't think I can handle a landing.

It's 8:35 p.m. We've touched-down and taxied to our gate. I'm in sorry shape.

I can hear all the passengers disembarking, but I'm still gripping my armrests. Queasy.

Eyes clamped tight and holding on for dear life.

Passengers are chuckling as they pass me, some rather loudly. That's not very nice.

Realizing that the jet has now totally emptied out, I slowly open my peepers. What's this big mess piled up all over my lap?

Dozens of air sickness bags. A mountain of vomit bags, opened-wide and ready for use. Compliments of my band, our soundman Jay, and Doc. Thanks a lot you bums.

In the terminal we are met by promoters Oswaldo, Ivan and Felipe from Adrishows. They whisk us through Venezuelan immigration and Customs. I'm immediately struck by the police officers strolling every hallway. They look cool, calm, collected - but they all have large, black military-style rifles clutched by their sides. Hanging from leather shoulder straps.

We retrieve our luggage and are all escorted out to the curb.

Incredibly, each one of us gets chauffeured to the hotel in a different luxury car.

Danny Hargrove rolls away in a Mercedes.

I'm in an Audi Turbo, driven by Rudy.

Conversing with my private driver, I learn that Adrishows is made-up of a coalition of car dealers centered in Miami USA and Caracas Venezuela.

Rudy has the car radio turned up loud.

Radio Capital is blasting Joe Perry music. Lots of it.

Nothing else but Joe Perry. Seriously.

And not just his Aerosmith hits, lots of Project tracks too.

It's the only thing they play. That sobers me up pretty fast.

Fighting heavy traffic, we finally arrive at the towering Anauco Hilton at 10:30 p.m.

Now it's 11 p.m. and Joe wants me to join him. We're driven to the studios of Radio Capital for a live interview. On the way to the station we cruise beneath a vibrant "Welcome Joe Perry Proyect" banner, strung across the main drag of the city.

Proyect? We're swept-up an elevator and enter the broadcast studios. We meet Ivan the deejay. A very nice young man who is overjoyed to meet Joe Perry. Ivan interviews both of us in english while he hypes the huge shows that we'll be performing locally over the next two nights.

The Admiral and I are escorted from the studio by booking agent Mark and guided into another waiting luxury sedan.

Now it's midnight in Caracas and I'm dancing with the most beautiful woman in the world. Her name is MaryBella.

Between dances she mentions that she has to be on TV in the morning. MaryBella is here for a late-night press cocktail party hosted by Adrishows.

The Venezuelan media are all at this downtown disco to meet the Joe Perry Proyect. It's a wild scene. Pounding music, rotating lights. As I spin MaryBella around the dance-floor I can see the Admiral and Adrianna, a very friendly-looking brunette, who is in charge of our hospitality needs. Both seem to be getting well acquainted rather quickly. Doc is slamming down shots with Richard, Wrabit's road manager.

Our manager Tim, along with Ivan, Danny Hargrove, Philipe and Mark are at the bar sitting beside Laura & Tania, who we just met. They're all schmoozing a bunch of news reporters and photographers. My driver Rudy is dancing with three extremely untroubled ladies who aren't shy about anything.

I guess Ron is back at the hotel banging his drum pad.

Tuesday July 20, 1982

It's morning and I'm rooming with the Admiral. He's out cold.
In an effort to sort out my brain, I switch on the hotel TV.
The first person I see is the most beautiful woman in the world.
"Buenos Dias Venezuela, I'm MaryBella."
Holy crap. That's the same babe I was dancing with a few hours ago. I stare at the tube for a few minutes, catching flies in my slackened jaw.
MaryBella is the Venezuelan equivalent of our Jane Pauley, the new morning girl on the NBC Today Show.
But even sexier. No offense to Ms. Pauley.
I make some coffee and switch on the radio. Let the Music Do the Talking is playing. Then Soldier of Fortune. I try to change the station. But there are no other stations. Radio Capital is the only station. And all they play is Joe Perry music.
At 10 a.m. Doc rounds us up.
Another fleet of German-built sedans are parked in front of the Anauco Hilton, waiting for us.
We are delivered to the offices of the Music Syndicate.
After having our passports carefully studied we are all given a "temporary affiliation" and are wheeled back to the hotel.

Some of the hotel bellman are telling us to be careful.
Don't stray beyond the hotel property or wander out into the neighborhood after dark. They also warn us not to use a common American hand gesture that means "I'm okay."
They demonstrate by joining their forefinger and thumb making a little *O*.
In Caracas that gesture supposedly means "I'm weird and very horny. Ready for anybody and anything."

We have an early soundcheck at 2 p.m. today.

So after lunch we get chauffeured through more dismal Caracas traffic, to El Poliedro, a gleaming, white-domed arena.
Built ten years ago. It has a capacity of 20,000. The Joe Perry Project will be headlining here - for the next two nights.

Operations manager Felipe and the director Oswaldo give us a tour of the gigantic arena. There are large, clean dressing rooms for each of the four bands.
A backstage kitchen and dining room are just off to the side.
Entering the huge hall I see our road crew up on the high stage, stacking our gear, which was flown-in two days ago. Woody is talking to one of the local spotlight operators.
The sound company is called Audiorama. Towers have been built on either end of the stage, packed with enormous USA-built sound reinforcement speakers. Not the very latest models, but plenty good enough for our brand of rock.
There is raised seating all around the perimeter of the venue, with upper balconies rising above that. The huge floor area is devoid of seats. But there's a little reviewing stand with comfortable seating set-up beside the stage.
A lady is sitting there.
Blonde. She seems to be staring at me.
Since we'll be closing the show, we get to soundcheck first.
After we're finished, the Wrabit crew will set up their gear in front of ours and do their soundcheck. Followed in turn by the next two bands. By the time the opening band gets to sound-check there won't be very much space left on the stage.

Following our soundcheck the blonde lady comes over and introduces herself.
"I'm Marlene. I'm celebrating my last day of school."
"College?" I ask.
"No. High school."
She's a lot younger than she looks. But she speaks English and she's very polite.
"How did you get inside this place?" I ask.
Marlene motions towards a cluster of Adrishows promoters.
"They all know my family."

Driving back to the hotel we see rows of posters plastered on walls and fences.

Super Auto Las Mercedes presents
Rock Show
Da la Bienvenida a su artista exclusivo
Joe Perry Proyect
Wrabit
Y también Arkangel y La Misma Gente
en El Poliedro
Martes 20 y Miércoles 21 de Julio
Entrada Bs. 80

Around here we are The Proyect.
We get back to our suites on the seventeenth floor in the Anauco Hilton and after a short rest, Doc rounds us up again. We fight more traffic and listen to more non-stop Joe Perry music on Radio Capital. Finally arriving back at the arena, which is now swamped with long lines of Venezuelans anxious to get in.

We make our way back to the dressing room. I can't believe my eyes. A handsome fellow dressed like a maitre'd greets us with enthusiasm.
He's standing in the doorway of that backstage dining room area I checked out just a few hours earlier. Only now, it's all laid out with white table cloths, silverware, napkin rings, the whole nine yards.
Standing at attention are white-coated men wearing clogs and chef's toques. In front of each chef is a gleaming silver domed platter. Servers are buzzing back and forth from the kitchen.
The maitre'd turns to me.
"We are so very honored to have Señor Joe Perry and his Proyect here with us tonight. I certainly hope you gentleman brought large appetites."
"Sure…thanks…I'm always starving…
What's for supper anyway?"
"I highly recommend the lomo vetado."

"Oh yeah? What's that?"
"Rib-eye steak sir. Have you ever sampled Chilean beef
before?"
The Wrabit and Proyect guys take full advantage of the
hospitality, the fancy atmosphere and all this incredible grub like
it's our last supper. The South American food is delicious and
different. Servers are pouring wine, chefs are ladling extra sauce
over our steaks and roasted mountain-grown potatoes.

Between courses, I wander out to the side of the stage to check
out the first band, La Misma Gente. I figure these are local guys.
They aren't flashy, they look like the kids who are swarming
into the general admission floor area.
Their songs are kind of like sing-alongs.
The audience is immediately chanting along on the choruses.
From the way people are reacting, I can only guess that there
might be a political message to these tunes.
Simple, but forceful, anthems along the lines of Power to the
People or Say it Loud (I'm Black and I'm Proud).
But I'm only guessing.
La Misma Gente finish their twenty-five minute set to loud,
jubilant cheers and applause.

Whoa, now that's really weird. I only just realized...
There's a division of the audience here. All the men are on one
side of the arena floor - the ladies are all on the other side.
There's a heavy cable running the entire length of the Poliedro,
from the center of the stage, all the way back to the entrance
doors.
Gender separation, enforced by more of those white-shirted
police officers we saw at the airport yesterday. The cops here
aren't conspicuous, they're hiding back in the shadows. But I
can see they're all still sporting military-type guns, strapped
over their shoulders.
Now I'm looking at that small reviewing stand area.
I can see familiar faces. Some of the luxury auto dealers that I
met at the disco last night. Members of the press.

TV star MaryBella is hard to miss. I can see Ivan, the deejay
from Radio Capital. My friend, the high school graduate
Marlene is up there too. Men can sit with women in the posh
section. It's all roped off with security guards on duty.
The class division is horribly obvious. The rich are seated
together up in the comfortable seats. All the rest are treated like
peasants, not to be trusted.
Arkangel are on next. These guys must be the Van Halen of
Caracas. The music is their own but they play and dress in the
Southern California Van Halen style. I've never seen Van Halen
live but if they're this entertaining I can see why folks like 'em.
Arkangel go down well with the crowd but not quite as well as
La Misma Gente. Now I'm even more certain that the first band
were singing about something real, something that connected
with and stirred the emotions of this crowd.

Wrabit hail from the Toronto area. I've been told that they're a
big band in Canada and their latest album is on MCA Records.
I've been so busy dancing with TV celebrities, doing radio
interviews, fine dining, and meeting cute high school grads that
I've barely had time to talk to this Canadian band.
It's 9:30 p.m. when they hit the stage.
A few songs in and the audience doesn't seem to be
overwhelmed with these guys.
Wrabit play melodic rock with an occasionally heavy edge.
They use a lot of keyboards and vocal harmonies.
Kind of like Styx.
I'm back in our dressing room when I sense the mood of the
audience beginning to change. I don't know if Wrabit did
anything specific to ignite it, but all of a sudden I hear cat calls
and insults erupting from the crowd.
Doc sticks his head into our dressing room.
"It's not looking too good out there, boys."
I sneak out to the side stage, just in time to see a wire
wastebasket crash up against the keyboard stand. Wet
newspapers and candy wrappers are flying by, soda cups roll out
onto the performing platform. Wrabit members are dodging
bottles and cans as they zip through the air.

I think to myself "Oh no. Not this again."

I don't think it's Wrabit's fault. They're good.

It's just that these crowds are very anxious to see

"Joe fukken Perry." The Admiral's the guy everyone came to see
and the anticipation is making people lose their minds.

Incoming. A sticky root beer bottle rolls across the toe of my
cowboy boot, I retreat to the dressing room.

It's 11 p.m. when the Ride of the Valkyries comes sweeping out
of the huge sound towers.

Now, with the equipment from those first three acts all cleared
away, the stage is deep and expansive.

Woody has men up in the rafters, running the Super Trouper
spotlights that criss-cross the floor of El Poliedro.

The entire arena is shouting, stomping in time.

The stage is blacked out.

Backstage, Joe gives the nod. Doc leads us out towards the
deafening roar.

If I was to add up the total attendance from our first 25 shows,
I don't think that number would equal the sea of people in front
of the Joe Perry Project at this moment.

As the Admiral hits the strings of his Stratocaster, Woody jams
open the lights.

We plow into Toys in the Attic.

Fists in the air. Girls crying out with ecstasy.

Did Joe ever play South America before? I don't know.

He sure has a lot of fans down here. Our sound is razor sharp,
deep and heavy. The lighting design by Woody is
brilliant. We power through the set as the crowd sings along.

In the middle of Life at a Glance - things get weird.

Fire.

People are lighting fires inside the arena.

Nobody stops them either.

From where I stand, it looks like kids are piling up trash on the
arena floor and lighting it up. I see at least three distinct bonfires
blazing. Way back, fifty yards or more, fans are jovially dancing
around the rising flames with their arms held high in the air.

The Admiral raises the temperature even higher as he breaks
into Walk This Way. As I sing the chorus, I begin to see human
beings flying through the air. What the hell?

On closer examination I see that some of the music lovers in the
back have unfurled big blankets. A crew of strong folks take
hold of the outer edges of the blankets. Brave ones take turns
hopping into the middle. They are then bounce, bounce -
Bounced high up into the air.

Some of these fliers turn somersaults and do backflips as they
soar ever higher. During Rockin' Train I'm watching multiple
human cannonballs silhouetted bizarrely against the red glow of
a half-dozen indoor bonfires.

I've been to plenty of arena rock shows - but they were never
quite like this one.

Ron is storming through his drum solo and the crowd is dancing
along in a frenzy. That's when the local authorities decide it's
time to make a show of force.

From the upper balconies and corridors they swoop.

Policia. Brandishing firearms. Shockwave.

The party-people down front, thousands of them, part, just like
the Red Sea in that Charlton Heston movie. The entire audience
rises-up as one, and vanishes. Where did they all go?

Into the upper stands? Under the seats? Hiding in the
bathrooms? Hallways? The coat room? Damned if I know.

Now I'm singing for the Venezuelan Police Force. Just the
Proyect and forty gun-toting riflemen, in an empty arena.

Some of the uniformed men stomp on the fires.

Others confiscate the big blankets.

Mission accomplished, they march back into the shadows from
whence they came.

Seconds later, 20,000 Joe Perry fans flood back onto the floor -
from wherever they were all hiding. And the band plays on.

I wouldn't believe it if I hadn't seen it with my own eyes.

Quickly, the fun picks up where it left off, cresting as Perry
straps on his clear-body Dan Armstrong guitar for

Let the Music Do the Talking, and finally, a blazing version of
Train Kept A-Rollin.'

"Thanks everybody. We'll be here again tomorrow night."

Later that evening:

When we arrived in South America the promoters gave us a notice which read:

"Water. The water/ice cubes is safe to drink, wash, lick and suck. It is suggested, though, that for drinking purposes utilize the hotel apartment's kitchen faucet, all of which have water filter. Otherwise stick to alcohol and Coke."

With the aid of our lovely hospitality girl Adrianna, the band and crew are taking that "alcohol and Coke" advice to heart.

Alcohol and Cocaine that is.

Straight from Peru and packed in medicinal-looking glass vials. Cocaine isn't for me but from what I'm hearing from a lot of other folks up here on the seventeenth floor, this is extremely good stuff. Wicked pure and wicked cheap. Adrianna seems to have a never-ending supply of the wonder drug.

So after the concert, everyone is hanging out on the hotel balconies, tooting away.

I watch in wonder as the guys and our guests make quick work of the stuff. Then, ceremoniously, they fling the empty glass vials down into the courtyard garden far below.

Wednesday July 21, 1982

I awaken to a sunny day. I think I'll go visit the restaurant for breakfast.

Walking through the lobby I see a familiar face.

Sitting on a couch. It's Marlene.

"Hey. What're you doing here?"

"Buenos Dias, I just came by to tell you that you were wonderful last night, Cowboy."

"Really? Thanks...uh, did you have breakfast already?"

"Yes. With my parents."

"Well, I was going to get something. Join me?"

"Gracias, Cowboy."

The main restaurant of the Anauco Hilton is mostly made out of glass. It looks out to a beautiful reflecting pool surrounded by palm trees and flowers.

The hostess asks if we'd like to sit outside. It looks nice.

She leads us to a glass table, under a sun umbrella, which the
hostess adjusts for us.

I try to study the menu. Coffee is 10 Bolivars.

"How much is this anyway?"

"A Bolivar is worth about 20 cents American" replies Marlene.

"So coffee...?"

"Two dollars, Cowboy."

I order some coffee and some muffins. No cherry pancakes on
the menu. The high school grad just drinks water.

I'm listening intently as Marlene tells me about her plans for her
future. That's when I notice the potted plant to my left.

One, two, three?...hell I count at least half a dozen empty
cocaine vials in there.

The crew must have been using this planter for target practice
last night.

After breakfast, Marlene hangs around for a while. I invite her
upstairs to see the view from the seventeenth floor.

Caracas is tucked into a valley, ringed by a small mountain
range, that borders the ocean.

Our hotel is one of several modern skyscrapers.

Marlene points the other buildings out.

"Oil. All the big ones are oil. The one over there might be a
bank. The oil bank."

Not far from this cluster of expensive high rises, I can plainly
see thousands of tar paper shacks and sad looking hovels.

Clinging to the surrounding hillsides. The contrast is startling.

The haves-nots and the haves. Living right on top of each other.

At 8:30 p.m. Wrabit and the JPP are driven back to the Poliedro
for tonight's concert. I'm anxious to enjoy another gourmet
dinner. I am not disappointed.

The show goes very much like last night's.

Happy to see that Wrabit's set is received a bit better.

Thanks to Marlene's math lesson, I've figured out that the 80
Bolivar ticket price to attend this concert equals $16.

I never know how much our band gets paid for any of our dates,
but from what's being rumored, our appearances at El Poliedro

are putting a large, sorely needed, stack of greenbacks into the
Project coffers.

Thursday July 21, 1982

Following the concert last night, the crew packed all our gear in
road cases and trucked it out to the cargo area at Maiquetia
Airport.
I'm back in my hotel suite, having morning coffee as the sun
rises over the mountaintop.
Our gear should be flying back to Boston right now.
Later, down in the lobby of the Hilton, I notice something odd.
Out in the courtyard.
I see our crew, all sitting around a table together.
Concentrating, heads down, working together.
Have the roadies suddenly taken up jigsaw puzzles?
I smile as I approach the table. No, it's not a puzzle.
They're all just writing postcards. Lots of cards. Probably to
their parents and grandparents. Such nice guys. As I move in for
a closer look, I'm confused to see the boys are addressing all
these cards to themselves. To themselves? What's going on?
It gets even weirder when I see the postage stamps. Not normal
stamps. No, these are big, colorful stamps. I mean they're really
big. That's when the vials come out.
I watch in wonderment as the crafty lads begin dumping little
mountains of white powder from their vials onto each of the self
addressed postcards.
Up in the corner, right where the stamp usually goes.
Then they begin licking the stamps.
But not the way normal people do.
No, instead of slurping across the gummed adhesive, they are
licking only the edges of these large stamps.
Carefully, they set the dry center part of each stamp over the
mound of powder.
Then they press down on the sticky stamp edges.
Pressing firmly. Sealing in the contraband hidden underneath.
You can bet these clever chaps will be checking their mail at
least several times a day as soon as they get back home.

Friday July 23, 1982

A horrible start to the day. Wake-up call at 5 a.m.
Twenty minutes later, we are marched out of our celebrity suites
at the Anauco Hilton.
At 5:30 a.m. the Project and Wrabit are transported via another
fleet of luxury sedans out of Caracas and back to Maiquetia
Airport. I ask my driver to turn on Radio Capital.
The Eagles "Hotel California" is playing.
The twilight zone has finally ended.
We spend time in the Venezuelan immigration line. Additional
time at the gate. We finally board Viasa flight #800 at 8:00 a.m.
I'm in seat 16A.
Right next to my favorite cousin, Danny Hargrove.
Lifting off the runway at 8:30 a.m. Sharp. Bound for JFK.
Adios, Venezuela. We all pass out.

The Viasa jet hits the tarmac in NYC. It's 1:10 p.m.
We drag our tired butts through the long line at USA
immigration and customs.
Wrabit is right behind us. An officer eyes the little crocodile
head keyring I bought in the Hilton souvenir shop. He waves me
through. We all board a transfer bus. It brings us to La Guardia
Airport. No more Proyect. We're the Project again.
We bid farewell to the guys in Wrabit and they all hop away to
catch an Air Canada flight back home. Seemed like nice guys.
We board the Eastern shuttle back to Logan.
In Boston, Doc is waiting for us curbside at the Eastern Airlines
terminal with the brown van.
No more German luxury sedans, we pile back into the mud-
streaked Dodge and our road manager speeds us through the
Sumner Tunnel, up 93, and then south on 95, over to Route 3
North. You guessed it. We're heading for the home of
Jack Kerouac - Lowell Massachusetts.

It's Friday night and the Joe Perry Project is headlining the
Lowell Memorial Auditorium. Due to our lengthy journey we
miss the soundcheck.

Entering the auditorium, I can hear the teen-beat of Hang on Sloopy, one of the first songs I ever learned to play on guitar. Rick Derringer and his band are halfway through their set and the auditorium is packed.

This is another Tom Kalil production.

That guy sure is making things happen.

We're escorted back to our dressing room in a daze. I'm greeted by Ric, Bobby and Steven from Thundertrain along with their dates. Our friend Frenchie is here too and I see Tabitha, a young photographer who helped me with Mag 4.

Rick Derringer lifts-off into Rock'n'Roll Hoochie Koo and the crowd eats it up.

That song wakes us up a bit. After a brief set change our ominous intro music rises up. Here we go again.

Saturday July 24, 1982

I'm back at Logan Airport in Boston. With the non-rested JPP. Nodding at the gate. Waiting to board an Air Canada flight to Toronto.

You know what we all need right now?

12 HOURS of ROCK

Yup, that's where we're heading.

The flight is short and we've all been shoved into another van along with Doc's friend, Zorn Ptomaine.

Something called the Orient Express has put together a 12-hour party in an expansive park area outside of Toronto Ontario.

Q107, the big rock station, is co-promoting the show.

Lots of local favorites like Rough Trade, The Spoons and Teenage Head will perform.

Plus the American headliners: Mountain and the Joe Perry Project. Zorn locates our target on his map, Courtcliffe Park. It's halfway between the cities of Mississauga and Hamilton. Our van rolls along a winding access road towards a distant stage. Groups of music lovers are strewn all over the grass. Frisbee-whipping, Molson-chugging, weed-smoking Canadian kids. The closer we get to the outdoor stage, the more densely-packed the crowd becomes. I can see Leslie West.

He's performing right now. Singing Long Red. Since they
appeared at the Woodstock festival, thirteen years ago, I think
Mountain have split up and reformed about a dozen times.
Not sure who's in West's line-up today.
Doc slows down the van and we slide open the side door,
picking up two radiantly smiling hitchhikers. They don't look
very dangerous, there's absolutely no room for concealed
weapons in those teensy bathing suits. The blonde one leaps
inside and lands right in my lap.
"You guys must be the band, eh? I'm Bridget."
"It's a pleasure to meet you. I'm Cowboy."
I can see the Admiral glancing back over his shoulder.
Covering his mouth and rolling his eyes. He tries not to laugh
out loud. Cue The Wanderer.
Just an hour later, we're up on that stage, and I am indeed
singing The Wanderer, while Bridget and her brunette girlfriend
Kathy, go-go dance over by the monitor mixer on the side of the
stage.
Having just played those out-of-this-world Venezuelan gigs a
couple days ago, I'm taking today's wild festival scene in stride.
Rocking out, alongside Joe Perry? Yup, Check.
Playing for thousands? Okay, Check.
Beautiful strangers falling into my lap? Of course. Check.

Back in my room at the Oakcliffe Holiday Inn, it hits me.
The Project just rocked three different countries in three days.

Sunday July 25, 1982

I wake up in the small town of Carlisle. Our Holiday Inn is right
down the road from yesterday's festival. After breakfast a few of
us take off in the rental van. We want to check out nearby Lake
Ontario. It's big.

Monday July 26, 1982

Jet back to Boston today.

Unfortunately, my sister Cathy is jetting out of Boston at the same moment, going back to her Air Force home base. So I completely miss out on seeing her.

Tuesday July 27, 1982

It's not very exciting this morning at the pink palace.
Julia is working in her office at SyncroSound.
I think being in a traveling rock band might be like being an astronaut. After a lot of preparation, you finally get to lift off.
Very noisy and exciting.
Then suddenly it's quiet again.
Silently floating around, for days or weeks until…Big landing.
You get to chase Martians around and blast your ray gun again.
Then…back into the capsule, waiting, wondering.
Living in suspended-animation, until your next big mission.

Wednesday July 28, 1982

Did I mention how it is becoming clearer to me why self medication is so rampant in rock'n'roll and other parts of this entertainment racket? I'm having trouble weaning myself away from that ultra-fantastic roller coaster I just got dumped out of.
The concerts, flights, people, spotlights, hotels, celebrities, cheering crowds, go-go girls.
All that stimulus. I don't want that electric-high feeling to stop.
That's the only way I can explain being out here in Holliston, sitting in front of my parents' liquor cabinet, drinking something really nasty tasting.
These same old, dusty bottles of Martini & Rossi vermouth, Hennessy brandy and Johnny Walker Red have been sitting in this cabinet ever since I was a Cub Scout.
I won't say my parents are tee-totalers but I will say that a single six-pack of Ballantine Ale can last my father a year or more. I might have seen my Mother sip a glass of wine but only on a few occasions. I think this liquor stash is here for my

grandfather Nelson. In case he ever stops by. Grandfather Bell
doesn't visit very often though. You're more likely to see a
moose climbing a tree than to see Nelson Bell in Holliston.

Thursday July 29, 1982

I haven't heard a peep from Elyssa.
I don't know where the Admiral is either.
Maybe he's staying at Tim's.

Friday July 30, 1982

I'm a show-off and a publicity hound.
It's almost noon, I'm eating breakfast at the palace, tuned to
WBCN as usual.
They're hyping a live remote broadcast happening this afternoon
from the Boston Museum of Science. The "BCN Blood Drive"
to be hosted by deejay Mark Parenteau.
I'm always looking for my next chance to be on the radio.
I hike over to Central Square. A Red Line train takes me to the
Park Street T, where I hop the Green Line up to Lechmere
Station. From there it's a bip and a bop to the Science Museum.
Haven't been here for awhile.
Hopefully, I'll see Spooky, the Great Horned Owl.
Spooky used to appear a lot on WBZ's Rex Trailer Boomtown
TV show. Rex was a good singer, with a Gibson acoustic guitar.
The WBCN van is parked out in front of the museum. Red Cross
signs lead me into a big room with a bunch of nurses and cots.
There's Parenteau. Center stage. Merrily jabbering away into his
mic. Uncle Mark sure is good at talking. Like a male Elyssa.
I waste no time rolling up my sleeve.
The nurse searches in vain for a vein.
I'm O negative, I've been told it's a valuable type.
I've been giving blood for years but it's always a struggle to get
the red stuff out of me. My veins are invisible and once tapped,
my flow is slower than a lawyer's mount to heaven. I'll watch
three or four guys come and go on the neighboring cot, while
my pint bag is still flopping around, only a quarter full.

I see the tall deejay approaching. His every word booms out over the airwaves to the masses who listen to the 50,000-watt Rock of Boston every weekday afternoon.

"Look over here. Can you believe it? We have a celebrity in the room. And he's donating blood as I speak. Wow, everybody.

It's the lead singer of The Joe Perry Project.

My good friend - Mach Bell.

Hey, Mach, thanks for stopping by and helping out the blood drive."

Parenteau and I chat for a minute, maybe more.

A single minute seems pretty long when you're talking on the radio. As usual, I try to throw in a few witty bits. I thought some up during my journey over here.

Plus I have a gig to promote.

"Hey everyone. C'mon down to Nantasket Beach tonight, I'll be rocking all night with the Joe Perry Project.

At Uncle Sam's. Don't miss the party."

Afterwards, I'm given some free juice, sugar cookies and a promotional Lisa Hartman album.

It's a huge relief to reunite with Joe and the whole JPP gang again. I'm a goldfish who just got plopped back into my bowl, after flopping around on the floor for a week.

Tonight's show goes well. Much better than when we played here four months ago. I wish *"Captured Live"* captured this one instead. I wonder when that show airs anyway? Tonight's opening band is called the Reputations, a good punky rock band. The group is led by singer Nikki. Little sister of Elyssa.

Saturday July 31, 1982

Last night, on the way home from the gig, I heard Rock This Town on the radio again. All the stations are playing it.

All the time. Stray Cat Strut too.

This business is too weird.

Was it really just four weeks ago that I watched these same Stray Cats get booed off the stage? They were unknowns and scorned by everyone back then.

Now they have this big hit album and everyone loves them.
Their picture is in People magazine this week. In color.
It reminds me of an Aerosmith concert at the Boston Garden in
the beginning of 1976. All the concert-goers were out in the
hallway inclines, smoking and getting prepped to cheer on headliner Joe fukken Perry and his Bad Boys of Boston.
I was one of the very few who stayed seated out in the arena, to
hear the under-rated Peter Frampton, the guy who quit Humble
Pie. That was the night that Peter first introduced the songs from
his new album to Boston, Frampton Comes Alive.

Sunday August 1, 1982

I go to the movies. *Fast Times at Ridgemont High*.

Monday August 2, 1982

My buddy Danny Hargrove comes over.
Sure am glad I have Danny to help me get through the slow
times between the fast times.

Tuesday August 3, 1982

A week from today we'll try it again.
Another chance at that Atlantic to Pacific to Gulf Coast road trip
- the one that got short-circuited last May.
This time we're prepared to get the job done.

Thursday August 5, 1982

WBCN keeps on playing Eye of the Tiger by Survivor, along
with those two Stray Cats songs.

Fri/Sat August 6/7, 1982

Tim booked us two days at the Cambridge Complex, to sharpen
up before the tour begins.
Rehearsal is at 1 p.m. both days.

Sunday August 8, 1982

The Compass Lounge in South Yarmouth is another of those
places Thundertrain always longed to play.
One of the happening rock bars on Cape Cod.
Other popular beach party places were Brothers Four in
Falmouth and the Mill Hill in West Yarmouth.
We're buzzing along Route 28 and there it is. The Compass.
It doesn't look like much compared to the Fountain Casino and
El Poliedro.
I've become very spoiled, very fast.
Andy is here with his girlfriend and Julia's here too. She hasn't
seen us play for a while.
Coming off two days of rehearsal, we sound really tight.
We do our dirty work - almost knocking out the walls of this
medium-sized rock room, packed with beach kids.

Monday August 9, 1982

I do the rounds of the local Boston dives and bars, bidding
farewell to one and all.
In truth, the way our trip is routed, we'll be sneaking back into
the Hub next week. But only for a couple of days. Following the
initial Midwest dates, we'll return but just to re-pack our bags
and catch flights out of Logan to the West Coast.

Caracas Venezuela   July 20/21, 1982

My original doodle art for the Joe Perry Project logo. 11/22/82

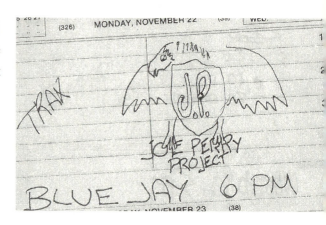

Ron, Mach & Joe in California.   Photo by Kyle Runge

IV
FOUR GUNS WEST

Tuesday August 10, 1982

I've got my blaster in one hand and my bag in the other.
Julia drops Danny and me off at the Annex at 8 a.m. sharp.
Doc is waiting in the Dodge van. Ronnie Stewart and the
Admiral have already taken their usual spots. We hit the road.
Driving west on the Massachusetts Turnpike I90. Traffic slows
as we pass Worcester. Clearing I84 South (the route down to
Hartford and NYC) our speed picks up as we roll toward the
Berkshires.
They aren't that big, as mountain ranges go, but still steep
enough to slow down the pack of 18-wheelers we're sharing the
highway with.
Crossing the New York State line we start making better time.
I90 West passes through Albany, Schenectady and Utica.
By this time everyone is starving. Doc fires up the CB radio and
polls some of the good ol' boys who are wheeling their White
Freightliners and Macks on both sides of us.
"Any fine-dining establishments around here?"
A few minutes later we grab seats in a busy joint near Rome NY.
A sign outside promises EAT.
As usual, the Admiral chooses the kind of manly, traditional
food I'd expect Rambo or James Coburn to select.
Like a ham and swiss sandwich on rye. Or some pea soup.
Meanwhile, I'm searching the menu high and low for a "Belly-
buster Special" or a mile-long chili dog with a side of cheese
worms.
Our first gig on this trip is set for tomorrow night in Detroit.
You can't drive from Boston to Detroit in one day with time left
over to make a show, so we're just pushing as far west as
possible. After lunch we slog past Oneida, Syracuse, Auburn,
Waterloo, Rochester, Batavia and Buffalo. After that, I90 dips
down, we pass Hamburg and Dunkirk and finally cross over the
Ohio state line.

Boston to the New York state line is around 140 miles. Albany
to Buffalo adds another 300 miles. By the time we roll into
Ashtabula Ohio we've totaled around 500 for the day.
We book into the Holiday Inn for the night.

Wednesday August 11, 1982

With Doc at the wheel, we continue to mush west in the trusty
Dodge van. Ronnie is blissfully bashing away to Toto and
Kansas tapes with his headphones on, while the rest of us listen
to AC/DC, Howlin' Wolf, Jimi, the Stones and of course,
the Sex Pistols.
I even try to convince Joe to listen to my Adam and the Ants
tape. No go.
Passing through Cleveland and then down past Elyria and
Sandusky. I was born in this state, Yellow Springs Ohio.
We moved to Holliston as soon as my father graduated from
Antioch College. I was just an infant then. Rod Serling and my
friend, Ric Ocasek, both went to Antioch as well.
Finally we hit Toledo and head north. Straight shot to Detroit.
Driving through city streets, rolling up Harper Ave and through
an alleyway into a grubby parking lot. Incredibly we're met by a
good-sized posse of Joe Perry superfans who've been
waiting for Joe to arrive. They're probably surprised to see the
legendary guitarist arrive in a dusty van. More likely they were
expecting a shiny tour bus, or maybe a helicopter landing on the
rooftop.
We pour out of the Dodge, a bit stiff from today's 250
miles. Ron and Joe are asked to sign a whole bunch of Project
records and photos. Some pretty girls ask Hargrove and me to
sign their autograph books. No problem. We happily oblige but
then I realize, I just wrote my name next to all these legitimate
stars like Chrissy Hynde, David Lee Roth and Sting.
I hope I don't get into trouble for devaluing those pages.
Harpo's Concert Theater is cool. It used to be a big movie house
called The Harper, probably because it's on Harper Ave.
Later, in the 70's, The Harper unfortunately became a disco.
In 1980 a brand new owner (a rock'n'roll guy) took over.

Wanting to distance the club from its shameful disco past, he renamed the theater Harpo's.

A clever choice, as the theater boasts an impressive, expensive-looking vertical marquee out front. All the new owner had to do was change the last two letters on the original Harper's sign.

Joe's dedicated crew has the amp-line all set up in front of a big velvet curtain. The stage is six feet off the ground and it's framed by heavy carved timbers. I think you'd call the style Gothic. There's a pit out front, surrounded by some tables and lots of open spaces. Long bars in the back and stairs leading up to a second level. Capacity 2000.

Now we're back from the hotel - it's almost midnight. Our dressing room is side-stage, but up above, on the second or third level, overlooking the entire stage set up. Ride of the Valkyries rumbles out of the house sound system.

Cheers erupt. Raised Bic lighters, stomping feet.

It's time once again to Let the Music Do the Talking.

Joe and I are working the stage together really well these days. At first I was afraid to do too much, I wasn't sure what my boundaries were. In Thundertrain I was known for climbing the amp-stacks and literally hanging from the rafters. The Project has a different vibe than my old band. I still put on an energetic show but I try to keep equal focus on what Danny, Ron and especially Joe Perry are doing.

A smart frontman has the power to move the eyes of a crowd to particular spots of interest at particular times. Lifting an already exciting show - to an extreme level.

Quite a scene in the dressing room after our performance and at the post-show party back at the Park Crest Hotel.

I meet two cute local girls named Terri and Chris who are very funny and nice.

Thursday August 12, 1982

Mark Hyman is the booking agent who flew with us down to Venezuela for the JPP/Wrabit shows. I'm out of the business loop but I assume Mark had a lot to do with putting that whole concert package together.

Right now we're in the van heading for the head office of DMA, an international booking agency based in Michigan that specializes in hard rock acts. It's the company Mark works for. We arrive at the agency offices and Joe Perry is led into a closed door meeting.

The rest of us stand around staring at gold and platinum records all over the walls. I'm briefly introduced to a DMA agent who was at our concert last night. I shake his hand and smile. "How'd you like the show?"

The guy shoots me a weird look and mumbles something. That bums me out. Maybe the dude was just mad about being left out of the closed door meeting with the Admiral. Who knows?

I tend to always assume the worst.

I'm not a very confident person.

We drive west to Niles MI and check into the Holiday Inn.

As I carry my bag through the lobby, I see a dark-haired girl staring at me. Nothing wrong with that. People always stare at me, because I look funny. But I could swear that same young lady was staring at me yesterday.

In the lobby of the Park Crest Hotel in Detroit.

Our next gig is tomorrow night. Just over the border in South Bend Indiana. Having the evening free, we decide to check out a drive-in movie theater out by Lake Michigan.

The whole band and most of the crew come along for the fun.

It's a double feature: *Blade Runner* and *Poltergeist*.

Friday August 13, 1982

Doc vans us onto the grounds of St. Patrick's Pavilion in South Bend IN. It's another outdoor event. On a perfect day. A concert for farm families and civilized music enthusiasts, not a free-for-all, reefer-fest like up in Canada the other day.

Headlining is the Marshall Tucker Band. These guys are from Spartanburg South Carolina. Everyone on the planet knows their chart topper "Heard It in a Love Song."

Like our pals, Duke and the Drivers, there is no one named Marshall in this band. The leader name is just a hoax. They named themselves after Marshall the blind piano tuner.

That's what I heard anyway.
Doc dumps us off behind the stage and we meander up the steps
into a dressing room with our name pasted on it.
"Hey, Cowboy."
Huh? Who knows my name in Indiana?
It's a sexy girl that I met months ago, side stage at the
Hampton Beach Casino in New Hampshire.
"Uh…hi. What are you doing here?"
"I told you I was going on the road, Cowboy."
Hargrove and the Admiral are watching this awkward exchange.
Nudging each other. Trying to stifle their laughter.

I'm a bit nervous launching our Boston rock-attack straight into
this hillside full of lovely Midwesterners and their children.
Thankfully and surprisingly, everyone seems to latch onto our
brand of aggressive rock immediately. Hands up, dancing,
shouting and carrying on. The South Bend crowd soaks in every
riff and cheers for more.
They seem to be loving everything we do.

Saturday August 14, 1982

I'm excited to be heading towards Columbus Ohio. I never got
to play the storied Fillmore West or East, but the current best
known chain of rock venues are the Agora Ballrooms. Originally
in Cleveland and then spreading to Hartford, Hallandale,
Tampa, Houston, Dallas, Atlanta, Akron and beyond.
I got to play at the Cleveland Agora once with Thundertrain.
The JPP is headlining tonight at another one of the outposts.
The Columbus Agora.
We arrive to find a beautiful 2000-seater, situated directly across
the street from Ohio State University. We get a good, dog-days-
of-summer turnout. I bet if school had been in session we would
have been turning people away.

Sunday August 15, 1982

This just wasn't my day.

I woke up innocently in a Columbus motel and got herded into the Dodge van for a rapid trip north. A quick 145 miles later, Doc pulls us into the Sheridan Community Center.
We're halfway between Ann Arbor MI and Detroit.
The Project is slated to perform here in the field house, for an all ages show, just a couple hours from now.
As I bumble around, a very nice person comes to my aid.
Showing me the layout of the place and pouring me a very appreciated cold beverage. I adopt her as my hostess and try to stick by her side. Danny rolls his eyes when he gets a load of my latest acquaintance-of-the-day.
Thankfully, Joe isn't around to shake his head at me.
I'm not sure what kind of gig this is. We're in Taylor. Lots of locals are pushed up to the front of the makeshift stage. Young kids, 4-H members, bikers, farmers, teens, older fans, juvenile delinquents, maybe some livestock too.
Basically everyone from this part of Michigan is here.
We put on a great show as usual, the ominous intro music, Joe emerges and unleashes his helicopter attack, the Lone Ranger theme and then we barrel into our deafening but highly entertaining set. My hostess is standing off to the side. Suddenly she's blowing me kisses.
 I try to ignore her and shake my maracas.
As we bang into Once a Rocker, Hargrove dances by and nudges me, he points into the front row.
Oh, no. What's she doing here? It's my sexy Hampton Beach friend from last night in Indiana.
She's dressed to kill and giving me the look.
I try to ignore the incoming cooties. Just keep on rocking.
We kick into Walk This Way, which has everyone, even the random livestock, up and moving.
I bend down to grab a sip from my water bottle and,
Oh, no. Really?
It's Terri and her friend Chris. Those two cute girls from Detroit.
Chris is jumping up and down. Wiggling her fingers at me.
Terri is playing with her hair and giving me smoldering googly eyes. What the hell?
I thought I kissed all you girls good-bye already.

This is really bad. On top of that, none of these lovebirds are
aware of each other.
What do I do now? Does this stage have a secret trap door?
Just gotta keep singing. I'll think of something.
The Admiral kicks me in the ankle and calls for The Wanderer.
Hargrove is laughing so hard, he's practically weeping.
The scene that followed, back at the Holiday Inn, was right out
of Three's Company.
I choose to think of myself as an old fashioned, honorable guy.
These lovestruck women weren't buying that crap for a second.
Once they met each other and realized what was going on,
they all banded together - against the Cowboy.
I hid in my closet for awhile and then I tried to make up with a
couple of them, one at a time. That dumb move set off catfights
and more tears. I ended up being chased through the halls and
hunted like an animal. I ducked into every doorway. I even
jumped out a window. The Jack Tripper of rock.

Monday August 16, 1982

It's Danny Hargrove's birthday.
We book out of Taylor MI (thank goodness) and head east.
Every time the Admiral looks at me he just covers his eyes and
shakes his head. Hargrove won't stop laughing at me.
I swear I was framed. Everybody knows I'm no playboy.
I have no luck pleading my case to these guys.

Tuesday August 17, 1982

The Dodge finally pulls up to the curb at the pink palace.
We drove straight through the night. No hotel.
I go upstairs and crash heavily.

Wednesday August 18, 1982

While I was away, the Commonwealth of Massachusetts sent me
a tax refund check for $109.

A windfall that will come in handy. I walk up Broadway to the corner laundromat. Today I'm laundry boy but tomorrow...

Thursday August 19, 1982

We're boarding American Airlines flight #199. Bound for San Diego. The JPP road crew jetted out of Boston yesterday.
At LAX, the crew picked up the instruments, cables and random gear that got shipped along as cargo. They rented a 14' truck, loaded-up and hit the 405 into Los Angeles. At Studio Instrument Rentals (S.I.R.) they grabbed a bass rig for Danny and a couple Marshall stacks for Joe.
Meanwhile, down in San Diego, our landing is exciting.
They have a very short runway here. The captain jams on the brakes, the aircraft shakes and screeches before jolting to a stop.
It's three hours earlier here than in Boston, the afternoon sun is still blazing, California is experiencing an unusually hot summer - with temps topping 100 degrees.
Doc is over at the rental desks trying to dig up a van.
The new ride doesn't compare to our brown Dodge.
I'm not sure what this is, a Ford, I guess. A lot smaller than our van. Not sure what you'd call the color either, dirty pink?
We pile in and Doc drives through San Diego, finally turning onto Clairemont Mesa Boulevard. Cruising along, studying the gig sheet carefully, suddenly he whips the vehicle into a strip mall parking lot. There it is, at the corner of the mall, right next to a nail salon, The Bacchanal.
You never know where you're gonna find the next great rock'n'roll venue. While not the most impressive looking place we've ever visited, The Bacchanal stands tall when it comes to booking a huge variety of national and international music acts.
We meet some really nice kids out in the parking lot. They've been waiting a long time for Joe Perry to return to this city. One friendly guy - named Thai - seems to be the happening, connected dude around here.
Inside the nightclub we find Jay, Ed and Woody. The stage set up looks a lot different. This rented amp-line is way smaller than what we're used to. Nice pro gear but not nearly as imposing

looking as our regular rock pile. Danny's Gibson Les Paul bass made it here. Joe will be limited to just four of his favorite guitars for the rest of this tour. Usually he sticks to his Tele-Rat, an upside-down axe, Frankensteined together from Fender Telecaster and Stratocaster parts.

Friday August 20, 1982

The show in San Diego went down well. The audience was definitely on our side.
Even after the longer than usual soundcheck, we still had a bit of a challenge dialing in our sound on this new gear.
Joe sounds different playing through stock Marshall amps.
Not bad, it's just a little different. After the gig we drove 121 miles up here, to Van Nuys, in the San Fernando Valley of L.A.
And now it's several hours later, almost 10 a.m.
I'm sitting here in my room at the Holiday Inn. Staring at a Sambo's restaurant right next door. Yum. It's just across the parking lot. Suddenly I'm in immediate need of cherry pancakes with red colored syrup and since everyone else is still sleeping, I decide to walk over there. Why not?
Sambo's looks to be only about 200 yards away.
As I dash out of the hotel, I immediately choke on a mouthful of dry, hot air. Like being thrown inside a clothes dryer on the highest heat setting. Yikes, it's dry.
Craving those pancakes, I forge on. Halfway across the lot, I feel the soles of my boots melting away. My lungs are burning.
I gasp, struggling for breath. The sun is baking down. Wiggly heat-waves rise from the scorched pavement. I'm still 50 yards away. My mouth is puckered and cracked, I'm weak, worried, feeling desperate. Can I make it?
I seriously think I might just pass out and shrivel-up in the middle of this skillet-hot asphalt lot.
Struggling the final steps - I reach the restaurant in the nick of time.
Thank you, dear Lord.

About five minutes later, the rest of the JPP touring party rolls up to Sambo's front door in the air conditioned van. Everyone comes barreling inside, laughing all the way.

Saturday August 21, 1982

Great news. Our show tonight at the Country Club in nearby Reseda CA has already sold out.
So, a second show is being added for tomorrow evening.
The Reseda Country Club is currently the number one showcase venue in the L.A. area. Promoters Wolf and Rismiller operate the 1000 capacity room. The building was formerly a Sav-On drug store. Right at the corner of Sherman Way and Reseda Bl.

Sunday August 22, 1982

We had a barrel of fun last night. Lots of activity in the dressing room. Terri Nunn, from the band Berlin, came back to meet Joe. I immediately recognized her from her MTV videos.
There were multiple reports of other stars sitting down at the bar. Heavy metal guys and dudes from upcoming Sunset Strip bands like Quiet Riot and Motley Crue. And some celebrities from XXX films too. I wasn't down there myself, so I can't verify. The show went really well, Perry showed the spandex SoCal crowd how we do it back in New England.
Danny and Joe have those rented amps all sorted out now.
We added Break Tune and Red House to the set.
Another change, that is proving to be very effective, is the pre-Ride of the Valkyries blasting of For Those About to Rock from AC/DC's current album.
Now we're heading back to the Country Club, to do it all over again, tonight.

Monday August 23, 1982

We're driving out of LA, south on the 405 when the rental van starts limping and banging. Flat tire.

Doc careens across seven lanes of traffic, finally landing in the ditch on the side of the freeway. What now?

The road manager starts digging around under our bags.

Looking to see if this pink van has a spare. Or a jack.

What a drag. Man it's hot.

The rest of us mill around, staring at the blow out. Cars fly by.

I hear Hargrove yelling. He's leaning over a guardrail, pointing down at something.

The Admiral and I go over to see what his problem is.

Hey, look down there, it's a funky little Mexican cantina with a cocktail lounge attached.

Danny leaps over the railing and crashes through underbrush-covered hillside. Joe and I are right at his heels.

Between cold Tecate beers, we get to know the very friendly barmaids. Joe asks the prettiest one if she'd like to come out to see our show down in Huntington Beach.

Eventually, our road manager drags his hot, sweaty, grubby self down to our happy hideaway.

"Gentlemen, time to start your engines.

Say good-bye to the ladies."

Back on the highway. Cruising south and…Damn.

We just blew out another tire.

Doc is pissed. He veers off the freeway with one hand, digging through his Halliburton briefcase with the other.

Looking for the vehicle rental contract and some dimes.

"I'm gonna go find a pay phone," he fumes.

We watch as Doc stomps away, back up the hot, noxious 405 freeway. Gonna be a long hike. So, we sit in the van and wait.

Vibrating from the eight lanes of traffic tearing past us.

It's starting to get really hot in here. This sucks.

"Hey, Cowboy."

"Yeah, Joe?"

"Remember all those hitchhiking stories you're always telling us about?"

"You mean when I hitched to Colorado with my girlfriend?"

"Yeah"

"Well that was back in '69. I haven't hitched in a while."

"So…We just sit here?"

A rumbling, stinking garbage truck passes by, rocking our van.
"No. Okay, Joe. Let's go."
With that, the two of us hop out, run a few car lengths down the
405 and stick out our thumbs. Cars and trucks fly by us even
faster. Some are blasting their horns.
"It's like fishing. Takes a little time."
"If you say so, Cowboy."
"Be patient. One of these guys will stop for sure."
We walk backwards down the freeway as we waggle our
thumbs.
Eventually we reach an overpass. The road down below us looks
a lot smaller. Friendlier too.
A two lane, divided highway.
"Look down there, Joe.
That road might be easier to get a ride on.
There're more places where a car can pull over safely."
Over the side we go, tumbling down an embankment. The road
below even has a sidewalk. We hike up the pavement in (what I
hope) is the direction of the Pacific Ocean.
This is like a neighborhood street. Trees, lawns. A dog.
Every so often a car approaches, I turn and raise my lucky
thumb. No takers.
Up ahead, I see this young guy out in front of a little house,
out in the driveway, hunched under the hood of a vintage
muscle car.
"Watch this, Joe."
 Nearing the house I stroll up to the grease monkey. The Admiral
stands back and watches me from the sidewalk.
"Excuse me...hey, nice car, man."
The kid pulls his head out of the engine compartment and stares
at me blankly.
My hair is a windswept mop, I'm wearing a blue bandana, a torn
radio station t-shirt, three studded leather belts, black jeans and
cowboy boots.
"Uh...thanks. What d'ya want?"
"Hey, look, I'm hoping that maybe you can help us out. We're
playing the Bear tonight - on Huntington Beach - and we need a
little lift...um, do you recognize that guy over there?"

I point straight at the Admiral, who shoots me a horrified glance.
"I dunno, should I?"
"I'll give you a hint. *Rocks, Dream On, Toys in the Attic*.
The kid squints at Joe.
"Oh, yeah. That's the guy from Cal Jam, right?
The Aerosmith guy?"
"Bingo, my friend. That's Joe Perry. The rock star. Standing
right here in front of you. How'd you like to drive Joe Perry to
his big concert tonight?"
"Gee, I dunno about that."
"We'll even hook you up with a backstage pass. Listen, my
friend, you're gonna be telling your grandkids about this day.
The day you got to cruise the beach with Joe fukken Perry of
Aerosmith as your co-pilot."
"Look man, I'd really like to help you guys out… but my car…
it's messed up…sorry."
"Really? Are you sure?"
"Yeah. Sorry dude."
I walk back to where Joe is standing.
As we leave Perry shakes his head,
"Cowboy, you came on a little strong back there. I think you
scared that poor kid."

Tuesday August 24, 1982

I wake up in my bed at the Huntington Beach Inn. Everyone
made it down here…eventually. Doc managed to get the lemon
van with the two blow-outs towed back to wherever it came
from. Then he rented a blue, hopefully better van, another Ford I
think, at nearby LAX. Looks better than that pink one.
After wearing down most of our shoe leather, Joe and I finally
gave up on hitchhiking. We counted up our pocket change and
grabbed a city bus that got us within a few miles of our
destination. Then we resumed the long march.
That's when a sedan glided up behind us.
"You fellas want a lift?"
It was the two barmaids from the cantina.

I got a little mixed up yesterday. We didn't have to play last night. Thank goodness.
So we had the remainder of the evening off, to hang on the beach and the Huntington Pier with the waitresses and to rest our worn out dogs. Fun, fun, fun.

I'm a hard rocker by trade, but a chunk of my teenage heart still connects to the surf-lifestyle promoted musically by Brian Wilson and the Beach Boys, guitarist Dick Dale, drummer Sandy Nelson, Jan and Dean and the Surfaris - with their inspiring hit, Wipe Out. Personally, I see myself as more of the beachcomber or beach bum type. In any case, I always gravitate to the nearest ocean. I'm in heaven, staying here at the Huntington Beach Inn on 800 Ocean Avenue. Beach movie memories take-over as I watch woodies, wahinis, hot-doggers, gremmies and hodads parading by. Anybody seen Deborah Walley sidewalk-surfing through here?
Fast forward, back to 1982, where the Joe Perry Project is playing right up the street at the Golden Bear. A storied venue directly across from the Pier. We're playing two sold out shows tonight.
Tim Bogert, the vocalist/bassist of both Vanilla Fudge and Beck, Bogert, Appice is the opener.

Wednesday August 25, 1982

Hated leaving that beach.
But I can't wait for our next adventure. We've got 400 miles to cover today and our drummer Ron is already plugged-in behind me. Hitting that little drum pad over and over and over again. We're pushing up the 5. A California freeway that bisects the lower half of the state. North of Los Angeles we pass the huge Magic Mountain amusement park before traversing a mountain range that finally opens up to desert sands and later on, farm lands. Passing Bakersfield, Avenal, Coalinga, Los Banos, Newman, Tracy and finally looping around into San Francisco Bay.

Thursday August 26, 1982

Once again, Doc manages to wheel us safely into port and book us into rooms for the night. We're at a place called the Berkeley House Best Western.

Sadly, whenever I think of Berkeley I always remember People's Park and "Bloody Thursday" a May 1969 incident where police aimed shotguns at student protestors and, following the urging of the frightened Governor, pulled their triggers. Over a hundred kids got sprayed with buckshot and were hospitalized. A student named James Rector was killed by multiple gunshot wounds. A lot of years have passed but I can't think of Berkeley without recalling that shooting.

I'm like that with Dallas, too.

Today, Berkeley is a happy, lively place. Students everywhere, cafes, galleries, book stores.

We're headlining the Keystone Berkeley, right on the main drag, University Ave, in between a copy place and a loan office. It has a capacity of 500. I'm betting on another full house.

I was right about the SRO crowd. I'm sure the kids tonight were expecting to hear the Project that recorded the last Columbia album. As a ticket buyer I would. Still, they seemed to accept Danny and me being up there instead. Of course, they mainly just came to see Joe Perry.

Seems there's no backstage door here, so post-show we get hustled through the crowd and out the front entrance. Out on the sidewalk the fans are clustered thick. Jay and Doc guide us toward our little rental van. It's perched on the curb. One by one we make our way into the vehicle. Fans are pushing up against us as we try to climb into the van. Joe's passenger door is still swung wide-open when he sees the girl.

We all see her. Tousled blonde hair. Blue, smiling eyes. A trim, tanned, curvaceous figure.

Doc is gunning the engine, time to hit it.

Joe reaches down into the surging crowd and plucks the girl up by her wrists, he lifts her up into the shotgun seat, she lands right on top of him, the van door slams - and we take off.

Her name is Kerstyn.

Friday August 27, 1982

The JPP tour moves to downtown San Francisco.
This hotel is imaginatively named Holiday Inn Downtown.
I'm all fired-up and racing around the city like the tourist I am.
Checking out Fisherman's Wharf, the cable cars, glomming
views of Alcatrazz and the Golden Gate Bridge.
Tonight we're at The Stone at 412 Broadway in the North Beach
district. Lots of Perry superfans have followed us here from last
night's gig.
These Keystone clubs aren't huge, which makes them easier to
pack. I'm riding high and Joe plays on a new level tonight.
Must be Kerstyn.

Saturday August 28, 1982

Wake-up call jolts me at around 10:30 a.m.
I saw an interesting shop down on Telegraph Ave yesterday.
So, today I swing by and pick up an embroidered black velvet
jacket before we blow town.
Lucky for me there's still another Keystone venue to visit up
here. This one is in Palo Alto. Doc is at the wheel. Joe has
moved out of his shotgun seat so he can sit beside Kerstyn. Her
skin glows and she looks and sounds really smart. Danny rides
shotgun. Tonight is the biggest of the three Keystone venues.
Turns out to be the most crowded of all.

Sunday August 29, 1982

I awaken at the Flamingo Motel in Palo Alto. There was an
after-party last night. I think I got to say "bye" to the Admiral
but I'm not sure. Anyway, he and Doc and Kerstyn are all gone
now and the rest of us have a lot of miles to cover.
I pack my stuff and meet Hargrove and Ron Stewart in the
lobby. Jay has taken over as our driver/road manager for the
next stretch.
I hate to say good-bye to the Bay Area. Fun people up here.
We aim south.

Stray Cats are on the radio singing Rock this Town.
We're hungry and Jay surprises us with a visit to meet his sister, Cathy. Her place happens to be just down the road.
Cathy has a home-cooked meal all laid out for us. We dine on her porch and enjoy the beautiful garden.
Then it's back to the freeway. We follow the dotted lines all the way back down the 5 until we finally hit the 10 in L.A.
We stop for the night in West Covina.

Monday August 30, 1982

Jay, Hargrove and I kept the bartender laughing all night here at the West Covina Holiday Inn. Sharing tales of endless cocaine in Caracas, Toronto go-go dancers, cat fights in Taylor Michigan and my attempt to hitchhike on the 405 with Joe Perry.
We're inside the rental van again, Jay cranks the stereo and about 475 miles later we arrive in Tucson AZ. We pull into the Sandman Inn.

Tuesday August 31, 1982

I'm not exactly sure where Doc and Joe and Kerstyn all disappeared to. I'd like to think Joe is in Hollywood, along with Tim Collins, taking meetings with major label executives who are all fighting over who gets to sign the Project to a multi-album deal with a huge advance.
On the other hand, Joe could be back in Massachusetts, appearing before some ornery judge who wants proof of his fiduciary responsibility. I really have no idea but I don't want to tip my hand by asking the others about it.
My father always advises me to "wait and see."
Jay drives us through 280 miles of amazing, wide-open American vistas today. Finally seeing a sign in New Mexico that says Welcome to Holiday Inn Las Cruces.

Wednesday September 1, 1982

For Those About to Rock.
So happy to find the Admiral and
Kerstyn down in the hotel restaurant this morning. The Project is
back in action.
Tonight we headline a big concert at the Pan American Center,
right here in Las Cruces.

Thursday September 2, 1982

That was fun.
Now let's drive 600 more miles through the desert.
Jay has rejoined the crew in the truck. Doc is back at the wheel
of our rented van. He and Joe are sipping bourbon from a Jack
Daniels bottle as we maintain a steady 100 mph.

Friday September 3, 1982

Ronnie Stewart went to buy drum sticks and these two ladies
trailed him back to the gig. We're at the Will Rogers Auditorium
in Fort Worth TX.
As we all know, I get pumped anytime I get to play on a stage
the Rolling Stones once performed on. This venue was a regular
stop for the Stones back in the mid-sixties. Hendrix burnt his
blue Strat on this stage at least once - and many other guitar
greats have appeared here. No wonder Joe Perry is booked here
tonight. The show goes pretty well, but the incredible reaction
from the California crowds last week has spoiled me a bit.
Ron's lady friends are backstage and they're totally smashed.
Turns out that one works at the music store and the other one is
her daughter. They both look younger than me.
Anyway, as our usual post-show fun and games commence, the
two drunks decide they both really like me.
Nothing wrong with that, except a few hours later the mom is
passed out on the empty bed in my room. That leaves poor
Cowboy having to squish into the other bed with her daughter.

Saturday September 4, 1982

Woody is pointing at me and guffawing.
That dirty dog spotted those two hungover Texas gals scurrying
from my motel room this morning.
Now he's telling everyone about what he saw. According to
Woody, the very same dynamic duo pulled the same stunt when
the band New England, another group Woody was touring with,
visited this same city about a year ago.
"Those two are notorious." cries Woody in hysterics.
The crew all grin at me and salute me with thumbs up.
"Forget it guys. Nothing happened." I sputter.
They all crack-up, howling, slapping each other on the back,
pumping their fists back and forth and arching their eyebrows at
me.
"Oh. Okay. Yeah right…Whatever you say, Cowboy…
We totally believe you."
It's no use.

Sunday September 5, 1982

Believe it or not, the mom and her daughter, now sober and
clothed appropriately, stop by the motel today and invite me to
join them for an outing to the local amusement park, Six Flags
Over Texas. I had fun, too. Except for the Texas Cliffhanger.

Monday September 6, 1982

It's been about three weeks since we flew out of Boston. I began
this swing with my $109 tax windfall plus a few dollars left over
from what Tim paid me for the Caracas shows and other recent
gigs in my back pocket. I've gone through all of it. Now I'm just
living on my $15 per diems. I have no credit card or any other
source of money. It's starting to get tricky. Sometimes, Doc will
give me a day or two advance on my per diem - but not
always. Eating enough on in-between travel days, when there is
no hospitality snack tray or free crew meal available, can be a

challenge. Especially if I spend too much at the bar or need to buy a band-aid or something else comes up.

Doc is beginning to get a little crazy too. He's been hitting the Jack Daniels bottles that Joe keeps beside the console pretty regularly. Pointed horns are pushing up through our road manager's skull.

I'm not sure if Doc digs it, now that Joe has moved to a back bench seat, so he can always be with Kerstyn. Speaking of her, she's a great traveling partner. Friendly but shy, she only speaks when spoken to. She's very respectful towards all of us in the band. Tonight we headline another Agora Ballroom. In Dallas.

Tuesday September 7, 1982

Waking up today in the Dallas Holiday Inn. After breakfast we gallop 200 miles due south on I35 where we find Austin waiting for us. I've heard tales of musicians who tour constantly for years, playing dozens of cities, without ever having to leave the Lone Star State. It's that big. We're booked at a really nice nightclub tonight, called Cardi's.

I wish I could say I've gotten over my lack of confidence on these JPP and Aerosmith songs. It must be so cool to open your mouth and sing the songs like they sound on the records.

I mean, I kinda know how that feels, my Thundertrain records got played on Boston radio and it was always more fun singing the songs once they were out as singles or on albums.

But when Hargrove and I hit the stage, I'm aware of people pointing, wondering, hey - what happened to David Hull? And Charlie? Or at least that's what I assume they're saying.

I'm a very insecure person.

Wednesday September 8, 1982

Doc was nursing that bottle of Jack Daniels as he sped the 166 miles over to Houston.

There's another Cardi's club here and I thought our stage show went over great. The crowd of several hundred responded well.

But then I snapped last night.

I'm not a violent person, I run from a fight. But some of my confidence issues came to a boil after our set.

I was being escorted by a crew member, back to the dressing room, when some wise-ass stepped right in front of me and said something along the lines of,

"You sucked up there.

Joe Perry should get back with Steven Tyler."

Normally I would have brushed it off - but not tonight.

I grabbed the dude by the collar of his jacket, twisted it hard, and lifted the guy right off the ground with one hand. Pretty high too. That's how pissed I was. The only person more startled than him was me. I let go and the guy came crashing down. I made a quick exit into our dressing room and stuck close to security for the rest of the night. That guy was big, he must have been drunk as a boiled owl, otherwise he would have clobbered me.

Thursday September 9, 1982

We have the day off in the Houston Holiday Inn. Joe leaves early for a short trip to Boston. Tomorrow's his birthday.

I'm sure he wants to spend it with his son.

Friday September 10, 1982

We've got 387 miles to cover today. I'm not thrilled about the way Doc is driving while drinking, maintaining speeds over a hundred. With the Admiral away, Doctor Feelgood Funk DDA comes out to play. I register several loud complaints from the backseat and he tells me to stick it.

I always heard about things getting crazy on lengthy road trips but I always brushed it off. I've got a lot to learn.

We get into Wichita Falls Texas and it's already way after dark.

I'm hungry but Doc doesn't want to take me anywhere. He's sloshed. The Holiday Inn restaurant has been closed for hours.

The snack machines are empty except for chewing gum.

The hotel is out on the highway in the middle of nowhere.

I only have ten bucks to my name and I'm famished.

I thumb through the Yellow Pages and start calling pizza places. All closed. Except for one. They're just about to shut down, so I quickly place my order and give them my room number at the hotel. My stomach won't stop rumbling.

I lie down and hope they deliver soon. Almost an hour goes by. No phone call, no knock at the door. I decide to go down to the lobby and wait for the pizza guy. Never been so hungry in my life.

As I head down the hallway I can hear commotion coming from Doc's room. His door suddenly flies open, and one of our crew tumbles out, pizza dangling from his mouth.

"What the hell?" Doc pokes his head out and grins at me.

"Whoops. Oh, hey, Cowboy. Was that *your* pizza we just ate?"

Doc laughs, flips over the empty box and flings it at my feet.

The dirty rat must have run into the delivery guy in the hallway, pretended it was his order, paid the bill, and ate the whole damn thing himself.

I pick up the greasy box and hurl it at Doc's drunken face.

Pissed, he charges right at me, gets me in a bear hug and throws me down. Crushing me as I struggle to get away.

Doc is easily twice my size. He's got me pinned down.

"Take off the dress, Cowboy. You're nothing but a pussy...and you can't even sing."

Back in my room hungry and hurt, not physically, but stung by Doc's carefully picked words. He knows my Achilles heel all too well. I'm so damn angry right now. No money, no food, Joe Perry's gone, I'm a thousand miles from home. I'm starving and I feel totally powerless.

Sobbing, I grab the lamp from the bedside table.

I heave it across the room and the ceramic base explodes all over the floor, shards of glass fly everywhere.

Two seconds later my telephone starts to ring.

"Fuck off Doc."

I tear the phone cord out of the wall and hurl the heavy telephone base into the air. It crashes into the dresser mirror, smashing it into smithereens.

Saturday September 11, 1982

It's just another Pleasant Valley Saturday.

Tonight we're playing an outdoor festival at the Pleasant Valley Speedway, here in wide open Wichita Falls Texas.

I'm still all worked up about last night. I camp out in the lobby, waiting for Joe to return.

Not long after his arrival, the Admiral kindly sits down with me and patiently listens to my grievances. He hears me out and nods his head sympathctically. That's as far as it goes though. I don't really know what I expect him to do. He's probably thinking to himself "Really, Cowboy? Doc ate your pizza? That's really tough...oh and by the way, I'm losing my house, my kid, all my possessions and I owe millions...But that's really too bad about your pizza."

Nothing like a great gig to turn the page. The scene out at the Speedway is really cool. They've built this big Altamont-type stage, facing out to throngs of bikers, teens and Texas party hounds who are all camped-out on the race track in total darkness. We can't see 'em, but we sure can hear 'em out there. Gunning their engines. Howling like coyotes.

My hero John Kaye and Steppenwolf go on before us.

I'll never forget the night in the Spring of 1969 when Merry and I hustled up St. Botolph Street in Boston. Headed for a wrestling venue called the Boston Arena, to see a dizzying show that featured The Youngbloods (Everybody Get Together), the Crazy World of Arthur Brown (Fire) and Steppenwolf (Magic Carpet Ride.)

All at the top of their game.

Tonight is, hands down, one of the most glorious performances by Mr. Joe Perry that I've ever witnessed.

His guitar excursions are mind-bending.

Talk about a magic carpet ride. Forget my current struggles, Joe is riding tall in the saddle.

Following our set, Point Blank, a popular band from Texas with the recent hit "Nicole" tops off a great night under the stars.

Sunday September 12, 1982

Doc has taken it down a notch, maybe Joe spoke to him.
He's acting more like a professional and cracking some good
jokes as he drives us east. I even laugh, a little. We cruise back
through Dallas and along I20, passing Gladewell, White Oak,
Kilgore, Longview and Marshall. Finally crossing the state line
into Louisiana. Shreveport is just a few miles down the road.
We make camp at the Bossier City Holiday Inn.

Monday September 13, 1982

We have gigs waiting up ahead, so we continue slogging
through the south in this little blue Ford van.
319 miles dissolve behind us.

Doc keeps telling us about the Fountain of Fire.
After a bit, we pull up to a hotel on Dauphine St.
Doc comes out with our room keys. Welcome to New Orleans.
It's already dinner time by now. Jay, Ron, Hargrove, the Admiral
and I all want to find out about Doc's Fountain of Fire.
It's a quick walk along Dauphine to St. Peter's Street, and there
at 718, we find Pat O'Brien's. The cocktail napkin says "Site of
the first Spanish theater in the United States, Built in 1791."
We are quickly seated in the crowded courtyard and damn, there
it is - a great big fireball, suspended within a fountain of
cascading water.
"Never mind the menu" coaches our road manager.
"Just order the Hurricane."
We do. And another. Now I'm feeling something.
This city of New Orleans, it's a little different. We wander out of
Pat O'Brien's and see Bourbon Street just down the block.
We join the crowds of people out on the sidewalks, sipping
cocktails and passing music bars without doors or walls. Some
really good bands too. Rock, blues and jazz is oozing out into
the street. Everyone is dancing, drinking, laughing and making
out with each other.
I see a little shop that sells black cat bones, voodoo dolls,

gris-gris bags and shrunken heads. Might be a good place to buy Julia a souvenir. Maybe not.

We turn the corner onto Toulouse St. and notice an eerie alley. There's a gruesome severed arm laying in front of a closed doorway. We have to check this out.

On the door it says *The Dungeon - Members Only*. Of course we all immediately want to join the club. Doc snoops around and is able to get somebody named Kimberly to vouch for us and issue us all temporary membership cards. But the Dungeon doesn't open until midnight. So we still have 45 minutes to kill. Luckily there's plenty to do around here. We duck up the block for some glow-in-the-dark shots and a bowl of foul-tasting alligator stew. Entering the Dungeon, we hear loud, horrible music playing. Cool. We pass through a hallway lit by torches gripped by frozen hands attached to dead looking arms protruding from the cement walls. Like the scene in Polanski's *Repulsion*. We enter a flame-lit bar crowded with bikers, dwarfs, deviates and unhealthy looking individuals. Definitely my kind of place.

I'm looking for a girl to dance with - but most of the girls are wisely dancing with the other girls.

I see the Admiral climbing a steep staircase/ladder that rises up from the dance floor. What's up there? I'm too scared to follow him. I go search for Hargrove. I find Danny at a smaller bar standing between a female body-builder and a creep. We drink a toast to our success. Music getting louder now. I notice that Ronnie isn't around. He must've ditched us, back at Pat O'Brien's after the first round.

Here at the Dungeon our bartender has a jagged spike stuck through part of his face. A cute girl walks by with her date on a leash. After a few more cocktails, Danny suggests we should check on our leader. We push through some perverts and grapple our way up the steep ladder. We enter the V.I.P. room. It's like a little flying saucer with a stainless steel dance floor. I see human forms grunting in the corner on sticky looking futons. Wicked cool. And then over by the bar we see our Admiral.

He's jiggling around. Trying to dance to an Alice Cooper track that's blaring. Danny and I rush to his side.

When you see Joe Perry attempting to dance - you know it's
time to get him home immediately.
"Joe, we gotta get you back to the hotel."
We try to escort Mr. Blotto but he pushes us away.
The Admiral staggers towards the steep staircase and...
He trips forward, falling head first, bumping his skull on every
other rung as he crashes to the bottom of the staircase.
Danny and I are too late to grab his ankles and save him.
Perry is sprawled across the main dance floor down below us.
Hargrove is by his side in a flash.
"Give him some air, folks. Keep on dancing."
Danny attempts to scoop up the Admiral. No go.
That's when Doc and Jay emerge from the opium den,
out in back.
With the help of the bouncers, they are able to carry the
sloshed superstar back up the block to his bed.

Tuesday September 14, 1982

It was past noon when I finally pried my eyes open.
If you ever become a band manager or a booking agent here's
my advice. Never book the New Orleans tour-stop in the middle
of your group's road trip. Save New Orleans for the very end.
We played a venue called Richie's tonight, right here in town. I
already can't tell you a thing about it. This place is dangerous.

Wednesday September 15, 1982

Now we get an entire day off? Here? In the French Quarter?
Danny Hargrove and Cowboy Mach are wild in the streets.
We don't plan on visiting any museums or libraries either.
Might as well cancel the rest of the tour right now.

Thursday September 16, 1982

As my friend Hargrove would say, "We're having more fun than
humanly possible." Not much fun this morning though. We get
rolled out of the Chateau LeMoyne Hotel and carted westbound

on Interstate 10 past LaPlace, Gonzales, Baton Rouge, Breaux Bridge and into Lafayette Louisiana.

Somewhere, somehow, in the midst of today's ride, our manager Tim Collins joins the JPP touring party. Doc books us all into the Lafayette HoJo's motel.

Tonight we're playing a big show with two other bands.

The opener "Toronto" is riding a top ten hit in Canada right now called Your Daddy Don't Know, and their line-up is very similar to Heart's.

Headlining is the hit-making Scottish hard rock band Nazareth. The Project will be going on second, between those other two.

The venue, Slick's Music Hall, is a gigantic, rusting steel warehouse down by the swamps. Something right out of a horror movie. The place is overcrowded, illegal looking and full of sweaty teenagers. The entire scene inspires me tremendously. Seemed like a great show too, but I admit I'm still hallucinating from gallons of Hurricanes and pails of alligator gumbo.

Friday September 17, 1982

Van Halen is playing on the cassette deck in the van. It's their third or fourth record, called Diver Down. I was with the Admiral when he bought this tape in one of those airport newsstands at JFK back in New York.

Not as raw as the usual stuff we listen to in the van. To me, this one doesn't sound as in-your-face as the game-changing first Van Halen album did. But MTV is playing their Oh Pretty Woman video to death and radio is eating up VH's harmony laden Dancing in the Street. Both are cover songs. Interesting. I can't help but analyze every rock hit I hear, always trying to figure out what makes it tick, hoping to crack the magic formula. Chart success is a moving target, especially for hard rockers, and Van Halen are scoring bulls-eyes right now.

Just like Joe and Aerosmith were a few years ago.

We're on our way to a venue impressively named The Spectrum, even further down into the bayou. We cruise through the steamy, sleepy towns of New Iberia, Jeanerette, Bayou Vista, Morgan City and finally throw out the anchor in Thibodeaux. It's only 95

degrees today, cooler than the 105 degree heat emergency that was frying Southern California when we visited a few weeks back. But the tropical humidity here causes sweat to roll down my spine the second my boots hit the parking lot pavement. And there it is. The Spectrum. Another rusty, tin shack.
But much smaller than Slick's last night.
The gig is nothing to write home about. No models or celebrities came to see us. Some guy who catches nightcrawlers for a living shook my hand, that's about it. Except for Joe, we're pretty much on auto pilot, playing a good tight set - but not adding new tunes or doing anything we haven't pretty much covered in the last dozen concerts. I'm feeling a little burnt out. I haven't eaten a vegetable in thirty days.
Horribly, in order to make the next show in time, there will be no hotel or shower tonight. Following our grand finale, we stuff our sweat-drenched selves back into the van and Doc burns rubber out of here.

Saturday September 18, 1982

My mother (and her mother) have birthdays today. I mailed both of them cards from New Orleans. At 550 miles, last night's (and this morning's) drive, across Louisiana, up through Mississippi and on into Georgia, was one our most uncomfortable yet.
We finally get showers and fall into welcome beds at the Sheraton Atlanta.
Savoy Brown is opening for us at Rumors tonight. I don't usually have very much to say to the other bands we work with but back in 1969/70, I was way into Kim Simmonds and Chris Youlden. *Raw Sienna* was always playing on my turntable and I followed the Savoy Brown Blues Band whenever they played the New England area. Cigar-chomping singer Youlden left long ago but lead guitarist Kim still looks a lot like I remember him. I strike up a conversation with the Welsh-born Mr. Simmonds. He seems pleased to hear some of my recollections of days spent chasing his band around.

Of course I'm sure he hears this stuff constantly, everywhere he tours. That's one of the reasons I usually keep my mouth shut when we're on the bill with a star I admire.

The show in Atlanta goes fine. Kim even joins us onstage at the end and jams with us, which is thrilling for me.

In the dressing room after the show I meet Prilla. She works at the Piggly Wiggly. She bakes cookies there. She even brought a little bag of her cookies to pass around the dressing room. She's a cute little rebel gal, so I invite her to the after-show party. But Prilla can't come - because she has to be back at the Piggly Wiggly by 4 a.m. to start getting the daily cookie dough ready.

I bring all this up, because later, back at the Sheraton, the cookie girl shows up - with her girlfriend in tow.

The Project is up on our floor with some of the room doors propped open. Crew and band members, still exhausted from last night's drive, are drinking shots courtesy of the hospitality liquor bottles we brought back from the club. My blaster is cranking away and I start to dance around with Prilla.

That's when Jay runs in, yelling frantically.

"Where is it? Who took it?"

I look up from my excellent dancing.

"What's wrong now, man?"

"Cash. I had it in a Shure mic bag. Where the hell did it go?"

About an hour later, I borrow the van to give Prilla a lift back to the Piggly Wiggly supermarket. Returning to the Sheraton, the missing money has been found.

Stuffed inside the handbag of cookie girl's *girlfriend*.

Joe Perry doesn't talk to me very often, but one of the first things he told me when we started traveling together was:

"Don't let girls into you room, Cowboy.

They'll steal your clothes."

Sunday September 19, 1982

Normally I bum out when a gig is cancelled. Hearing that tonight's show in Daytona Beach has been scrubbed doesn't phase me in the least. I get to stay put.
Right here in the Atlanta Sheraton. Crank up the AC.

Monday September 20, 1982

Back out on the highway to hell. Doc is bombing down I75. We pass Valdosta GA and blow into Florida. It's a gray overcast day. First time the sun hasn't cooked us in weeks. We pass Lake City, Alachua, Gainesville and I doze off.
Waking-up, as we push past Kissimmee, Kanansville, Yeehaw Junction (look it up) and on down to Port St. Lucia.
We're looking for a town called Stuart. Somewhere along the line Kerstyn went missing. She's so quiet I don't really know when it happened. Maybe the Admiral has her stashed up in Boston somewhere. Maybe she returned to California.
I like Kerstyn and hope to see her again.
But it's a good thing she isn't around today because we just pulled into the HoJo's motel in Stuart - and guess who's waiting here for Joe? Elyssa Perry.

Tuesday September 21, 1982

Kim Simmonds is on the bill with us again tonight, I'm psyched. I think they usually have a lead singer, but Kim is doing the singing right now. Savoy Brown is currently a power trio.
A guy named Mark is on bass and Tom is on drums.
We're at Stage East and Joe delivers another very strong show. Ronnie is still challenging the Admiral to musical duels, seeing who can get the final lick in on a lot of the songs. The lengthy song-ending battles sap a bit of the forward energy out of our set, but they allow Ron and Joe to free-form musical ideas that don't fit into our regular repertoire. Kim Simmonds comes back out and joins us for an encore of Going Down. Elyssa watches the show. She gives me a curt hello but keeps to herself.

Wednesday September 22, 1982

Hargrove and I relax poolside at the HoJo's motel in Stuart FL.

Thursday September 23, 1982

Hooray for Hollywood. Hollywood Florida that is. I'm in a
Ramada Inn at Hallandale Beach. We're headlining at yet
another nightclub called The Agora. They're all big but they
don't resemble each other at all. Not like how Kodak Fotomat
booths or Sam Goody record stores all look exactly the same
everywhere you go. I don't know, maybe these Agora clubs get a
better choice and price on touring acts by banding together
under one name, and buying talent in bulk.
Not our biggest crowd of the tour, just a hundred or two, but
definitely some hardcore, longtime Perry fans, all pushed up
against the stage front. The Admiral is hanging out with his
Project again. Elyssa must've headed back up to Boston.

Friday September 24, 1982

We roll up into Tampa and skate out to Tarpon Springs. Just
north of Clearwater, on the shore of the Gulf of Mexico.
We've got a gig booked here at the AstroSkate Park.
Amazing, the places I get to sing with the Admiral. In the past
few months we've hit racetracks, vaudeville houses, amusement
parks, tin shacks, 4-H barns, movie theaters, arenas, roadhouses
and even a bank - but this is our first roller-skate rink.
On arrival, little kids are gliding around while Olivia Newton
John sings Xanadu over the AstroSkate PA system. The birthday
party skaters are ushered out as we begin the soundcheck. Not
the best acoustics I've heard. We'll need to draw at least ten-
thousand fans to soak up all these reverberating soundwaves.
A local music writer is interviewing Joe. I listen in.
*"I wasn't looking for the sweetest voice in town. I was looking
for the right chemistry. Now it's starting to happen again.
It feels great...for the first time in a long while."*
That makes me feel good.

We rock hard for the enthusiastic crowd, not the thousands I'd hoped for, but several hundred at least. Later, out in back, a kid on a bicycle points across the street and tells me,
"I live right over there. I couldn't believe it when I heard Joe Perry was gonna play here at the AstroSkate.
I still can't believe it. Right here. In my backyard."

Saturday September 25, 1982

Waking up in another HoJo motel. In Tampa this time.
Seems like we aren't staying in Holiday Inns very much anymore. Not since I trashed my room at that Holiday Inn back in Texas.
We load-up the Ford and hit the road. South to nearby Sarasota.
Good-bye rental van. So long for now, Florida.
At Sarasota/Bradenton International Airport the JPP boards People Express Flight #168.
We'll be back in Boston in time for supper.

Sunday September 26, 1982

Dazed. At the pink palace in Cambridge. My ass is kicked. I'm too tired to sleep. Wired from 100 mph drives, screaming teens, Doc, Sambo's, the Dungeon, Sex Pistols, Texas Cliffhanger, not eating or sleeping, getting wasted and dancing with a cookie girl. Still having the same emotional and mental battles inside my head. Still no word of any record deal on the horizon.
I finally pass out and sleep for a week.

Friday October 1, 1982

We rehearse at 4 p.m. at the Cambridge Complex. Looking to develop some new material. Joe's banging away on some half formed riffs. I've been messing with lyrics in my notebook.
We had gigs booked this weekend at the Rusty Nail and another down in Providence but I guess they both got moved back.

Oh yeah, Tim called me to the office and showed me this letter:

Holiday Inn Wichita Falls-Downtown Texas
September 11, 1982

To: Mr. Mach Bell
This is an official letter regarding damages to personal
property of the Holiday Inn on the 10th of September, in Room
#307
1 Broken Lamp = $50.00
1 Broken Mirror = $45.00
TOTAL DUE $95.00
We are not charging you for the disconnected phone from the
wall.
Payment is due upon check out
Thank-you.
Sincerely,
Mary
Front Office manager

Tim docked the $95 out of my pay. For all those CA, NM, TX,
LA, GA, FL shows, I ended up grossing around $1,525 and that
includes my daily $15 per diems. It's a long way to the top.

Tuesday October 5, 1982

We're back at the Complex working on new songs.
Getting acquainted with our own amps again. Joe has this new
hook that is unique. A fast moving, brittle sounding riff that calls
and responds to itself. It has a different feel. I've got some lyrics
tentatively titled Across the Borderline - but they don't fit.

Wednesday October 6, 1982

*"Flight to Caracas / I was half-way gone
By the time we landed / I could do no wrong
I could do no wrong / I could do no right
Big Mercedes / Drives into the night"*
These lyrics flow nicely over Joe's cool new riff.
Here comes the chorus:

"Adrianna tell me / When do I sleep?
Haven't passed out yet / Been in town for a week"

With the addition of bass man Danny on high register
backing vocals and Ron's pulverizing beat, When Do I Sleep?
sounds like a winner.

Thursday October 7, 1982

2 p.m. rehearsal at the 'plex. We change gears and rock through
the regular set for the first time since the AstroSkate Park.

Friday October 8, 1982

We headline E.M. Leow's on Main St. in Worcester. The same
room I was breathless about playing six months ago. My scope
has widened since then. Don't get me wrong, I'm still thrilled to
play this huge theater, but it isn't the apex of my career
anymore. My dressing room guests include Andy Bell,
Mr. Silva, Rickey Gallagher, Tabi and an ex-girlfriend from
Holliston named AnneMarie who is currently employed by
Bill Graham Productions out in Marin California.
AC/DC's For Those About to Rock rings out of the house sound
system and the crowd fastens their seatbelts. In the months since
we last visited Worcester, the Project has become a beast.

Friday October 15, 1982

Back in the trusty Dodge van and out on the road. Not much
action since the last show in Worcester. No rehearsals. I hung at
the palace and messed around with my lyric book.
Looks like Tim wants us to cut some fresh demo songs soon.
Doc is at the wheel, needling Danny Hargrove.
"How've you been cuz? Long time no see."
"I'm not your cousin."
"No need to get sore hommes, I only wanted to know how
you're doing."
"I'm doing fine and I'm still not your cousin."

The legend of Doc has been whispered in the bars of Boston for
years now. I think I know most of the tale but I'm not sure what
parts are truth and which parts are fact.

As I understand it: Doc was formerly a cop named Dan. A New
Jersey State Trooper. He fits the profile physically and he sure is
quick on the CB radio. Doc drives and acts like a cop and he still
throws around terms like "alleged perpetrator" whenever he can.
Anyway, Doc was a police officer and he had a family.

Something shitty must have happened because Doc suddenly
ditched everything and everybody and joined the Army. Or
maybe it was the Coast Guard. Or the French Foreign Legion.
I'm not totally sure about that part.

Anyway, Doc was in the armed forces and aboard a military ship
that was anchored out in Boston Harbor. Something shitty must
have happened again because Doc suddenly decided to go
AWOL. He dove off the ship in the middle of the night and
managed to doggie-paddle all the way to Jimmy's Harborside
restaurant down on the waterfront.

Doc didn't know anyone in Boston. He grew his beard and hair
long so the MPs wouldn't catch him. He started getting really
high and I guess that's when Earthquake and the rest of the
Drivers found him.

Next thing you know, he's playing drums with Boston's favorite
party band, under the alias Doctor Feelgood Funk D.D.A.
The rest you can read in your history books.

After a lengthy stretch, riding through the Allegheny Mountains,
we finally pull into Altoona PA. Doc gets us rooms in the
Holiday Inn - so I guess I'm off their shit list.

Saturday October 16, 1982

We forge on, due west. In Pittsburgh we drop our bags off at the
GreenTree Holiday Inn before heading over to the Stanley
Theater. This place was a movie theater before it started booking
live shows like Frank Sinatra, back when Frank was a teen idol.
Movies must have been pretty popular in the olden days because
this place seats 3,800.

It's enormous - and we're the headliner tonight.

I'm really nervous about playing to thousands of empty seats.
That would look pretty weak.
Thankfully, some stage hands start pulling ropes and a bunch of
curtains and partitions fall into place, closing off the far end of
the venue. We're suddenly in a much more reasonable space.

Sunday October 17, 1982

We head north on I75 and exit onto I90 just before we fall into
Lake Erie. Running Northeast along the Great Lake we pass
Shore Haven, Dunkirk, Lake Erie Beach, Hamburg and Buffalo.
We continue on up to Niagara Falls and the nearby town of
Lockport.
New York audiences, in every part of the state, are always good
and rowdy. Joe fukken Perry is right up these kids' alley.
We give 'em what they're looking for, a powerful, no holds-
barred show tonight at the After Dark. Doc loads us back into
the van and checks us into rooms at the HoJo's in Buffalo.

Monday October 18, 1982

We've been driving a lot these past couple days.
We have tonight off.
If I was smart I would kick back at the HoJo motel and maybe
catch up on some HBO. We're gonna be camped here for
48 hours. But me - smart? Never.
I look at a map and realize that Buffalo is just over the border
from Ontario. Wow, I wonder what those two little go-go girls,
Bridget and Kathy, are up to?
After a quick call to Mississauga I make a very sneaky border
crossing into Canada with nothing but a few bucks in my
pocket. The go-go girls manage to round up some guy with
wheels and they all meet me in nearby St. Catharine's.
We joyride back up to Mississauga where Bridget lives. At the
top of a high-rise building, no less. The doorman greets her with
a big smile and gives me a sly wink. Kathy giggles and the other
guy pushes into the elevator behind us.
We get up to Bridget's pad and there's a party going on.

On a Monday afternoon? Kids are slithering around in slow motion. Smoking weed. Funneling Molsons.

The stereo is blasting Loverboy or Survivor or maybe it's Wrabit. There's a fully stocked bar. What the heck?

Blonde Bridget looks to be maybe 22 at best. How can she afford all this? Her penthouse looks like it was decorated by Hugh Hefner. Is she some kind of a high-end call girl?

Could be, she's over there dancing on the coffee table with her shirt undone down to her belly button.

A popular stripper or porn star maybe? She's alway bopping around and wiggling her bum in everyone's face.

Does she have a sugar daddy or is she a trust fund kid?

I have no idea. But I see more free spirits are entering this fun house. Suddenly I'm drinking shots and dancing around like the rest of the teenagers. At 29, I'm the adult here, but I try to fit in with Bridget's mod squad.

Then suddenly - I get horribly, horribly sick.

Tuesday October 19, 1982

Bridget, Kathy and that guy with the car, helped me get back down to the border and dumped me in a wooded area. I truthfully don't know how I crawled back into the USA. I'm a wreck. I had a dime left to make a phone call to the band. Somebody in the JPP van fetched my body and toted my sorry ass back to our encampment at the HoJo motel in Buffalo. Everybody gives me the business.

"What were you thinking, Cowboy? Drinking shots in Ontario? Dude, you're a lightweight. No way you were going to keep up with those two crazy chicks. Don't forget you have to sing tonight...Hey, did ya get any?"

I just want to stick my throbbing pumpkin inside the ice machine. Or flush myself down the toilet. Ouch, my brain is killing me. I sure hope Julia doesn't find out that I'm a stupid moron.

I really let Joe down this time. Not to mention the crowd who came to see us at the Purple Moose in Hamburg NY.

Of course Perry and Hargrove can cover my vocal parts no problem. Danny, in particular, has been doubling my lead vocals for a while now. He has all the lyrics down. When my voice is shot, which is often, especially if we're out for multiple days in a row, I'll just give Hargrove the secret signal that means "You take the high road and I'll take the low road."
The crew basically has to carry me into the venue tonight. I'm that bad. Still out of control. Reeling around and crashing into things. Straight-arrow Ron shakes his head and smirks at me as if to say "Are you ever going to grow up?"
That's when I kick my cowboy boot through the dressing room door and begin lurching towards the stage.
All around me, the rest of the Project is sure-footed as ever. I fall numerous times during the concert. On my ass. On my face. Off the stage. The crowd meanwhile, who are pretty wasted themselves, seem to be getting a kick out of watching me stagger around and flame-out in front of their eyes.
It's only rock'n'roll.

Wednesday/Thursday October 20/21, 1982

I'm not feeling much better. What's wrong with me? We drive to Boston for a minute and turn around again. Wednesday was Woody's birthday.

Friday October 22, 1982

Now we're back in Bergenfield NJ at the Circus. I stride out onto the stage with much bravado. The band is tight and Joe is playing miles above where he was last time we visited this joint. He leads the charge.
The Admiral has a new thing going on these past few weeks. I notice that he reads books on occasion, and when he does, it always seems to be stuff by Hunter S. Thompson.
Joe's even been smoking his cigarettes using a holder recently - one of Hunter's trademarks.

The rumor I heard, is that the Admiral and Hunter have been in contact and are plotting some kind of joint endeavor. The thought of those two drugged-up, gun-toting, wild-men doing *anything* in tandem has me fearing and loathing.

Saturday October 23, 1982

Brad Whitford sits in with the Project for a ballsy show at Mr. C's (the Commodore Ballroom) in Lowell MA. Afterwards I have dinner with John V and his wife. Besides being physically sick, I'm still very conflicted about going out on stage every night and singing other guys' hit songs. I'll never sound like the originals and it's an uphill struggle. I want to promote a record with my own voice on it.

Sunday October 24, 1982

Julia tries to help, but I'm in knots. Bed ridden for days.

Thursday October 28, 1982

We meet up at the Cambridge Complex for a 6:30 p.m. rehearsal. A little bird tells me that the JPP is about to be evicted from this practice room.

Friday October 29, 1982

We're down in Roslyn New York at My Father's Place and I'm very thankful to get to play on this famous stage. As a teen, I used to subscribe to the Village Voice, just so I could follow the weekly ads for great venues like the Fillmore East, the Steve Paul Scene and this place. I think it had just opened back then. Brad Whitford sits in with the Project again tonight.

Saturday October 30, 1982

We cruise up to The Chance in Poughkeepsie. The steadfast patrol of JPP fans are still waiting by the

backstage door - as if they hadn't left since last time we visited.
My friend Joanie comes to see the show too.
She's very cute but she doesn't bring lasagna anymore.

Sunday October 31, 1982

We're in Rome NY at Coleman's.
Everyone in the crowd looks strange. Probably because this is
Halloween. The Project looks strange everyday.
During the set I sing:
"Took a boat to China / Took a jet to Rome..."
The crowd cheers. They all know this is the Rome that I'm
singing about.

Monday November 1, 1982

I've been trying to fight it but I'm still really ill. I have fluid in
my lungs, I'm hacking, coughing and bumming.
Tim sets me up with one of Joe's physicians, Dr. Rees.

Tuesday November 2, 1982

At 11 a.m. I meet Dr. Rees. He's a lot older than me.
He might be almost 50.
He talks to me for a while and checks me out pretty thoroughly.
"Asthmatic bronchitis." he concludes.
Riding in the JPP van is like riding in a bong. But there's more
to it than that. I admit that I have a weird history with the illegal
drug marijuana.
As a young adult I was the Frank Zappa of my town.
Like Zappa, I was probably the freakiest looking guy in
Holliston, but also like Frank, I didn't use drugs.
I never smoked cigarettes either. I tried inhaling a butt once as a
kid and immediately wanted to puke.
I just wasn't down with inhaling anything and I had no need for
it. I didn't like the illegality of pot or drugs either and I always
had my music to keep me busy.

Years passed. Kids would throw joints to me up onstage during my Joe Flash, Biggy Ratt and Thundertrain shows.

I'd just hand them off to my crew. I drank a little beer but smoking reefer was a no go.

Then, years later, on a crappy Thundertrain gig up in Lake Placid NY it finally happened.

We were stuck in a cold, dark band house for a week.

Except for Joanie, our one loyal NY fan, nobody up there gave a damn about us. We performed night after night to zero response. "Play some Aerosmith you a-holes."

At 27, I'd still never touched weed. But then, during that frigid, miserable week, I needed to escape. So, our longtime light man Mick gave me a "shotgun."

That is, he got me to hold a joint in my mouth.

Mick lit it, put his mouth around the lit end and puffed - sending smoke back up into my lungs.

The rest of my stay at Lake Placid suddenly spiraled heavenward. Comfortable, smooth, warm and magical.

So began my late-in-life fling with the killer weed.

Unfortunately, I am extremely allergic to smoke and probably marijuana too. I could tell from the very start. Wheezing, itching, congestion. Back then I was broke, so there was never much of it around. It wasn't a big problem.

Since joining the Project, that's changed. I'm still broke but now we go to more parties, meet more people, fans hand us stuff almost everyday. There's always a joint being passed around. Everywhere we go we're living in a cloud of smoke.

Dr. Rees sets me up with a little inhaler and I go on my way.

Saturday November 6, 1982

I've been puffing my new asthma inhaler but I can't promise I didn't puff on some other stuff too. We headline at Northeastern University tonight here in Boston. I strut across the stage wailing Charlie's I Got the Rock'n'Rolls Again and kicking my heels into Ralph's Rockin' Train.

Holding court like the cockiest, most carefree singer in Boston. But I'm just a showman. It's show and nothing more.

Sunday November 7, 1982

My health takes a turn for the worse.

Tuesday November 9, 1982

I'm back at Dr. Rees's office. Tim is really trying to help me get
better. I have some physical ailments but the big problem is
inside my head. I'm tormented.
When it comes to producing the vocal sound of those earlier
Project and Aerosmith records I fall flat every single night. I
can't help it, I'm nothing like those guys. My voice is instantly
identifiable and totally different from anyone. I need to
establish my own identity in this band. If only I could get these
new songs that I've been co-writing with Joe out on a record.

Thursday November 11, 1982

The Dodge van departs Porter Square in Cambridge at 10 a.m.
Doc wheels us up the Mass Pike straight into New York.
Halfway across the state, Danny Hargrove takes a turn at the
wheel. I'm not sure if Danny has a driver's license but he has
good aim. He keeps the van on course all the way to Ohio,
where Doc takes over again and I finally fall asleep.

Friday November 12, 1982

We pull up at the Park Crest Hotel. I dash to my room and crash
out. A couple hours later I get roused for soundcheck.
In the lobby I see that mysterious dark haired girl again, staring
my way. We head over to Harpo's, pull into the alley, and see
our great gang of ever allegiant Joe Perry followers waiting for
us. Joe is mobbed as usual, Ronnie too.
As I step down from the van, Terri and Chris suddenly swoop
towards me chanting "Gigolo, gigolo, gigolo." Who, me?

The first time I played Harpo's or the Keystone or the Chance, I figured that these were just random kids, in random cities, on random days, never to be seen or heard from again.
Cowboy has a lot to learn about this small world.

Saturday November 13, 1982

Midwest girls sure do hold a grudge.
We're cruising west on I94, road manager Doc is at the controls. We pass the famed cities of Ann Arbor, Battle Creek and Kalamazoo, finally sighting Lake Michigan and dipping down through a bit of Indiana and then into Illinois. Prospect Heights is a suburb north of Chicago, next to Wheeling. Doc manages to locate Haymaker's, a concert club that looks inviting. Good sized stage and decent backstage area.
The first thing I always do is set up my blaster in the dressing room and pop in some AC/DC, Stones or James Brown to create the appropriate atmosphere. Tonight's performance will probably fade into memory but something else happens here that could set our ship on a different course.
A woman.
With eyes for Ronnie. It all happened in an instant.
Ron is suddenly all over this attractive stranger and vice versa.
Frankly I'm startled.
I've seen most of the other guys I'm working with talk to, or at least look at a girl once in awhile. Never Ron though. He only has eyes for his drum kit and that practice pad of his.
Things are about to change.

Sunday November 14, 1982

We set sail from the Flamingo Motel in Prospect Heights and head due south. We cruise back down through Chicago. Doc is at the wheel, the Admiral in the shotgun seat. Hargrove and I ride in the first bench seat. Something is missing. It's strangely quiet in here. The never-ending patter of Ron, beating his drum sticks along to Toto and Asia tapes in the way-back seat has been such a constant in this van that I hardly even noticed it anymore. Until it stopped.

Approaching East Chicago, Doc turns off I90 South onto Route 83. Behind us, riding in a small sedan, are Ronnie and his new girlfriend.

Not far down the highway, at the junction of Route 83 and Route 30, in the small town of Lynwood, we see the "The Midwest's Ultimate Rock Club." A big box of a venue called the Pointe East rising up out of the middle of a large, potholed lot.

We make our way inside. The JPP crew is working on the stage, getting things ready for soundcheck. The Admiral joins them, carefully going over his rig with Ed the guitar-tech. Scanning the posters on the walls I see that Ruby Starr played here a few nights ago, The B'zz, a local Illinois band on Epic, were just here last night. The Iron City Houserockers and Rare Earth will both be here next week. Ronnie and his lady friend are huddled together at a corner table, immersed in conversation.

Monday November 15, 1982

We sleep through every wake-up call at the Coachman Best Western. The housekeepers are banging on the doors when we finally emerge, over two hours past check out time. We load up the van and hit the first diner we see for coffee and breakfast. It's 2 p.m. when we leave the diner, making tracks for Boston. We drive all day and all of the night.

Tuesday November 16, 1982

Doc drops me off in front of the pink palace at 9 a.m.
Time: Lansing IL to Boston in 19 hours.

Wednesday November 17, 1982

Doc's birthday.

Thursday November 18, 1982

We rehearse at the A.Wherehouse in Waltham today at 5 p.m.
I'm dying to see it. Aerosmith's famed rehearsal hall/recording
studio/merchandise headquarters/club house.
It's a big building behind a hardware store. I guess Aerosmith
isn't using it right now, so Joe figures "why not me?"
Turns out to be a roomy place, pretty rundown but perfect for
our rave-up needs. More like a teen center than the Playboy
Mansion I was hoping for.

Friday November 19, 1982

Back at Dr. Rees's office in Boston. Still reeling.
Ever since my idiotic day trip to Canada a month ago.

Monday November 22, 1982

Following a couple days of bed rest, I'm back on my feet and
out in the sticks with the Project. We're at Blue Jay Recording
studio in Carlisle MA. Last time we visited, we had Brad
Whitford in the line-up and Danny and I hadn't even played a
single JPP gig yet. We return as a band with scores of concerts
and thousands of miles under our belts. The plan is to re-record
a few of the best songs off our first demo and add some of our
newer material as well.
We have no time (or budget) to mess around.
After setting-up and mic checking we begin laying down basic
tracks for six songs.
The top hits of the day are Eye of the Tiger by Survivor, Jack &
Diane by John Cougar Mellencamp and Who Can it Be Now?
by Men at Work. Our stuff sounds nothing like any of that.
There's no way Joe and I are gonna write a Don't You Want Me
Baby? We just stick to what we know. Rebellious, riff driven
rock'n'roll. My lyrics are often based on the true adventures of
the JPP. Otherwise I just try to put what I hear Joe's guitar
saying to me into words.

As the session winds down, I'm sitting in the studio lounge doodling in my daily diary. My style is cartoonish. I make a little shield with two snakes on it, the snakes form the letters JP, behind the shield I draw a bird of prey, a hawk, with its wings outstretched and its beak cocked to the left. Joe walks by and glances down at my drawing. "Not bad, Cowboy."

Tuesday November 23, 1982

We return to the studio at 2 p.m. to overdub all our vocals and the Admiral's lead guitar parts.

Thursday November 25, 1982

President Reagan reads a proclamation of thanksgiving on this, our national day of Thanksgiving. Personally I'm thankful to be up here at the Cumberland County Civic Center in Portland ME. The Joe Perry Project are opening up for Nazareth tonight and it's been a while since we played one of these big arena shows. Nazareth has their tour bus parked alongside the stage door.
I watch a parade of anxious groupies trooping into that vehicle. Nazareth must be a bunch of dirty dogs.
Several thousand are already in their seats to hear the Project play. The headliners know that Perry is a big draw around here and have left plenty of room on the stage for us to do our thing. They let us play a full hour set too. Joe goes way back with Nazareth, they have a good relationship.
The show goes great - but it feels weird to be all done for the night at 9 p.m.

Friday November 26, 1982

Tim Collins fired Doc.
Our road manager is done. Gone. Just like that.
I don't know what happened last night.
Some big screw-up?
Maybe just the final screw-up in a long line of screw-ups.

Monday November 29, 1982

We're mixing the new songs out at Blue Jay. We began at 6 p.m.
and this will be an all nighter. Joe is at the controls throughout,
working closely with the engineer.
We end up with some great recordings.
They'll Never Take Me Alive is a new thing that we just put
together at the A.Wherehouse a couple weeks ago. A mid-tempo
number, built around an atmospheric, arpeggiated riff from the
Admiral, with a desolate, haunted vocal from me.
Walk with Me Sally, on the other hand, is a balls-to-the-walls
rocker. Fast-paced and fiery.
Next we have the true tale of our South American adventure,
When Do I Sleep?
It's only now, as I study the playback, that I realize that beneath
the thunder of the drums, my urgent
vocalizing, and the groovy bass/guitar interplay - this song is
actually riding bare-back atop a disco dance beat.
Disco sucks - but this song is pretty hot.
Remakes of Once a Rocker, When Worlds Collide and
Black Velvet Pants round out the six-song demo.

Friday December 3, 1982

Managers Tim and Steve have put together a string of dates for
us up in Ontario Canada. Tim has also been busy making some
changes following the departure of Doc.
I'm on the front bench seat of the van, next to Hargrove.
Lovestruck Ron is with us again, his headphones are in place
and his practice pad is being punished in the way-back.
Joe is in his usual shotgun position.
At the wheel is our brand new road manager - Jay.
He's still our soundman, too. Jay is a smart, nice guy. Not nearly
as fearsome as Doc. Jay is smaller than Doc, he's not all that
much bigger than me. He's a few years younger than me too, but
when he wears a blazer he looks business-like.

We're headed west. Cutting through Mass, across New York
state, buzzing through upper Ohio and up into Michigan.
In Detroit we make the border crossing up into Canada.
First stop is Wallaceburg Ontario and the Webber Hotel.

Saturday December 4, 1982

Our concert in the ballroom of the Webber is intense and goes
down great, but the crowded after-party in the hotel lounge gets
way out of hand.
Ed, the Admiral's longtime guitar technician, just got married
and he is suddenly feeling terribly homesick for his bride.
To console himself, Eddie decides to lay his head back-on-the-
bar while our Canadian fans pour assorted drinks into his
open pie-hole. The hotel lounge has a special indentation carved
into one end of the maple bar-top for this sport.

Thirst quenched, our crewman suddenly shows his evil side.
Shit-faced Ed leaps atop the center table, and starts to do an
extremely rude dance as he flips off our neighbors to the North.
He proceeds to hurl insults at the roomful of "foreigners."
One by one the locals begin to berate our bombed roadie.
In retaliation, Marine veteran Ed tears open his trousers and
begins to gyrate lewdly.
Danny and I can hardly believe the spectacle unfolding before
us. Hargrove nudges me astonished,
"I never knew Eddie was such a good dancer."
Ordered by the hotel management to leave the public area,
intoxicated Ed races out of the bar and down the hotel corridor.
Half-naked and cursing loudly. We watch as Ed pries a large fire
extinguisher off the wall - and gallops away, around the corner.
Next thing we know, thick foam is spraying everywhere,
dripping off the walls and across the ceilings.
I duck into my hotel room as the fist-fights begin.

Sunday December 5, 1982

The Joe Perry Project is laying low, somewhere in Ontario,
following the partial-demolition of the Webber Hotel the
previous evening.
We have a new kid on the road crew named John.
He joins Woody, who runs our concert lighting (as well as
tending Stewart's drum kit), Ed, the dancing guitar-tech, and our
new road manager Jay (who also does the house sound mix).
This kid John looks really young and really stoned. From what
I've seen so far, his job is to smoke and talk to girls.

Monday December 6, 1982

We motor east on Route 2 passing Kent Bridge, Thamesville and
Middlemiss before arriving in London Ontario where we rock a
downtown bar called Fry-Fogels. The girls are amazingly
beautiful in this city (home of a recent Miss Universe winner)
but our band is more interested in watching John Carpenter's
The Thing in the club's comfortable, downstairs screening room.

Tuesday December 7, 1982

Jay checks us out of the Park Crest Hotel in London and we
continue our Canadian tour, rolling past Woodstock, Brentford,
Hamilton and Mississauga. Next stop is Toronto. Once again I
will have the thrill of playing a stage that the Rolling Stones
once roamed. The club is El Mocambo. The night the Stones
played here in 1977 is legendary. We've already sold out both of
the two shows we'll be performing tonight. And yes,
Kathy and Bridget are here to go-go dance to their favorite band.

Wednesday December 8, 1982

El Mocambo was a trip alright. The room holds around 500 so it
was packed for both performances - and they dug what we
dished out. We've made some changes to the set list.
Not a single Aerosmith song in the bunch.

Life at a Glance
Discount Dogs
Ain't No Substitute for Arrogance
Once a Rocker
When Worlds Collide
Heartbreak Hotel
Manic Depression
Soldier of Fortune
Red House
Black Velvet Pants
East Coast, West Coast
When Do I Sleep?
Rockin' Train
I've Got the Rock'n'Rolls Again
Let the Music Do the Talking
Encore: Walk With Me Sally

We're set up at the Oakfield Holiday Inn, just south of Mississauga. We have another show tonight at a nearby rock venue in Burlington Ontario called the Orient Express. The same Orient Express that promoted that festival last summer at Courtcliffe Park. Our new roadie has earned a nickname by the way. I'm not sure why - but everyone is calling him Phuck.

Thursday December 9, 1982

We're still holed up at the Oakfield Holiday Inn outside of Toronto. Ed has finally had enough. Missing his new wife, our trusty Marine turns in his resignation letter to the Admiral and heads back to Boston.
Bye, Ed. Everyone is sad to see him go.

Friday December 10, 1982

Barrymore's in Ottawa is another top flight venue. A converted movie theater that books really good bands. Later this week they've got the Psychedelic Furs and Roy Buchanan coming in. The staff is top notch and I must note - they have two of the sexiest cocktail waitresses I've ever seen. Wanting to impress the help, I put on an extra special good show.

I also help out a bit on Joe Perry's side. Now that Ed is gone, I jump into action in between some of my vocals. Dashing side-stage, slapping on the guitar tech's headset and running the Admiral's guitars through the Conn Strobotuner - since nobody else on the crew has guitar tuning skills.

Following a searing show, I go outside to cool down. Not too much time passes before I see headlights slowly coming my way, aimed right in my eyes. The vehicle approaches and swerves to a stop, right in front of me. It's a red convertible sports car.

In the front bucket seats sit those two incredibly attractive cocktail waitresses.

"Hey, you. Wanna have some fun?" they coo.

They're stunning - but for some unknown reason I say "no thank you." Can you believe I said that? I can't.

From the startled looks on their faces, it's obvious that these two lovelies have rarely been turned down for anything.

They try me one more time, but seeing that I'm a party-pooping dud, they hit the gas in disgust and book it out of there.

Saturday December 11, 1982

Busted.

The Joe Perry Project fail the USA border crossing.

The Admiral, Ron, Danny and I, along with Jay and Phuck, were all traveling together in the Dodge van. At the Canada/USA border we got detained, They escorted us out of our vehicle and into a drafty holding area.

We can tell that computer background checks are being run on all our I.D.s. Hunched over their glowing screens, we see the agents pointing and whispering. We try to eavesdrop from the next room. It's cold but I'm sweating.

Now a border patrol officer gets on the phone. Shit. He's calling the State Police. One of us is about to get arrested.

We sit squirming, each feeling guilty as sin.
Of course we've all been indiscreet and unlawful all week, all
month, and for most of our lives.
Ron looks innocent, but is he really?
Hargrove definitely looks like someone who belongs in the city
jail. I have unfinished court business involving my arrest at a
Thundertrain gig down at Framingham South High that's been
haunting me for years. And what about the Admiral? You can bet
Joe Perry has a closet full of skeletons.
Cop cars screech in, blue lights flashing. The Admiral is glaring
at the floor. Hargrove is gritting his teeth and turning white.
My nose is running and my feet smell. The cops sweep in. They
take out the hand cuffs. Pulling him to his feet and spinning him
around they cuff the teenager who only joined us this week.
Phuck.
They escort the kid out to the paddy wagon.
The rest of us high-tail it back to Boston.

Monday December 13, 1982

The bad news is there was some sort of arrest warrant out on the
kid. Breaking and entering or something like that. The good
news is that Phuck's dad is a big wheel in law enforcement.
He's the district attorney of New Hampshire or maybe a police
chief, I forget which. Anyway, Pop should be able to spring his
kid out of jail sooner than later. Other than that, I've been busy
kicking myself in the ass for turning down those two cocktail
waitresses in Ottawa.
I'll take this shame to my grave.

Tuesday December 14, 1982

Jay drives the band down to Wilkes Barre PA where we spend a
couple nights in this off-beat hotel made out of old train cars.
All linked together on a siding of track.
The railway cars have been remodeled into cool hotel rooms
with brass beds, velvet upholstery and Victorian furnishings.

The Cowboy is living it up like James West on the Wild Wild
West TV show.

Wednesday December 15, 1982

Next door to our train-car hotel is a venue called The Station.
More of the railway motif here too. We're the headliner and
maybe we should bring back Train Kept A-Rollin' as the
kick-off for this show.
Now that Phuck is in jail, we have someone filling in. Another
teenager, this guy looks even younger. His name is Sean.
Taking over Ed's position we have another new recruit who
claims he used to be on The Ramones crew.
A shady looking character - named Zakowski.

Thursday December 16, 1982

Our show this evening in Philadelphia got 86'd.
We stay in our train-cars for another night.

Friday December 17, 1982

I find a pay phone and give Julia a call, back at the palace.
Today she is flying home to London (the one in England not the
one in Ontario) to spend the Christmas holidays with her family.
The band is heading over to New Jersey, where the Joe Perry
Project delivers a bagful of rock to the kids at Somerset College.

Saturday December 18, 1982

We roll into Riviera Beach MD where we headline The Sandbar.
I don't know what it is about this place that I love so much -
or to put it a better way - is there anything about this place NOT
to love?
Right on the shore, big crowd, loud reception.
These kids really dig our new tunes too.
A fitting way for Hargrove and me to celebrate our 80th and
final Project show of this totally unexpected, unforgettable year.

Sunday December 19, 1982

We make the ride from Baltimore back to Boston in 9.5 hours.

Monday December 20, 1982

I attend a Christmas party at the Rat in Kenmore Square.
Everyone buys me drinks.

Tuesday December 21, 1982

Ron Stewart departs for Chicago to spend the holiday with his
new lady friend.

Wednesday December 22, 1982

Joe Perry leaves for Sedona Arizona to spend Christmas with his
mom and sister.
I hit the Christmas Party at Storyville in Kenmore Square and
then the Metro Christmas party on Lansdowne St. behind
Fenway Park. Everyone buys me drinks.

Thursday December 23, 1982

Tim Collins closes up the office for the holidays.
He heads up to NH for Christmas.

Friday December 24, 1982

I go home to Holliston MA to spend Christmas with my parents
and siblings.

The Dungeon

738 TOULOUSE
(DOWN AN EERIE ALLEY)

- Guest -

THE UPSTAIRS IS FOR MEMBERS ONLY

Kimberly

Thursday January 6, 1983

The Admiral returns to Boston from his holiday getaway in
Arizona. Julia returns to the pink palace from London.
Unfortunately, this is also the day that another of Joe's longtime
crew members resigns. Woody bids farewell to the JPP.
I can't help but wonder if the recent departures of Ed and
Woody possibly had something to do with the loss of Doc as our
road manager.
I figure that when Jay got elevated to the road manager position
it might have been difficult for his mates Woody and Ed to
adjust to Jay's new status as the boss.

Rock'n'Roll slows down in the month of January. Colleges are
in recess, it's cold and dark, blizzards threaten.
People (around here anyway) just don't want to go out so much.
Our managers focus their efforts on finding the Project that
elusive record deal, and booking shows for the year ahead.

Saturday January 22, 1983

At 3:30 p.m. I meet with the Admiral at the A.Wherehouse. The
Project has been using it as a temporary practice space.
We toss around a bunch of new song ideas.
Joe riffs on his guitar and every time he gets into a new groove -
I flip through my notebooks and try to match my lyrics to his
music.
Choose Your Poison, Help from the Devil, Little Girl Lost,
Thin Red Line, Four Against the House, Riding Shotgun,
Captive Heart, Twelve'o'Nine, Maypole Song…
On and on it goes. Just jamming in circles 'til something clicks.
We take a break and begin pipe-dreaming about renting a house
out in Hollywood and moving the Project west to get out of all
this snow.
We'll be hitting the road next week, hungry as ever.

Thursday January 27, 1983

Phuck is at the wheel of the ice-covered van as we depart
Cambridge for Cleveland Ohio. Joe and Ronnie are manning
their usual posts. Danny and I are relieved to be back on the
path to adventure. Normal life is hard to cope with after cruising
for months with the Project.
We motor 11.5 hours before finally checking into the notorious
rock hotel Swingo's. Danny and I drink a toast to Ed back in
Boston. It's Eddie's b-day today.

Friday January 28, 1983

Headlining at the Cleveland Agora. The Godz open.
WMMS co-promotes. Psyched to play the Project's first show of
the new year. Our revamped crew is green.
We have juvenile delinquent Phuck, who drove us here
yesterday, as stage hand.
Teenager Sean is now our lighting director.
Shifty looking Zakowski, who is around my age, is looking after
the Admiral's guitars. Zakowski is checked into Swingo's as
Lance Charger and he raises my suspicions immediately.
It's that deranged glint in his eye. I'd hate for him to lead the
newbie crew kids astray. Following a sensational and satisfying
Agora show, we recess to the after-party at Swingo's.

Saturday January 29, 1983

Checking out of Swingo's, road manager Jay is back at the
wheel. Flying down I71 passing Ashland, Mansfield and
Berkshire before hitting Columbus.
Swingo's to the Columbus Red Roof Inn = 2.5 hours.
We headline the Agora Ballroom tonight and it's my pleasure to
get to know local JPP fans Susie, MaryLou and Elaine.

Sunday January 30, 1983

Super Bowl Sunday at the Downtown Cincinnati Holiday Inn.

The Alexander's Massacre.

Cops in the halls, Blood on the walls.

I'm not a big sports fan, but what the heck. The Project is here in Cincinnati for a concert tomorrow night. I figure I'll ride the elevator up to the city-view cocktail lounge and check out Super Bowl XVII.

It's playing on a big 27-inch color TV, mounted over the bar.

The Dolphins are battling against the Redskins.

Playing out in Pasadena, at the Rose Bowl.

As I sit munching pretzels and sipping my Bud, our new JPP road crew is down the street at a local bar called Alexander's.

Why or how it all went down I haven't a clue.

For some reason, a fist-fight breaks out at Alexander's and some people get hurt. Including at least one of our crew guys, who starts bleeding profusely.

Meanwhile, back at the city-view lounge, the Redskins are whipping the Dolphins. Final score 27-17. I leave the bar and head back down to my room to crash, totally missing what happens next.

The JPP crew were tracked back to the Holiday Inn by police officers who responded to the massacre at Alexander's.

Cops follow the bloody trail that leads back to our hotel and through the lobby. The blood stains end at one of the elevators. After a quick bit of sleuthing, the Cincinnati police determine our floor. It's the level with blood splattered up the hallway. The trail of blood continues around the corner and straight to one of the roadie's rooms.

Case cracked. Thankfully, mercifully - no arrests are made against the Project this time.

Monday January 31, 1983

Welcome to the greatest night of my life.

We're mid-set at Bogart's when our road manager Jay waves me towards the wings.

"Bunnies." he gasps.

"Huh?" I yell back through a pipeline of guitar feedback.

"Down in the dressing room, Cowboy. Playboy Bunnies."

I briskly wave adios to my bandmates and vault down the back stairs...and Jay isn't kidding.

A bevy of shapely and enchanting young ladies are clustered in our changing room. I squeeze myself inside as the rabbits push up against me, warmly introducing themselves. "Bunny Kim" and "Bunny Jill" and "Would you and your band like to be our guests back at the Club?" Heart-pounding and eyes-on-stalks, I suddenly hear the count-off into Rockin'Train.

I rocket back up the stairs, slide across the stage, and hit the mic. Almost on cue.

During Ron Stewart's extended drum solo, I hustle Hargrove and the Admiral downstairs to meet my new pals.

The remainder of our concert is performed in double-time.

We proceed over to the Cincinnati Playboy Club, for a party that lasts past closing.

Then the whole party moves back to our floor at the Holiday Inn Downtown. I just turned 30. It sure feels great to be 30.

Tuesday, February 1, 1983

Last night didn't end. After a restful 25 minutes of sleep I get my wake-up call. Time to get back to work. Down to the lobby, where I'm escorted to my waiting limousine.

Yup. Besides enjoying the company of the oh, so friendly Bunnies last night, we also made friends with their limo driver. Rick. Not only that, Rick owns the limousine company.

Since this is his day off, Rick borrows one of his fleet of stretches and temporarily joins the JPP tour as our new driver.

We're gliding up I74 through Indiana. It looks really cold out there but it's plenty warm in here.

Rick has the stereo system grooving. Ronnie is in front, gazing out the window at the iced farmland flying by. Hargrove and I are sprawled out in our leather seats, enjoying our overnight success immensely. Great to get out of the grubby van for once.

The Admiral is having an even better time.

He grabbed a souvenir back in Cincinnati.

Bouncing in his lap is cuddly Bunny Kim.

We pass through Batesville, Greensburg and Shelbyville, finally pulling up to the American Inn North in Indianapolis IN.

It's early enough that I can grab a desperately-needed nap before the 5 p.m. soundcheck.

There's a gaggle of loyal Joe Perry fanatics waiting by the stage door of the downtown Vogue Theater. Our limousine pulls up, and Rick - who has changed into his official driving-suit and cap - rushes back to open the rear doors.

Danny and I emerge and wave to the crowd, like two Oscar Award nominees. Joe Perry and his buxom, smiling Playboy Bunny alight from the limousine to booming cheers.

The assembled kids watch and nod to each other knowingly. "See? I told you. That's how the Joe Perry Project rolls."

Wednesday February 2, 1983

Jay is at the wheel of the van. We're all listening to the radio bulletins coming in. The entire midwest is bracing for a major storm. Snow is already falling at a rapid clip as we hit the Illinois state line, still on I74 West.

Following a standout show at the Vogue last night, we had a short after-party at the hotel. After that, Rick drove Bunny Kim back to her hutch in Cincinnati.

Our road manager Jay looks like hell. His eyes are watering and he's coughing. I've been suspicious about what's going on in the crew rooms ever since guitar tech Zakowski came aboard. It's obvious that the sex and drug activity has increased. Our crew is suddenly looking like the Manson family.

Danville, Urbana, Bloomington, Peoria. The snow plows are up ahead of us, clearing the way. Jay is on the CB radio and drivers are being advised to leave the highway.

By the time we hit Galesburg we're in the midst of a full-scale blizzard. Almost impossible to see up ahead.

We cross the Mississippi River (can't see it though) into Davenport Iowa, finally stopping at the Budget Plus motel.

Jay wades through a snow drift and into the lobby. We wait. Too many minutes go by. Jay returns with bad news.

Our rooms have already been sold.

Because of the snow emergency, they figured we'd never show up. Then it gets worse.
Jay finds a pay phone and calls around to the Holiday Inn, Ramada, Best Western, Red Roof, Super 8, Motel 6, you name it they're all packed, full of stranded motorists.
We're the lone vehicle on the road by the time we skid into the Tall Corn Motel.

I'm rooming with my buddy Danny Hargrove. We sled our gig bags through a three-foot snowdrift and unlock the door.
A herd of cockroaches stampede towards us.
We flip on the lights.
The filthy bugs scatter in every direction. Into the tattered furniture, squeezing into moldy cracks in the walls, they even disappear into the stained mattresses.
We bolt out of there, terrified.
The Project somehow makes it to the gig at StageWest, where we proudly rock for three whores and a midget. Nobody's coming out in this weather. Later, we sneak back to our infested room at the Tall Corn. Freaking-out with fear.
There is nowhere to escape. Every hotel in Iowa is packed due to the storm. It's way below-freezing outside, with snow drifting eight feet high in places. We have no choice.
Danny and I get to work. Inside the room, we turn on every lightbulb and remove every lamp shade. Bright light is the only thing that can hold the swarm of vermin at bay.
We lay down on top of our tightly made beds with all our clothes and jackets on. Our pant legs are tucked snugly inside our boots. We attempt to sleep in the fully-lit room by wearing blindfolds that we fashion out of our bandanas.
Is this why traveling rock band guys are all wearing bandanas these days?

Thursday February 3, 1983

Heading back east towards Chicago. The snow won't stop falling, it's windy and miserable.

We mush our way into Kankakee IL, about fifty miles south of Chicago.
"Hey. I have an idea. Let's book a big rock show.
Out at the fairgrounds, in the middle of February."
What were they thinking?
Some local promoter thought it would be fun to have the Joe Perry Project play at the County Fairgrounds today - as the snow falls and frozen gales whip down from Lake Michigan.
At least they didn't ask us play outside in the field.
No, we're set-up in some kind of indoor goat pen.
Nobody comes to see us. The promoter looks suicidal.
After the final note rings out to no applause I slip on the ice and my right elbow begins to swell up.

Thursday February 4, 1983

Back up the highway to Haymaker's. The club where Ronnie fell in love. She's here. Of course. Ron puts on his best show ever. A much better crowd tonight than at the frozen goat pen yesterday.
We're staying in Prospect Heights at the Flamingo motel.

Friday February 5, 1983

Joe Perry Project returns to the Motor City. Arriving today at Harpo's in our road-salt encrusted van for the 5 p.m. soundcheck. Nobody meets us at the backstage door this time. Too damn cold and windy.
Ron arrives separately in that little sedan, along with his girlfriend. We book into the nearby Park Crest Hotel. Teenagers Chris and Terri stop by the hotel, dressed-up like bimbos. They flounce around in a strangely entertaining way. WRIF-FM is promoting our concert tonight. Rick Derringer played here last night and Johnny Winter a few nights before that. This is the biggest crowd we've seen since Indianapolis.

Saturday February 6, 1983

Joe Perry needs these concert fees to satisfy court orders and to keep out of jail, we press onward. Travel day for the JPP.
We leave Detroit, bound for the Red Roof Inn in Rochester New York, 400 miles. Along with me in the van, we have Phuck, the Admiral, road manager Jay, and Dan Hargrove. Up ahead, in the Ryder truck, are Lance Charger and Boy Sean. I guess Ron went off somewhere with his girl.
Along the way we stop for some fun at the Buffalo Playboy Club - but get turned away for some reason. The friendly bunnies in Cincinnati hooked us up with Playboy Key Cards but these NY doormen won't let us inside.
So instead, we go to a place called Cassidy's and discover something new called Buffalo Wings. I think these things are actually chicken wings - cooked in hot sauce. They're pretty good too, Cassidy's could be on to something.

Wednesday February 9, 1983

The band regroups in Rensselaer NY for a headline show at the Hulla-Baloo. This town is right across the Hudson River from Albany. I've played this room before. Thundertrain opened here for the David Johansen Group back in 1978.
Bands like Dire Straits and the Police worked this venue too. But the club is most famous for Tanya, the big jungle cat who lives in the upstairs office, chained to a post at the top of the stairs. You have to pass right by her to get to the dressing room. Tanya is full-sized and has spots. I guess she's a leopard. I watch most guys stride right past her, no problem. Some might even pat her head. Not me. I'm scared to death of the beast and will do anything to avoid walking up those stairs.
My friend Joanie is here for soundcheck. After the check, Joanie and I try to figure out a way to get up to the dressing room without using the stairs - and crossing Tanya.
That's when we see this little hole up in the wall. Up on the second level. It's where the spotlight is set up. Joanie and I push and pull each other up the wall and manage to squeeze

our bodies through the little spotlight porthole. A dark, winding passage opens up into a hallway and the hallway leads straight to the dressing room door.

Tanya shoots me a hungry glance and licks her chops.

After the show we're back at the Budget 90 motel. Joanie slips a purple cassette into my blaster. "Mach, you gotta hear this."

Thursday February 10, 1983

On our way to Long Island. We're listening to reports of serious bad weather headed this way tomorrow. We play to a pretty good crowd at Nassau Community College in East Garden City. Then we hit the Coliseum Motor Inn, not far from Nassau Coliseum. I'm rooming with Hargrove.

"Hey Danny, check this out." I pull out the purple cassette tape that Joanie gave me yesterday - and load it into my Panasonic. *"Don't Worry. I Won't Hurt You.*
I Only Want You to Have Some Fun."

Friday February 11, 1983

As we leave Long Island it's already coming down. We slog up Route 9 North. Straight into another blizzard. The best Jay can do is to get behind a platoon of slow moving plows. Every so often a spreader truck passes by and pelts our van with another round of road salt. We're all staring out the window intently, struggling to see up ahead through the fast falling snow that's blanketing the windshield. We don't even have the stereo turned on, it's too distracting. A drive that we'd usually complete in under three hours takes a full nine hours.

We just make tonight's show at The Chance.

"Hello, Poughkeepsie." I shout out to a crowd that might total two dozen.

No way is anyone, except maybe Joanie, coming out in this weather. Snow is still piling up. Over two feet of fresh stuff. Once again we have trouble getting a room. No Vacancy signs are lit up everywhere.

We have to settle for the Dutch Spittoon.

It's probably really called the Dutch Doubloon or the Dutch Brigadoon, but my name fits the place better.

Saturday February 12, 1983

Yesterday it was north again, today we're headed south again. We're spinning like a yo-yo on this road trip. Back to Bergenfield NJ and the Circus. Down here they just got pummeled with over a foot of fresh snow. Still, Admiral Perry proves his box office power when several hundred iced maniacs show up to cheer us on.
I half expect them to be waving sap buckets and ski poles in the air. We stay at the Paramus, Holiday Inn, where Danny and I are once again blasting Joanie's "Prince 1999" tape. We are literally jumping up and down on the beds grooving along to Delirious.

Sunday February 13, 1983

The highways are clear but the roadside snowbanks are over six feet tall as we motor back towards New England.
Joe has his Sex Pistols tape blasting. Danny and I look at each other nervously. Should we? What if he hates it?
As the final Pistols song, E.M.I., draws to its vicious close, I hand the cassette up to the Admiral.
"Check this out Joe." I have the tape cued-up to Delirious.
The Admiral shoves in the cassette. Danny and I immediately start bobbing our heads to the infectious beat. No sign of motion or emotion up in the shotgun seat. The tune closes with the baby coo and the Admiral glances back at us.
"Not bad."
Joe let's it roll…Let's Pretend We're Married, D.M.S.R., Automatic…
Danny gives me a nudge. Joe's digging it.
Once the tape ends, Joe flips it back to the top and hears 1999 for the first time. And then, Little Red Corvette.
Game over. That clinches it. Danny and I are overjoyed that the Admiral is onboard. Move over AC/DC and Sex Pistols.
Prince has officially joined the Project playlist.

Saturday February 19, 1983

Back in Boston, Julia and I attend a record release party for
Ministry, who just put out a new album With Sympathy on
Arista. The LP was recorded at SyncroSound, where I got to
spend a little time talking with lead singer Al Jourgensen. Al was
very easy going and very interested to learn more about Joe
Perry and the gear he uses and about Joe's philosophies on
music. I was a little surprised that young Jourgensen, in his wide
brimmed Boy George hat, would be so interested in the Admiral
and our unsettling, unpolished sound. Al struck me as more of a
Duran Duran, a-ha type of guy. I've still got a lot to learn.

Sunday February 20, 1983

Winter is starting to get a bit redundant. I spent all last week
shoveling out Julia's car and clearing the sidewalk in front of the
palace. Over and over again. Every time I finish, the city plows
splash by, re-depositing old snow on top of the new snow that
keeps falling.
Today we're out in Brooklyn New York, at a club with a vibe.
Another ex-disco. This one is called L'Amour.
This place has been booking rock for a couple years and they
specialize in these upcoming heavy metal acts like Metallica,
Slayer and Megadeth.
Ten years ago, heavy metal was a term my friends and I used to
classify albums like Machine Head by Deep Purple.
Music's gotten way more metallic and heavy since then.
I take the stage and give these Brooklyn kids the best hard rock
show I can. Some of our numbers, like When Worlds Collide,
border on metal. Ron Stewart's aggressive attack - brutally
smacking his Eames drum kit - definitely gets the headbangers
going. They all love Ronnie.
One way or another, the Project scores big tonight at the
"Rock Capital of Brooklyn."

Tuesday February 22, 1983

Ron Stewart gives notice to Joe Perry.
Drummer Ron is the longest-running member of Joe's Project.
He was a founding member in 1979. He served with distinction
for nearly four years. After completing a couple more weeks of
engagements - March 12th will be Ron's final day with the JPP.

Thursday February 24, 1983

I go out to a local club to see Rick Berlin's band, Berlin Airlift.
They sound really good but I'm really here to check on their
drummer - Joe Pet. Before I recommend Pet to the Admiral and
Tim, I want to make sure he's still playing as hot as I remember.
Driving back to the pink palace, I'm listening to the Carter Alan
show on WBCN. I nearly hit a tree when I hear the intro chords
of Once a Rocker come over the airwaves for the first time.

Saturday February 26, 1983

I celebrate my one year anniversary in the Project by going out
for a few pints with the Admiral. As far as I know, it's pretty rare
for Joe to go out in public when he's on his home turf. In the
middle of the afternoon no less. We find two empty bar stools at
the Inn Square Men's Bar: Ladies Invited, a great old pub in
Cambridge. We drink a toast to our futures. For the past few
months Joe and Kerstyn have been living in a rooming-house
over in Boston's North End. In a little flat that looks out towards
the Paul Revere house.

Sunday February 27, 1983

I'm at a nightclub with Tim Collins and Joe Perry tonight.
Waiting to see Berlin Airlift again. They have a new album out
on A&M. They also have a talented percussionist named Joe Pet.
He's Italian - so I'm sure his real last name is a lot longer than
Pet. I can see the Admiral is impressed by Pet's drumming.

On the way home from the club we hear Once a Rocker on the radio. This time it's on WCOZ. Just the demo tape - we're still chasing that big record deal.

Monday February 28, 1983

Tim has put together an audition/rehearsal for Joe Pet. At an unlikely spot, a country club in Millis. Like that fancy place in *Caddy Shack*. Glen Ellen Country Club is just over the line from my hometown, Holliston. We're all set-up in a function room near the ice cream freezer. Pet dives straight into the music and puts a whole new spin on the sound of the Project.
Where Ronnie Stewart pounded through our tunes like a pile-driver, Pet is lighting sky-rockets underneath us and launching our jams skywards. Into the upper-part of the Stratosphere. After an uplifting and energetic jam session, Mr. Pet helps himself to the ice cream.
I heard Once a Rocker on the radio again today.
The bad news is that the trusty JPP Dodge van is messed up.

Tuesday March 1, 1982

We wanted to rehearse with Joe Pet at the country club again today. But we can't, because our van is in the shop. Tim Collins is trying to dig up some wheels for us. We have a four city road trip coming right up. I caught deejay Mark Parenteau playing Once a Rocker again this afternoon.

Wednesday March 2, 1983

Joe Pet officially joins the Joe Perry Project today. His first live date with the band will be on St. Patrick's Day, March 17.
Until then, we'll be doing some final shows with Ron Stewart. Every time I turn on the radio I hear Once a Rocker. WCOZ and WBCN both have the demo tape on regular rotation. Makes me hungrier than ever to have a real JPP album with my voice on it.

Thursday March 3, 1983

Headed for Poughkeepsie in the Silver Snake. A big old sedan
about the size of the space shuttle. Where did Tim Collins dig up
this boss ride?
It's the un-official Farewell to Drummer Ron Stewart Tour.
Beginning here tonight at The Chance. No blizzard this time, Joe
is greeted by his steadfast crowd of superfans at the stage door.
Joanie is pleased to hear that the whole Project is digging her
personal discovery, Prince.
We're staying at the retro Po'Keepsie Motor Inn this time.

Friday March 4, 1983

Jay makes tracks up I93. We're doing a personal appearance at
the InnerLight Records store in Manchester NH. Kinda weird,
since the Project doesn't have a new record to promote.
Or even a record deal.
Anyway, lots of kids show up to see us. The Admiral and Ronnie
sign a bunch of the first two Project albums. Perry signs old
Aerosmith records and related paraphernalia. Danny and I sign
some photographs the fans have taken of us at recent shows and
a few autograph books too.
Afterwards, the crowd of fans gaze in wonder as we all cram
back inside the rusted-out Silver Snake and go roaring off for
Concord NH. Headed for a big Project concert at the Capitol
Theatre. After the show we drive back to Boston - where we
crash for a few hours.

Saturday March 5, 1983

Snaking west to Middleton NY where we serve up more
undiluted Boston rock'n'roll at JB's Rock Palace. Not exactly a
Palace in my opinion, but a good place to play. A noisy,
energetic crowd turns-out to cheer us on. Not only that but we
get to stay at the local Super 8 motel too.
I talk to Ronnie briefly after the show. Asking him why he
decided to quit the Project.

Ron looks at me with a sad smile,
then he shakes his head.
"Look Cowboy. I love you guys. It's nothing personal…but…"
I'm waiting. Ron's grin grows wider.
"It's just that you guys. You're like…you're like children.
I joined this band to make music. Not to play games."
The drummer chuckles and continues,
"I don't know…it's like being at summer camp…
or a kindergarten…"
He shakes his head and laughs out loud.
"You guys can fool around and do whatever you want,
but I'm done."

Sunday March 6, 1983

On to Norwalk CT and a roadhouse called Players.
Stewart is playing great, like always, on these, his final few
weeks with us. After the concert we Silver Snake straight home
to Boston. Arriving at 6 a.m.

Monday March 7, 1983

After a couple hours of sleep, we spend the afternoon rehearsing
the set with our other drummer, Joe Pet, at the country club in
Millis. The Once a Rocker demo is still being played daily.
I already heard it twice today.
I think Kerstyn has gone back to the West Coast. That girl was
good for Joe. She kept him warm and occupied and tried to
divert him from some of his worst instincts.

Tuesday March 8, 1983

Back at Glen Ellen with the band and Joe Pet. This new
drummer is clever. He's charted-out all our arrangements on
staff paper, like a real musician. He sounds really tight on every
song after just a few sessions with us. We plan for another rehearsal tomorrow at noon, out in Shirley, at the Mohawk Club.

The club owner at the Mohawk is letting us use the empty venue prior to our headlining gig there this Thursday.

Wednesday March 9, 1983

Rehearsal in Shirley is cancelled. Why?
Because Phuck lost the damn keys to the Silver Snake.
That's why. Everyone is ticked-off because this was our very last chance to rehearse with Joe Pet before our national tour begins out in California next week.
Tim Collins goes ballistic. He fires Phuck.
Then he hires Joe Pet's friend Fred to be our new driver.
I remember Freddy as a nice, preppy-looking guy in a Polo shirt.
He used to help out Thundertrain on occasion.
Meanwhile, Mr. Perry is over at WCOZ at 7:30 p.m. doing an interview, promoting the two big Boston shows coming up this Saturday. Ron Stewart's final JPP gigs.

Thursday March 10, 1983

We're on our way to play the Mohawk Club out in Shirley. This big room used to always be packed - with servicemen and hookers - until nearby Fort Devens got closed down.
We're all over Boston radio, the demo tape of Once a Rocker plays continuously. WCOZ is sponsoring tonight's show and the airplay and promotion helps a lot - The Mohawk is packed.
When we launch into Once a Rocker, the kids are singing along as though it's a hit song.

Friday March 11, 1983

We're in Laconia NH.
Joe Perry Project plays an unusual venue today.
The Memorial Middle School. We stopped along the way so the Admiral could do a 2:30 p.m. spot on WBOS and a 4 p.m. interview on WBCN promoting tomorrow's shows in Boston.
Now we're playing for this little peanut gallery at the Middle School - where we meet a ton of new, very young fans.

Saturday March 12, 1983

It's our road manager/soundman Jay's birthday today.
At 1 p.m. the Admiral and I do an in-store meet and greet in
Quincy at the Rock'n'Roll Market. Then it's on to Boston for
Ron's grand finale. We're at the Channel concert club, a place
that holds about a thousand - and both shows are crammed full.
For the afternoon 3 p.m. all-ages show (Hargrove's and my
100th performance with the band) we take the stage at around
5 p.m. Then it's the evening 20+ concert, 8:30 p.m. doors with
showtime around midnight. It's broiling onstage and both Perry
and I are stripped to the waist by the time we play the final
encores. After an emotional farewell to the great Ronnie, our
crew loads up the truck and hits the road for California.
The Project begins a cross-country tour with new drummer
Joe Pet in 72 hours.

Monday March 14, 1983

The Admiral wants to get his hair trimmed before we set out on
what Tim Collins is calling the "Do or Die Tour."
I happen to know a great barber. I bring Joe out to Coolidge
Corner in Brookline where I introduce him to the cutest girl in
town. Glenda has hypnotic eyes, surrounded by ringlets of long
blonde hair. She's tiny, like a nymph illustration from an old
fairytale book. Smart and talented, a great dancer, and she
knows how to cut hair too.
Of course I'm sure Glenda will swoon when she sees Joe and I
am certain that Joe will dig Glenda immediately.
She's irresistible.
I've been concerned about the Admiral these past few weeks.
He's become homeless again. Spending too many nights at
deejay Mark's high-rise apartment on Mass Ave. Hanging with a
coked-up crew who don't take care of themselves.
Perry needs a lover to look after him, to cook him some hot soup
and hopefully provide some stimulation that doesn't involve
bourbon and narcotics. Everything goes exactly as I figured.

By the time the haircut is done, Joe has moved into
92 Pleasant St. with Glenda.
Not so much that he moves in - he just doesn't leave.

Tuesday March 15, 1983

We all meet up at the Collins/Barrasso office in Allston at 5 p.m.
Tim hands out itineraries for a tour that is about to begin.
Then he reads the riot act to us.
"Listen, you guys. We've been spinning our wheels for too long.
It's imperative that we break through to the next level. Or else.
This is the Project's last shot. There's no way I can make a deal
if you guys continue to screw things up. You've gotta prove
yourselves to these business people. It's Do or Die.
There can be absolutely no BS on this trip. No arrests, no
wrecking hotel rooms, no drunken accidents, no falling off
stages, no hitchhiking, no brawling... no NOTHING."

Thursday March 17, 1983

At 6:00 a.m. the whole band, along with road manager Jay, are
boarding an American Airlines flight departing Logan and bound
for San Francisco. After touching down in California and
collecting our bags we hop into a rented station wagon.
Station wagon?
And head merrily down the coast to Monterey.
Nobody likes the station wagon.
It's St. Patrick's Day. Celebrity drummer Joe Pet is making his
debut with the Joe Perry Project tonight at "The Peninsula's
Hottest Night Spot!" an oceanside joint named The Club.
We initiate our new drummer by stranding him alone onstage at
the end of his Rockin' Train drum solo. When Mr. Pet realizes
that we aren't coming back to finish-up the song, he just digs in
and plays a second drum solo.
The green-beer swilling St. Patrick's Day crowd loves both
solos.

Friday March 18, 1983

Jay wheels us back up to San Francisco in the crappy station wagon. We're booked into the York Hotel on Sutter St. This place is old and stodgy, with a flop house vibe. Is this whole tour gonna be done on the super-cheap? We do go out for an excellent meal though, at Don Ramon's, a swanky Mexican restaurant where I steal an ashtray.
Then it's off to play in Berkeley at The Keystone. On this tour the West coast crowd will get to hear Perry play on his own kustom gear - not that stock, rented stuff from L.A.

Saturday March 19, 1983

It's a rainy morning in San Francisco. I do a little bit of sight seeing before we head down to Palo Alto to play at another Keystone venue. The one that's shaped like an airplane hangar. Having a fun time onstage. Pet's beats are heavy but weightless at the same time. He makes everyone want to get up and move. No more of those drum/guitar duels at the end of every number either. That leaves room for more songs in our sets. We've been jamming on the Rolling Stones' blues nugget You Got to Move and the T.Rex groover, Get it On (Bang a Gong).

Sunday March 20, 1983

Having lunch in Sausalito with my former Thundertrain lighting guy Mick Martins and his sister AnneMarie. Both are Holliston kids, like me. The siblings are working here for Bill Graham Productions. AnneMarie and I head back down to San Francisco and visit the tourist trap Fisherman's Wharf before the Joe Perry Project bangs a gong at the Stone in North Beach.

Monday March 21, 1983

The JPP tour has the day off in San Francisco. Micky and I climb Mount Tamalpais overlooking the Golden Gate Bridge and the Pacific Ocean.

Tuesday March 22, 1983

The road manager has finally traded in that lousy station wagon for a club van. It's not as roomy as our brown maxi-van back home but a lot better than the wagon.
Walking out of the York Hotel onto Sutter Street (right across from Hard On Leather) I head down to Aardvark's Odd Ark, a vintage clothing store, where I buy an old jacket that has the words Fort Lewis 53 embroidered into it.
Then I go visit this place called the Hard Rock Cafe. I know the name but have never actually seen one.
The famous one in London started about ten years ago but they only just began opening a few of these burger joints in the USA. The sandwich is okay but the memorabilia hanging on the walls is really interesting.
An attractive lady that we met at our gig the other night invited us all out to a party tonight, at her place in Walnut Creek.
When we arrive, the doll eyes my Fort Lewis 53 jacket and gets all mystical. She tells me that Fort Lewis has something to do with Walnut Creek. So, I tell her that 53 is my birth year. This is apparently some kind of magical miracle - and the hostess immediately becomes a witchy Cowboy fan.

Wednesday March 23, 1983

We finally check out of the cruddy York Hotel and hit the road in the rental van that Jay nabbed for us. Headed for Merced, where we headline tonight at the Crazy Horse Saloon.
We book into the local Best Western. Musically things are going great. Joe Pet is an easy-going jokester and his rhythms are energizing and enlivening.

Thursday March 24, 1983

Did I ever tell you how I always get pumped up anytime I can stand on a stage where the Rolling Stones once performed?
We're booked at the Palace in Hollywood tonight.
The very same venue where I once watched Dean Martin

introduce (and tease) the Rolling Stones on the "Hollywood Palace" ABC TV show, back when I was a kid.

Things start out amazingly today. We arrive at the Sunset Marquis hotel. This is where the A-list celebrities stay. Somehow we got booked to stay here too. This ain't no Tall Corn or Dutch Spittoon. The Admiral's sister Ann meets us in the tastefully appointed lobby.

Ann will be visiting her brother while he's in town.

Later, while being driven over to the 5 p.m. soundcheck, I see a shirt in the window of a store on Hollywood Boulevard. For some reason I need to have this shirt. So after soundcheck I hike around the corner and there it is. In the window of a place called the Rock Star Store. I should have run away right then, but no, I'm an idiot, a rube from the sticks of East Holliston. I walk inside and purchase the dumb shirt. It's got this bold red sun pattern and some Japanese writing all over it.

Costs like 15 bucks.

After soundcheck at the Palace on Vine Street, the band is driven back up the Sunset Strip to the Rainbow Bar & Grill.

The Joe Perry Project have the best table reserved for dinner. The Admiral causes a real stir when he enters the Rainbow. Wow. Nearly everybody at the crowded bar and attached dining room cranes their necks to catch a glimpse of the legendary lead guitarist from Aerosmith.

Things sure are going great.

After dinner we head to our big show at the Palace. Jay pulls the van into the backstage entrance. Danny and I gawk at the Capitol Records tower, all lit-up - it's right across the street. Famed guitar maker Bill Lawrence greets the Admiral as we enter the venue. I'm on cloud nine. Ride of the Valkyries is welling up. I pull on my brand new shirt.

Time to rock Hollywood. Storming out onstage, I look up to see nine other guys in the front row, all wearing the same dumb shirt as me. Every kid in Hollywood shops at the "Rock Star Store." Oh Watta Goo Siam.

The other weird/horrible thing about this gig is, there isn't even a stage. This venue is set up for TV productions.

The entire floor area is level, so giant film and tv cameras can glide around as firetrucks get driven onstage or elephants march around. Some of the audience are up in a raised seating area, others are higher-up in a balcony.

But most of these tall, blonde California kids are standing right in front of me, looking down at small Cowboy in his dumb shirt.

Friday March 25, 1983

Joe Perry has his own personal endorsement deal with the Nike sporting apparel company. The Admiral has been requested to stop by the local Nike Promotion Center today at 1:30 p.m. and the company kindly invites Joe to bring along his band members too. After a quick tour, we're all allowed to pick out a bit of free merchandise.

The Admiral, Danny Hargrove and I each carefully choose a couple pairs of sneakers and a sweat shirt or two. Perry picks out one extra pair of tiny running shoes for his son.

Over in the other corner, brand new drummer Pet is stacking-up nearly a dozen boxes of shoes, a half-dozen running suits, multiple pairs of shorts, shirts and hats, in several sizes and colors. The pile grows higher as we watch, stunned.

Jay helps Pet the Pirate stuff his crates of Nike loot into the back of the rental van.

The Project performs two sellout shows tonite at the Golden Bear in Huntington Beach.

Saturday March 26, 1983

We're in sunny San Diego and it's 90 degrees. Seems like only two weeks ago we were fighting multiple blizzards. A friendly limo driver named Jay is driving the band to tonight's gig for free, because he likes Joe's music. The Admiral has sold-out two more shows here at the packed Red Coat Inn. Big Kahuna Thai, who we met last year, brings along party-girls and party-supplies for the post show celebrations.

We're headquartered at the Hotel San Diego.

Sunday March 27, 1983

During the bash last night, Zakowski (Lance Charger) took
drunken teen crewman Sean to get tattooed. They both ended-up
getting inked, and neither of the designs are in good taste. The
tattoo parlor is across the street from our hotel, right next to the
Can Can Club.
I'm not happy about the way Zakowski is influencing the
youngest kid on the crew and messing with him.
I find Lance and give him a piece of my mind. About twenty
minutes later, he kicks open the door to my hotel room, and
comes barreling towards me.
Problem is, Zakowski doesn't have a stitch of clothing on.
Nothing. His willy is flapping in the breeze as he slams his
sweaty body against me, hard. Yuck. I'm no fighter, but how am
I even supposed to push him away? I don't want to touch the
naked goon. I'm screaming at him to back-off, but he just
throws his body against me and laughs in my face.
Luckily, Hargrove comes to the rescue and kicks the gross
Zakowski out of my room.

After breakfast, Jay hands me a Shure mic bag full of cash.
He has to accompany Perry back to Hollywood for business.
I'll be in charge of the band for the next few days. Zakowski and
Boy Sean leave with the equipment truck.
At 2 p.m. the band departs the Hotel San Diego. Fred is our
driver. I'm in back with Danny and the luggage. Joe Pet rides
shotgun. We need to cover 1,431 miles by Tuesday.

Monday March 28, 1983

Fred is ultra-smooth at the wheel. We head east on the 8 out of
San Diego. Passing El Cajon, Jacumba, Ocotillo and El Centro.
Riding just north of the Baja Mexico border into Yuma Arizona.
Which reminds me of the months I spent on the road with Circus
Vargas a couple years ago.

After Thundertrain broke-up, and John Lennon was shot, Bobby Edwards and I ran away to join the circus. We started as roustabouts in Phoenix. Yuma was the second town we set up the big-top in, and performed, while working for Mr. Vargas. I kept a diary of that whole remarkable experience too.

Fred sparks-up another joint as we wheel through Ligurta, Mohawk, Aztec and Gila Bend. In Casa Grande AZ we join up with Interstate 10. Fred rolls another as he wheels by Eloy, Marana, Tucson, Mescal, Willcox and Bowie.

Danny winds down the window to let some of the smoke escape. We all look like extras from a Cheech & Chong flick.

Still on I10, we cross into New Mexico, passing the Shakespeare Ghost Town, Gage, Deming and finally at 2 a.m. we arrive at the Las Cruces Holiday Inn. San Diego to Las Cruces = 12 hours.

Morning comes quickly and I get my first sunburn of the year, laying out at the pool alongside a wholesome blonde who I met when the Project played the Pan American Center last summer. Drummer Joe Pet dares me to eat some weird green salsa that he got at the gas station. We pull out of Las Cruces at 3 p.m.

Tuesday March 29, 1983

Man am I sick.

I know it was that salsa Pet made me eat yesterday.

We drive all day and all of the night. Into El Paso Texas, through the Apache Mountains, Fort Stockton, into Crockett County and Ozona, then past the Caverns of Sonora. Eventually, Interstate 10 takes a dip to the south and we hit San Antonio, Fred tokes up and keeps pushing east.

Finally, we pull into the Manor House motel in Houston TX. It's around 4:30 a.m.

Wednesday March 30, 1983

The Admiral and Jay (everyone just calls him Dickman these days) jet into Houston from LAX. The Joe Perry Project is headlining here tonight at Rocker's.

Jim Dandy, of Black Oak Arkansas, is staying in the same motel
as us and today is Jim's birthday.
I'm still sick, but that doesn't stop me from swigging down
some early morning Coors with my hero Jim Dandy.
Along with Jagger, Rod Stewart, Daltrey, Tyler and Johansen -
Jim Dandy is a frontman who made a major impression on me.
The first time I saw Black Oak Arkansas play the Orpheum in
Boston, they were just another unknown opening act.
This was probably around the same time I first witnessed
Aerosmith, in early 1971.
Dandy sprang onto the stage, wearing eye-popping, skin-
rippin'tight white-leggings - strutting shirtless - but with white
suspenders and a washboard strapped to his tanned chest.
Ridiculously fantastic.
Whipping his blonde hair in circles and smirking just enough to
show the large gaps between his pearly-whites, Dandy and his
BOA gang were pure entertainment, with unforgettable numbers
like Hot Rod, and Hot and Nasty. Unforgettable drummer
Tommy Aldrich, plus three furious guitar players and
Jim as ringmaster…impossible to follow.
I can't even remember who the headliners were that night.
Maybe the Kinks? Or even Beck, Bogert, Appice? Didn't matter.
Jim was the guy everyone was talking about the next day.
Happy Birthday, Mr. Dandy.

Thursday March 31, 1983

We drive up to Dallas and book into the GreenLeaf Hotel on
South Akard St.
Surprise. Chauffeur Rick is here with his black limousine.
The same Rick we met at the Cincinnati Playboy Club a couple
months ago. He's waiting for us in the lobby.
At this moment I only have eight dollars left to my name but
who cares, I have a uniformed chauffeur to deliver me to my
next concert appearance. Once again we make a grand entrance
for a waiting pack of autograph hounds and groupies. As far as
these Dallas fans are concerned, this must be the luxurious and
stylish manner in which the Project travels the world. Why not?

The gig tonight is at Nick's Upstairs. A happening place with a pretty big crowd.

Friday April 1, 1983

Back to the humble rental van. Freddy drives the Project down I35 to San Antonio today. Of course we all need to visit The Alamo. It's a nice 80 degree day and we get there in time to take the official Fort Alamo tour. I'm still sick but it's a really interesting place to hang around in. Plus we're all staying at the (Davy) Crockett Motel. How cool is that? I call my little sister Cathy. She and I both wore coonskin caps growing up. Now she's stationed at Lackland Air Force Base, which is near here, but she can't make our show.

We're headlining at Daddy's. I saw this John Travolta flick called *Urban Cowboy* when it came out a couple years ago and they could have filmed it right here tonight. The bar is full of cowgirls and cowpokes all done up with big belt buckles, pointy toed boots, pearl-snap cowboy shirts and cowboy hats. Plenty of mechanical bulls for everyone to ride around on, too.

Saturday April 2, 1983

Pushing further south on I37, past the towns of China Grove, Thelma, Christine, Peggy, Three Rivers, Edroy and Odem and straight into Corpus Christi. We check into the Airport Holiday Inn. I call my sister again and we talk for a while.

I eat some solid food for the first time in almost a week.

We're headlining at The Yellow Rose tonight and a local video crew shows up to catch our act.

Sunday April 3, 1983

It's 84 degrees outside. We're still at the Corpus Christi Airport Holiday Inn. Right now I'm watching the TV3 News and they're showing video taken at our show last night. The Admiral looks and sounds great in this report.

I've never seen a video of our band before.

I'm still feeling ill. I'm glad we'll be cooling-out down here for 48 hours. The next JPP show is on Tuesday.

Tuesday April 5, 1983

Every time we book into a motel or hotel, lists with all our room numbers are distributed to us by our road manager. The Project touring party is often cryptically referred to as the O.O.A.Group. Our Own Army? Joe Perry is usually registered under the pseudonym Clyde Barrow. That makes sense because Joe's a star, very private, and doesn't want to be bothered.
Even though the paparazzi have zero-reason to care about me or the rest of us, we all get listed under false names too.
I'm always Cowboy Beeps. Hargrove is usually Mahogany Kane. The new roadie, Boy Sean, is Fawn Leebowitz (from *Animal House*). Road manager Jay is, of course, Larry Dickman. Zakowski, the sadistic roadie we inherited from The Ramones, is listed as Lance Charger.

Looks like we got out of Corpus Christi just in time. Lance got our road manager Dickman tangled up in some nasty business involving a local girl last night. It's getting way too hot around here. We're in the van headed for Beaumont Texas. We'll be headlining at Cardi's later tonight.

Wednesday April 6, 1983

The promotion department at local KIX-FM Radio thought it'd be fun to do a "Come to Dinner with the Joe Perry Project" contest. So after our soundcheck at the Oasis in Killeen Texas, the JPP gets delivered straight over to this local eatery. A table full of contest winners are inside at a long table, eagerly awaiting our arrival.
We've been cooped up, sweating in the van all day, smoking, hallucinating, drinking, being loud and obnoxious.
All I want to do now is to hit the shower at the local Budget Inn. But no.

Our road manager herds us into the dining area. Local rednecks
are craning their necks, like in the last reel of *Easy Rider*.
"Is there a freak show playin' round here?"
Pet and Hargrove rush in the direction of the contest winners,
but continue to rush - down to the far end of the table. They grab
all the bread baskets as they go.
Even on a good day, the Admiral never has much to say, and
he's already put away most of a fifth of Jack on the dusty drive
into Killeen. Not exactly in a chatty mood.
That leaves our always smiling road manager Dickman and the
Cowboy to try and make small talk with these lucky winners.
But the words just won't come. I'm fried. Thirty days in the hole
with the Project has put a damper on my social skills.
The band chows down while the winners stare at us.

Thursday April 7, 1983

Joe Pet somberly scans the horizon as we drive through the Lone
Star State. He's always on the lookout for the "brown i." Pet has
this odd bank card that (according to him) lets him take money
out of an "automatic bank teller machine."
I've never seen or heard of anything like it myself, but Pet
claims he found a machine back in San Francisco - and actually
got cash out of it.
"Keep looking for the brown i" he says. I think he means the
logo for Interstate Bank (?) the company that supposedly has a
few of these money machines located around the USA.
I doubt they'd have any down here in Texas.
As for Hargrove and me, neither of us have a money machine
card, or a credit card, or any saved-up dough. I've never really
seen the Admiral with any money or a credit card either.
I doubt he owns a wallet.
Last night somebody with really bad taste stole that dumb shirt
with the Japanese stuff written on it that I stupidly bought at that
idiotic Rock Star Store on Hollywood Blvd. But someone else
gave me a pretty nice Levi's denim jacket. Lucky, because it's
cold out here in the desert before the sun comes up.

We're doing a steady 100 mph in the van. San Angelo is 200 miles away, so I guess we'll be there in two hours.

Friday April 8, 1983.

The Joe Perry Project is the opening act tonight at the San Angelo Coliseum.
I phone my little brother, Sam, back home in Holliston. Sam is twelve years younger than me, an unexpected but happy surprise for the Bell family. Sam doesn't play a musical instrument but he's an avid record collector. Good stuff too. 60's psych, Syd Barrett, Beatles and Kinks. The last time I checked, he was way into Lene Lovich and Siouxie and the Banshees. Sam draws the line at hard rock, but I think he's proud that his big brother is out here entertaining the planet with Joe Perry.
Today Sam is turning 18.
The Project will be opening for Huey Lewis and the News. Huey's been all over radio and MTV ever since I joined the JPP. Workin' For a Livin' and Do You Believe in Love? were two of the biggest hits of 1982.
After hitting so many nightclubs on this trip, I'm excited to play for thousands in a great big arena tonight.
But once we arrive, it doesn't take too long to understand why the Admiral got sick of constantly playing massive sporting facilities.
The scale of everything is too big. The dressing room is a cold cement cavern. There are union guys and cops lurking all over the property. In front of the stage I see barricades and big gorillas wearing Staff shirts, getting ready to push the fans back out of the aisles and away from the performers.
Like most musicians, Huey is a Joe Perry fan. His crew gives us plenty of room to set up our full backline in front of his gear and we've been allowed a generous 50 minute set. Funny doing our show so early. The sun is still up.
We hit the stage at 8 p.m. sharp, as the arena starts to fill up. Opening big with Train Kept A-Rollin' then strutting into Once a Rocker.

We crunch through Ain't No Substitute for Arrogance.

During the guitar break, the Admiral performs the new trick he's been perfecting for the past few months. While Hargrove and Pet keep the song grinding in high gear, Perry turns on a dime and starts playing a totally different song from the rest of us.

The song? *Dream On.*

Perry stands there in the spotlight, playing his famous guitar intro from the all-time Aerosmith classic and sacrificing it, indelicately, into the turning gears of the nasty-sounding Project favorite that Pet and Danny are still wailing away on.

It takes a few seconds for the audience to catch on.

Joe is playing their favorite slow dance - but it's jarring, it's not right, it's...and that's when Pet bashes out the drum build-up that leads us back into the final chorus of Arrogance.

The piece makes a powerful statement.

To me, it sounds like the Admiral is pushing the Steven Tyler ballad through a meat grinder.

The arena is almost full now, so we clobber them. The Admiral tears into the riff of his 70's smash Walk This Way and suddenly Texas remembers who the "F" Joe fukken Perry is...

As always, I feel like an imposter singing it. I mean, I had nothing to do with the record being a worldwide smash, but it sure is nice to have it in our repertoire when needed. It never fails. As the ovation dies-down, we chug straight into the Rockin' Train and for all Joe Pet's antics, he's one hell of a show-drummer. His solo tonight keeps the entire Coliseum (now packed) roaring.

Time for a few more and then we rip into Let the Music Do the Talking and suddenly we're being hustled down the long corridor back into the antiseptic-smelling visiting team dressing room. It's not even 9 o'clock yet.

A big iron-rimmed door slams behind us - and suddenly I can't even hear the crowd anymore. Is that all there is?

After the concert lets out, the Project meets up with Huey and his News at a local bar where the resident cover band invites us up to do some midnight jamming for a surprised and enthusiastic house.

Saturday April 9, 1983.

We're leaving Texas under Sheriff's orders.
This whole situation is so unnecessary and it makes zero sense
to me. It goes something like this. Lance Charger (Zakowski)
was messing around late last night after he got back to our hotel
(Inn of the West), following the concert we just played in San
Angelo. Instead of sleeping, like a normal person, Lance dialed
up one of those "Talk With a Real Live Girl" phone sex-lines.
A bit surprising, since Lance never has any problem luring
unsuspecting women back to his room.
Anyway, he managed to intimidate the sex operator and got her
to confess her real name and her whereabouts to him.
Charger then took off from our hotel with the JPP van.
As I heard it, he arrived at the sex phone-bank place, forced his
way inside and by the time the police got there, Zakowski was
punching holes in the walls. I don't know how, but somehow
Lance managed to avoid arrest. We've all been ordered to leave
the County pronto. The Joe Perry Project has a 600-mile drive
ahead of us today. Heading to Shreveport Louisiana.

Sunday April 10, 1983

Yesterday's long drive ended up here at the Bossier City Holiday
Inn in Shreveport. JPP road manager/soundman Dickman and
my nemesis Lance are sharing a room. Clean-cut Freddy shares
with the Admiral. I'm starting to figure out that those two share
similar toxic tastes. Not sure where teenager Boy Sean sleeps.
Danny Hargrove probably bounces between Pet's room and the
crew rooms most nights, because I'm being pretty much left to
my own. Nobody wants to share with Cowboy anymore because
of my social life. I don't mind partying with a fan or two when I
come to town.
I didn't get around to mentioning it last time, but this Holiday
Inn is famous for its swimming pool. It's where the owner keeps
his large collection of live Snapping Turtles. Snappers are
floating all over the courtyard cement-pond, big and dangerous-
looking.

Over these past few weeks, the Project has accumulated a good collection of liquor. Leftover bottles from the hospitality bars that are usually set up in our dressing rooms. The Admiral claims all the bourbon for himself and the vodka goes pretty quick. Some rum and a few liters of tequila haven't been opened yet, so this afternoon we set up a shots-bar by the Snapper Pool. After an hour or so of swilling in the sun, the crew sees something that looks like a baby rhinoceros rustling in the bushes. A wild rodeo ensues.

The crew capture a couple of raccoon-sized armadillos.

We herd the odd looking creatures inside the Holiday Inn and stake-out a dragstrip down the gaily-carpeted hallway.

Following some friendly wagering, the Armadillo Races begin. The armored animals scamper down the corridor, bouncing off the walls. Chambermaids, emerging from a guest room, shriek with surprise as the tank-like critters stampede past their house-keeping carts.

We return the befuddled but unharmed animals back to nature and continue our tequila party as the Snapping Turtles eye us suspiciously. No gig tonight.

Monday April 11, 1983

Over breakfast, in the Bossier City Holiday Inn, the Admiral tells me that our manager Tim is about to finalize a recording contract for us. With our new drummer Joe Pet settling into the Project nicely, and all tour dates accomplished as contracted, the long awaited deal is nearly in the bag.

"Tim told me it's between EMI, MCA and Geffen," confides the Admiral.

I spend the rest of breakfast begging Joe to ask Tim to do something about off-the-rails Zakowski.

"Lance is bad news. He could get us all into a lot of trouble. He's a dangerous influence on Boy Sean and Dickman. Lance is constantly taking advantage of you, Joe. And the Project."

The Admiral listens to my beef. He says little. As usual.

Joe Perry doesn't expect his Project crew to be choirboys.

Truth is, this road trip has gone relatively smoothly. The villain
Zakowski has gotten away with his obscene, violent behavior
and self-made messes. I just hope his luck holds out until this
vital record deal gets wrapped up. Lance's impulsive,
destructive behavior gnaws at me. I feel a bad moon rising.
We leave Shreveport Louisiana at 1 p.m. and travel 650 miles in
the van with a long dinner stop. The JPP finally pulls into
Atlanta GA at 2:30 a.m.

Tuesday April 12, 1983

The day started okay. Waking up at the Shoney's HoJo Down-
town Inn in Atlanta Georgia.
The Joe Perry Project is headlining here at Rumours tonight.
We show up for the 5 p.m. soundcheck.
I'm just bopping along, following the Admiral into the venue,
checking out the stage area.
Then we hear this loud southern-accented voice exclaim,
"Hey? Who the hell let that n__ in here?"
My head spins. What did I just hear? Who said that?
There she is. Leaning on the bar. Glaring right past me.
Staring at Danny Hargrove.
I charge over her way. Yelling at her to shut up and get the hell
out. She gets right up in my face, drawling
"I ain't goin' nowhere, sweetie. I work here."
I stomp back into the dressing room. I can see the Admiral and
Hargrove huddled back in the corner. Talking privately.
Both are looking down. Danny silently lights up a cigarette.
Seemingly unfazed.
Hargrove and Perry are like soldiers. Sent down here to Atlanta
just to carry out an objective. Totally professional guys.
Men on a mission.
I'm not like that at all. I have a short fuse and I'm ticked-off.
Steamed and pissed as hell. That stupid slur unleashes a whole
tornado of anger that's been building up inside me over the past
few weeks. Evil Cowboy is no longer in the mood to be
professional, or to sing for that loudmouth, jackass rebel gal.

Or anyone else South of the Mason Dixon line at this particular moment.

I race back out to the JPP van. Bust open a bottle of booze and begin chugging like an A-hole. It's hot and wicked humid.

In no time I'm blotto. Staggering drunk. I get called back inside Rumours, where I make rock'n'roll history, committing the sloppiest soundcheck in the annals of rock'n'roll.

Wednesday April 13, 1983

Today is Earthquake Morton's birthday. The guy who drafted me into this Joe Perry Project in the first place.

Thankfully, our show for tonight at Playground South in Jacksonville FL has been cancelled. I need time to recover from my self-inflicted/ill-advised/headache/hangover from yesterday at Rumours. I have no memory of last night. I must have managed to find the stage and stay somewhat upright. I guess. Most of the time at least. Anyway, the show happened as contracted. We got paid. I know the Admiral is glad to get out of that town too. He was disappointed and embarrassed by the hateful way Danny was welcomed at the venue.

So it's a drive day.

For some reason, Lance is riding with us today in the JPP van. Looks like he must have found out that I've been urging Perry, and anyone else who will listen, to get rid of him. After a couple hours of holding it in, Charger begins harassing me.

"Cowboy gossips about me like a chick. But he's the one who messed everything up last night. Beeps is a wimp."

I hiss back at him, but my head hurts too much to put up a good fight. Lance gets in my face, pointing at me,

"You're a pussy. You'll never be hardcore. You can't hold your liquor. Beeps is a lightweight. Cowboy sucks."

He starts cracking himself up. His routine is so lame, it actually sounds pretty funny. On and on he goes. Joe Pet and Danny Hargrove can't help chuckling at some of his dumb put-downs. But the Admiral has heard enough.

He jams Never Mind the Bollocks into the tape deck and cranks the volume all the way up. Followed by Back in Black,

followed by Prince 1999 and then back to the Sex Pistols again.
We finally make it to Bradenton Florida. Road manager
Dickman checks us into the Holiday Inn-Sarasota. The nicest
looking hotel we've stayed at since the Sunset Marquis. I'm
lugging my bag and my blaster to my room when I notice Lance
Charger, he's heading up the stairwell - carrying several large
bottles of Bacardi 151.

Thursday April 14, 1983

I awaken to pounding on my hotel room door.
I pull-on some clothes and peer outside. Seeing nothing, I stroll
down the outdoor walkway. I can hear a ruckus going on and a
familiar voice hollering. Turning the corner I see a huge mess,
all over the Holiday Inn swimming pool area.
The chaise lounges, planters, tables and chairs are all over-
turned. A trash can is half-submerged in the pool. The loud
yelling continues and now I see a concerned group of guests,
dressed in respectable attire, cowering over by the
cabana area where the hotel breakfast buffet is set up. People are
pointing upwards, staring in disbelief.
That's when I see the naked guy.
About twelve feet off the ground, in a palm tree. Urinating with
impressive force. It rains down towards the horrified crowd.
It's Zakowski.
Now the hollering guy comes into view. Oh, no. It's Dickman.
Yelling for his pet dog, 1000 miles away back in Massachusetts.
Next I see the Holiday Inn managers and staff, buzzing all
around and trying to calm the guests.
Sneaking up, still closer, I see the scattered pool furniture has all
been tagged with a black marker pen. Everywhere I look I see
the same slogan, scrawled across each toppled white table,
chaise and chair.
"Cowboy Sucks."
I know the local police will arrive at any second, I race back to
my room, lock the door and hastily jam my belongings into my
bag. The telephone is ringing. It's Hargrove.

Danny's already on top of what's going down and he's rounded
up our drummer Joe Pet.

Hargrove snarls, "Lance started it. He and Dickman were in the
Admiral's room all night. Drinking 151. The Admiral's still
passed out."

Someone's banging on my door again. I pray it's not the cops, I
fasten the security chain before I ease the door open an inch.

"Cowboy. Lemme in. C'mon man."

It's Lance. Naked, slobbering, drunk, almost crying.

"Beat it, Lance. Get out of here, you idiot." I slam the door.
The nature boy scoots away, balls bouncing.

I meet up with Hargrove and Pet in the Admiral's quarters.
Hargrove has already located and commandeered the all
important Halliburton briefcase. The case our road manager
always carries. Inside is the cash, Tim's American Express card,
receipts, gig sheets and the contracts for all our concerts.

The nerve center of this pirate operation.

Joe Perry is sprawled across his king-size bed. Face down. Stone
drunk and passed out cold.

We try to revive the boss but he's in Candy Land.

Glancing out over the balcony, we watch as most of the
Bradenton police department arrive. A platoon of cops are down
by the swimming pool inspecting the remarkable amount of
property damage. Other officers are hand-cuffing drunk and
disorderly Dickman. Gloved cops are trying to pull bare-assed
Lance Charger out of still another tree.

The hotel guests shake their heads and stare in dismay.

"We gotta get Joe out of here," orders Hargrove, as he flips
Perry over onto a floral-patterned bed cover. Pet and I each grab
an end. We roll-up the Admiral inside the Holiday Inn bedspread
like a big Italian sausage. Hoisting the guitarist's limp body, the
three of us make a dash for the JPP van.

The parking lot is awash in blue flashing lights. We duck and
dodge our way across the pavement, trying not to drop the
rolled-up rock star. Hargrove rummages through the Halliburton
and finds the keys to the van.

Pet and I shove the Admiral's lifeless carcass onto a bench seat in back. Danny jumps behind the wheel.

We book out of the Holiday Inn guest parking area. The Admiral is flopping around in back, totally unaware that he just got kidnapped out of his own bed.

A mile up the road we see a sign for the Resort Inn - Best Western.

"They'll never find us here," shouts Joe Pet.

Danny runs into the lobby and books three rooms. I dump my bag in my new room, turn, and run back outside to help Pet and Hargrove smuggle the Admiral's body inside the hotel.

A high school field trip is checking into the hotel at this very moment. It's the school's drum and bugle corps along with a dozen majorettes. They're all assembled out in the parking lot, waiting for their chaperones to return.

Looking up, the youngsters are stunned and frightened when they see Hargrove and Pet dragging a human form, wrapped tightly in bed covers, up the exposed rear stairwell.

Joe's carcass is finally deposited in the room right across the hall from mine.

While the Admiral lays lifeless, I dial-up our manager Tim Collins, back at the office in Allston Massachusetts.

"Hi, Tim. It's me, Cowboy."

"Mach? Great to hear your voice. Hey, I've got some really great news."

"Listen, Tim. We're having some trouble down here."

"Trouble? No problem. Put the road manager on the line."

"Can't, Tim, the police just arrested him."

"That's a good one, Cowboy. So how's Florida? Are you guys enjoying the hotel I booked?"

"Well...we're actually in a different hotel now."

"What the heck are you talking about? Put Joe Perry on the line."

"Joe's unconscious."

"Quit joking around, Mach. The lawyers from MCA are on their way over here right now. We've got a deal."

"That's great, Tim. But we might need some help down here. Zakowski and Dickman are both on the way to jail."
"You're kidding…Aren't you? Tell me you're joking, Mach… Please."
"Listen, Tim. We're at the Resort Inn - Best Western. I'll have the Admiral call you if he sobers up."
"Oh my god. Stay right there, Cowboy. Don't go anywhere. Don't say *anything*, to *anyone*, about *any* of this."
"No problem, Tim. Talk to you later."

When Joe Perry finally comes out of his coma, he's bewildered as to why his stuff isn't where he left it the night before. He wonders why his room looks and feels backwards to how it was when he checked in.
I find the Admiral stumbling around out in the hallway.
He squints at me in disbelief as I try to explain everything that's been going on since he conked out.
Believe it or not, the Joe Perry Project somehow goes on to play our concert tonight at the Rock'n'Crown in Bradenton Florida.

Friday April 15, 1983.

I wake up at the Resort Inn-Best Western in sunny Fla.
Yesterday seems like a nightmare, but Dickman and Lance really did get carted away by the Bradenton police. They both spent last night locked in cells at the Manatee County Jail.
But (good news), yesterday the Joe Perry Project finally scored the recording contract I've been praying for every day since I joined this band, well over a year ago.
We're gonna be on MCA Records. The home of Lynyrd Skynyrd, Tom Petty, Joan Jett, The Who, Nazareth, Olivia Newton John, Night Ranger and Elton John among others.
Immediately after securing the deal, our manager Tim phones my good friend Earthquake Morton.
Tim has a belated birthday gift for EQ. A jet ticket straight to Florida. MCA has taken-on the Joe Perry Project, based largely on Tim's assurances that the Admiral's reputation for illegal

activities, car crashes, toxic excesses, collapses and arrests are all in the rear-view mirror.

Earthquake's mission is to mop up our latest Project mess and keep a lid on the Bradenton busts. And to try and salvage the final remaining dates of this cross country road trip.

What follows is how I think it went down today:

Arriving at our hotel in Bradenton, Earthquake relieves Danny Hargrove of the Halliburton briefcase (wise idea), thereby assuming the tiller and rudder of the battle-scarred JPP pirate ship. EQ then rounds up what's left of our touring party and relocates us all over to the Governor's Inn/Best Western in New Port Richey.

While we make ourselves comfortable in the lounge, EQ and Hargrove head downtown where some magic is performed at the Manatee County Jailhouse. After buzz-buzzing with the local Sheriff's Department, a deal is finally struck and our shame-faced crew members get bailed out and released.

Then it's time to Let the Music Do the Talking.

JPP headlines tonight, with the help of a make-shift crew of locals that Earthquake rounds up. We're at another Rock'n'Crown. This one is in New Port Richey. These R'n'C clubs are really strange. I'll tell you more tomorrow.

Saturday April 16, 1983

This morning the rotten apple Zakowski got his bare-butt sent home. Last we'll be seeing of Lance Charger.

Dickman is in the doghouse big time but we still need him here to mix our house sound. With the JPP crew down to just the demoted Dickman, Boy Sean and Fred, we're very lucky to have Earthquake Morton on our team.

We're headlining at still another Rock'n'Crown tonight, this time in Pinellas Park.

I'm from New England where everything is normal. I think these Rock'n'Crown venues are really weird. Each location is a huge discount liquor warehouse store, with an adjoining concert club attached to it. There's a pass-through door between the giant booze store part and the vibrating showroom part, where the JPP is rocking out tonight.

I'm not sure how it all works but the fans are showing their appreciation. Phenomenal to see Joe Perry rocking in a wild joint like this. Tonight marks the final date of this 20-city road trip, dubbed the "Do or Die Tour" by our manager Tim Collins.

Sunday April 17, 1983

Right after the last encore at the Rock'n'Crown in Pinellas Park, the JPP crew packs up the truck and hits the road.

Heading back up to Boston with a Ryder truck stacked-high with Project gear. When the rest of us return home, we'll all be busy for the next few weeks, or maybe even months, writing and recording the new Project album.

On this national "Do or Die" tour we were able to achieve both of the goals that our manager Tim Collins set out for us.

1. We got really comfortable with our new drummer Joe Pet, who only joined the band about six weeks ago on March 2nd.

2. We (almost) proved to the music industry that the Project can complete a road trip without falling off the stage or getting locked up in jail.

After lunch, Earthquake drives Joe Pet and me out to the Tampa Airport. He dumps off the rental van and tells us that our crew should be in Georgia by now and that Hargrove went along for the ride.

EQ hands us our tickets home.
Pet and the Cattle Youth (that's what Pet usually calls me) are riding coach on People Express, Flight #454.

Well, it's now 5:30 p.m. Joe Pet is tipsy and the jet just touched down at Logan Airport in Boston. I'm missing the road already.

Hargrove, Bell and Perry. Somewhere in America. Mark V. Perkins

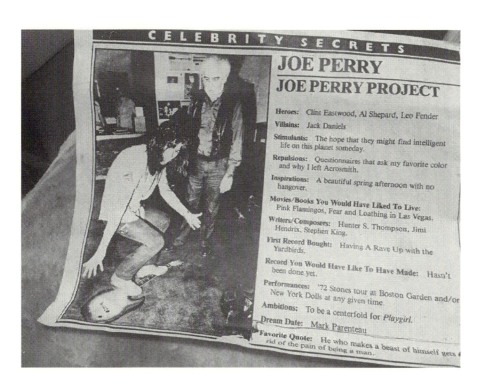

Joe Perry, Jim Dandy and Cowboy Mach in Houston Texas.

Danny Hargrove- most handsomest man. Photo credit: Henry Sancho

Rock singer Mach Bell (left) tries some of owner Robert Rooks' ice cream at Emack and Bolio's in Brookline. GLOBE PHOTO BY FRANK O'BRIEN

What's law next to ice cream?

By Bill Blanning
Special to The Globe

Rook, who is 39, hardly pictured himself lapping at success in the ice berry, cantaloupe, cranberry and chunky coconut.

My grandfather was baffled when he saw my mug on the front of the Business section of the Boston Globe.

Hampton Beach Casino   photo by Steve Pimpis

IV

BLACK VELVET PANTS

Monday April 18, 1983

I didn't even get to say "bye" to the Admiral. Not sure where he went. Maybe he stayed down in Florida, or went back to L.A. He might even be here in Cambridge.

Hard to tell with that quiet dude.

Tuesday April 19, 1983

The remains of our crew arrive back in Boston with our gear today. I file my income taxes. I can't even start adjusting to not rocking every night, not traveling everyday and not being in constant motion.

Wednesday April 20, 1983

Dinner with my parents in Holliston.
Then I go see Johnny Winter at the Paradise in Boston.

Thursday April 21 - Wednesday April 27, 1983

Lying on the couch in Cambridge MA at the pink palace. Watching Bob Barker, with announcer Johnny Olson, on The Price is Right. I'm prize-show pointer Dian Parkinson's biggest fan. Messing around with more song lyrics, new song titles and other ideas for the album.

Thursday April 28, 1983

It's our ex-drummer Ronnie Stewart's birthday today.
The Project gets together for the first time in over a week, at a 5 p.m. band meeting in Tim Collin's office. Tim lays out the upcoming schedule for us. We'll spend the month of May writing and rehearsing. With some scattered local concerts thrown in. The gigs will give us a chance to test out some new song ideas in front of a crowd.

The completed MCA record contract is set to be officially signed next week. At the beginning of June we'll book into a smaller studio for a week of pre-production. The actual MCA album sessions will begin six weeks from now.

Friday April 29, 1983

Playing the first Project date since the "Do or Die Tour" wrapped in Florida. Today we're at Dean Junior College in Franklin Mass. Our temporary road manager Earthquake is here with us. Except for Dickman (barely hanging in) and Fred, all the other crew members are new faces. Andy Bell is here tonight as is Bobby Edwards. I saw someone out in the audience video-taping our concert tonight with a huge camera.

Saturday April 30, 1983

We're down at Roger Williams College in Bristol RI. Same roadie situation as yesterday, Earthquake Morton is managing the new JPP crew. Our pal Mad Mississippi Buffalo aka Tom Swift, the vocalist/organist from Duke and the Drivers, is in the house tonight.
We are on a deja vu bill, with headliner sax-player Clarence Clemons from the E Street Band plus Gary U.S. Bonds.
Gary is riding a comeback hit This Little Girl is Mine and I know him from his huge 1961 hit, Quarter to Three. I wish I knew more about Mr. Bonds, he's sitting right over there, but I don't want to say the wrong thing and bother him.

Wednesday May 4, 1983

Universal City CA: it's official, MCA signs the Joe Perry Project to a record deal. I have to admit, I never could understand why multiple labels didn't jump to grab the Admiral a whole lot sooner. I know he was in bad shape early last year but ever since then he's been rocking and writing and recording new material. Criss-crossing the map with his new band and making every

single date. He draws fans everywhere, he signs autographs, and
he does press and interviews wherever he can.

I used to think it was tough to land a recording contract back in
my Thundertrain days, but I never imagined that even a proven
rock star, with a history of success and huge earning-potential
like Joe Perry, could get passed over for so long.

Thursday May 5, 1983

Yesterday, at Pet's apartment we worked up pretty good
arrangements of Eddie Cochran's Something Else and the
T. Rex number we've been jamming on, Get it On (Bang a
Gong). We can try them out onstage tonight, we're headlining in
Wallingford CT at a roadhouse called Boston McGee's.

A very dedicated, but meager, cluster of kids show up.

A couple hundred at best.

A lot of our audience is usually made up of rock musicians.
Especially guitar players. Makes sense, I guess the audience at a
ballet probably includes plenty of dancers and the folks who go
to rodeos might be riders and ropers themselves.

Beginner guitarists will push up to the front, along with the
superfans and stare at Joe in wonder.

Intermediate guitarists are poking their buddies,
"Hey, that's just a barred B7 chord, right? Why does it look so
different when Joe Perry plays it?"

The self-appointed top guns, the ones who play like lightning
but never made it beyond the county line, are back at the bar and
laughing, "See, I told ya he's nothin' without Brad Whitford."

The Admiral doesn't care. Just as long as they all keep showing
up and paying the admission fees.

Saturday May 7, 1983

I'm a participant at the "Boston Rock Music Seminar" this
morning. I get to wear a name tag that says Mach Bell and sit on
a panel with some other musicians, agents and radio people.

Then I return to my element - performing tonight at Uncle Sam's
on Nantasket Beach in Hull MA with the JPP.

A word about showmanship.

I stole plenty of my moves from Mark Lindsay, Wilson Pickett, Roger Daltrey, Rod Stewart, Keith Relf and a few more from Jim Dandy. I learned an awful lot from watching Steven Tyler. Steven opened my eyes to so many tricks when I'd go see Aerosmith in my teens. Playing at the local town halls and youth centers, Tyler was only a few feet away and easy to observe. Steven is five years younger than Jagger and there's no doubt Tyler spent many hours studying the master. I'm five years younger than Steven, so it figures that Tyler was the guy I wanted to learn from. I'm not sure how old David Johansen is, he's another guy I modeled my stage activities around, and David obviously attended Jagger University as well. Meanwhile, Mick copped plenty of his act from the Godfather of Soul - James Brown.

Tuesday May 10 - Friday May 13, 1983

Everyday at 2 p.m. the Admiral, Danny and I travel up to Medford. A town just a few miles north of Boston. It's a nice family neighborhood of double and triple deckers. This is where Joe Pet lives with his wife and son. Their upper level apartment has a small room in the front that Pet uses as his drum studio. His practice kit takes up most of the space. There's just enough room left over to cram in a couple Peavey practice amps. Lucky we're all skinny.

I think we've worn out our welcome at the Cambridge Complex and at the A.Wherehouse. We're lucky that Pet has a place for us to work.

We spend hours jamming with a tape recorder going. Searching for gold. Joe has come up with a grinding Cream-ish riff that we go round and round on for a while. Then there's a wide open Angus-type power chord progression. In reality they don't really sound like Cream or Angus, they just sound like Perry. But in order to keep track of his ever-growing mountain of riffs and structures, I give them all code names.

While Hargrove and Perry duck outside for a cigarette, Pet and I get into it.

Pet starts ribbing me, it's pretty obvious that when it comes to the Admiral, I'm star struck.

I admit it. From the first time I saw Joe playing at Lakeview I immediately knew I was in the room with a unique presence.

After more than a year on the road with the Admiral, nothing has changed.

I'm still totally awed by Joe Perry.

"Get over it, Cowboy. He's just like you and me."

"Oh c'mon, Pet. You've got to be kidding."

"The Admiral puts his pants on every morning. Just like we do."

"What's that got to do with anything, Pet?"

"He's just a good guitar player. That's all."

"Yeah, right, dude. Good guitar player? So that's why kids stand outside for hours in the rain and snow waiting for him? And pay ten bucks so they can stand at the front of the stage every night to yell Joe fukken Perry?"

"You're nuts, Cattle Youth."

Saturday May 14, 1983

Great to get out of that little room and play to a crowd again.
This show is called the "WAAF May Day Beach Party."
It's out in Hubbardston Mass.
The openers, The Stompers, are hot right now.
A local bar band who write, play and sing catchy songs in the currently popular Asbury Park/Stone Pony style, they have a new album on Boardwalk Records and are getting plenty of airplay around here.
Andy Bell and Steven Silva arrive along with some of their friends. It's a nice day for a beach party. We're set-up on some flatbed trucks in front of a lake, with a little sandy beach. Kids in bathing suits. Bikers, babes, rockers. I get a little carried away in the hospitality area.
But I thought the show went okay.

Tuesday May 17, 1983

Laundry boy time again. I'm walking up Broadway to the
corner laundromat when I see a gorgeous blonde bouncing up
the sidewalk, coming straight towards me.
Wait. I know that girl.
"Hey, Billie."
"Mach. What are you doing here?"
"Nothing. Laundry. Hey, how's Willie?"
"Good. He's okay."
"So...did you see the show last night?" I ask.
"Motown 25?"
"Yeah. Did you see that backwards, forwards thing he did?"
Billie starts shuffling her running shoes backwards, while
attempting to glide ahead.
"I can't figure it out. It was so crazy," she laughs.
"He's gonna be even bigger than he was with the Jackson 5.
So what're you doing around here anyway, Billie?"
She points to a big brick apartment house, across Broadway.
"I live here. Right up there."

We were at Joe Pet's home-studio again yesterday, and today
we're back. Making a tape of some things we're considering for
the record. Something Else, Never Gonna Stop, Instrumental,
Bang a Gong, Into the Night, Funky Pagans.
The Admiral is planning to meet with an MCA A&R man who is
flying up from Nashville tonight.

Wednesday May 18, 1983

I get called into the office. Tim throws a copy of the Worcester
Telegram down on his desk. "Read this."
It's a review of our beach party gig the other day. After a
glowing review of the Stompers, the writer blasts the "preening,
strutting, unwatchable performance of Joe Perry's egomaniacal
vocalist Mach Bell." The review gets a lot worse from there.
"Aw c'mon, Tim. I was just messing around. Everyone on the
beach was having a blast."

Tim glares at me. "Listen to this."

Our manager turns on a small cassette player that is sitting on his desk. What begins playing is dismaying.

Hargrove, Pet and the Admiral sound tight as ever, but when the vocal comes in…I'm singing in an entirely different key from the rest of the guys. And I hold that wrong key painfully, not straying an inch. The song is in A and I'm nearer to F#.

The result is unlistenable and embarrassing.

"What's wrong with you, Mach? I'm sending you to a doctor."

I scamper out of there with my tail between my cowboy boots. At 6:30 p.m. I go to see Dr. Jonas. I'm advised to knock off all the partying. The doc injects me with a Vitamin B12 shot.

Thursday May 19 - Friday May 20, 1983

Leon Tsillis, that's how he spells it, the A&R executive from MCA, gave the Admiral a song the other night. We're back at Pet's studio and listening carefully.

The tune is called Women in Chains. The lyric has a nice twist, it's not a story about whipping your girlfriend and chaining her up in the kitchen. No, it's just the opposite, a protest against male domination of the opposite gender.

The demo tape sounds really good too. Probably cut in one of those big Nashville studios. The vocalist sounds a bit like Sting.

Later, I ask the guys to jam some more on the Admiral's Cream-sounding lick and I begin singing.

"She's a dream in the night / the Queen of the streets
And when we walk / I'm the King of the Kings"

Friday May 21, 1983

Brockton is a working class city, about twenty-five miles south of Boston. Adjacent to the Westgate Mall is a large rock room, called Scotch'n Sounds. Johnny A's Hidden Secret opens the show. Johnny is a damn good guitarist and his former band, the Streets, were an opener on Aerosmith tours a few years back.

 From the dressing room we can hear 1999 erupt out of the sound system. Our current entrance ritual goes like this:

1999, For Those About to Rock, Ride of the Valkyries, and finally, the William Tell Overture fanfare.
That mix-tape takes about fifteen minutes to complete, giving us fair warning for last minute preparations. I'm being careful to avoid the substances being handed around.
I'm in the doghouse with Tim Collins right now.
We pull a big crowd and I sing like a bird.

Tuesday May 24 - Thursday May 26, 1983

Back at rehearsal, the Admiral has adapted Women in Chains to his guitar style and he leads us through it.
I'm singing it more like Alice Cooper than Sting.
Perry has another new, really exciting staccato riff that we all latch onto immediately. Pet adds a sprinting groove that incorporates a clicking clave counterpoint, something I've never heard on a hard rock song before. On Wednesday, we're joined by Harry King, a pianist who will help us make the record. We manage to wedge King's electric keyboard into Pet's small studio. Jamming along with us, Harry quickly learns the changes to all the material that we've been crafting.

Friday May 27, 1983

It's Friday night and people are crowding into the Hampton Beach Casino. Harry King is here to see what the Project is all about. The show begins early, with short sets from local bands the Reflectors and the Lines, followed by special guest Zebra, an excellent power-trio who have a new LP coming out on Atlantic. Our former crew member Phuck is celebrating with us tonight.
We put on a hell of a show for the birthday boy.
Dickman has been relieved of his duties. We have a new man, named Rob, as road manager and a biker-looking cat, named Rick, running the sound. Boy Sean and Fred are the only hold overs from the Do or Die tour.

Saturday May 28, 1983

Salem is the coastal town where the gruesome witch trials were held back in 1692.
Flashing forward almost 300 years, the JPP headline at the Salem Theatre, an old movie house with just the right acoustics and perfect seating for a rowdy Joe Perry crowd.
Pet's friend, Brother Brown, arrives backstage with a tank of nitrous oxide and we do a bit of scientific research - laughing it up before the show. Whoever promoted this gig did a great job.
Every seat is sold. A frenzied crowd of young crazies greet us.
The vibe tonight is magical, and this gig stands out as one of my favorite evenings so far with this amazing rock band.

Sunday May 29, 1983

We've got our work cut out for us today.
Two shows in two different states.
We begin up in Bridgton Maine - about 70 miles north of Portland, over by Sebago Lake.
Watch out for black bears and bobcats.
The gig is creatively titled Outdoor Festival. Good line-up though. Along with the Project they've got The Stompers, Bill Chinook, the Pousette-Dart Band, Midnight Traveler and NRBQ.
I especially want to catch NRBQ but due to our schedule we have to play early and scram the minute our set ends. The festival has a surprisingly great turnout. I bet attendance could have been doubled if the show was held closer to civilization.
Now we have to make a gig on Cape Cod.
Fred books it down Route 302 and hits I95 South in Portland. In New Hampshire we have to sit in several miles of back up, waiting to pay a buck at the dreaded Hampton tolls.
From there we drop down into Massachusetts and connect with Route 93 South which takes us through Boston, via the Central Artery and straight into abysmal traffic on the South East Expressway. Fred finally breaks free at the Braintree Split and we rocket down Route 3.

We pass Plymouth (where the Pilgrims landed) and finally
join the queue crossing the Sagamore Bridge onto the Cape.
Exiting onto Route 130, we enter the village of Mashpee.
Very recently, the Channel (back in Boston), bought a venue
here, and re-named it the Cape Channel. This large room was
previously well-known as On the Rocks. A place where all the
most popular cover bands and the prettiest beach girls would
spend their summers. Thundertrain would dream of getting a
booking here. Waiting to cheer us on tonight at the Cape
Channel is Kersti, the little sister of the counter girl from the
Holliston Music'n'Things store. The store where I first
encountered the name Aerosmith, a dozen years ago.

Tuesday May 31, 1983

In honor of the rekindling of the Citgo sign high above Kenmore
Square...Mr. Joe Perry requests the pleasure of your company
down below Kenmore Square.
The Pagans
At the Rat
Tuesday May 31, 1983
For one night only
Come Get the Rock and Rolls...Again

So reads the invitation distributed to the press, radio and our
fans. Following the gasoline crisis, back in the mid-70's, the
famous Citgo sign was shut-off to conserve energy. Being a
Boston landmark and a notable feature on all Fenway Park
telecasts, the public demand to relight it finally wins out.
We're playing the Rat under an alias: The Pagans.

Sitting in the disaster area known as the Rat dressing room,
I recall the night I once sat here with a guy named Steve.
It was early in 1977 when Rat owner Jim told me that a new
band from Cleveland would be opening for Thundertrain.
I had never met these guys but a few months back both our
bands shared a page in Rock Scene magazine, spotlighting
"Bands to Watch For." His group was called Frankenstein then,

but now they've changed the name. Steve's about to change his
name too. Interesting, because I want to do the same thing.
There's this other guy, named Mark Bell, he's making noise as
the drummer of Dust. So I'm thinking of "Mach."
It's basically Mark - but pronounced with a Boston accent.
"Yeah, Mach is good," nods Steve.
 "Go with something like Mach, or Fabian, or Liberace, or
 Hercules. So everybody knows you just from the first name."
"Okay, man - that settles it. From now on I'm Mach."
"Nice to meet you, Mach. You can call me Stiv."
That's how I first met Stiv Bators, and his (renamed) band the
Dead Boys.
Tonight's crowd at the Rat includes the Admiral's roommate
Glenda, Andy Topeka (the master technician from The Cars and
formerly with Aerosmith), Bunny Patty from the Boston
Playboy club and WBCN afternoon-deejay Mark Parenteau.
This is our final show before recording begins.

Wednesday June 1 - Thursday June 2, 1983

The last stage of pre-production commences in Newton at a
recording studio called White Dog. Phil Adler engineers and
Harry King assists production. We show up at 1 p.m to begin the
slow process of setting up the gear, choosing mics and getting
sounds. On Thursday, we lay down basic tracks for the Cochran
cover song Something Else and the original Into the Night.
Things are rolling along smoothly.

Friday June 3, 1983

"MCA Drops the Joe Perry Project."
My heart stops beating when I hear the news.
What? Are you serious? Why?

We're in the middle of today's session at White Dog when the
call comes in. I'm numb.

As I understand it, there's been a shake-up at the label. A new president has been elected/appointed. Music-biz heavyweight Irving Azoff, manager of the Eagles, just took the reins at MCA. Irving's first official move is to dump Joe Perry.

Saturday June 4, 1983

Tim keeps his cool. He tells us to keep working on the record and he'll think of something. I'm not sure how we're going to proceed, studio time costs a lot. And what good is a record if there's nobody to release and distribute it? I want to trust Tim, but I'm downhearted. Of course I've also been spending the last two months marching up and down the street, bragging about my big record deal to anyone who'll listen. What now?

Sunday June 5, 1983

The Admiral doesn't seem very fazed either, I know he's been through a whole lot worse. He keeps the session right on track, and today we mix the White Dog demos. When Do I Sleep?, Into the Night, They'll Never Take Me Alive and several more. The office calls. Tim has managed to put together some private financing with two of his friends. Tim isn't taking Irving Azoff's action lying down either. He's preparing to do battle with the label. A deal's a deal. In any case, we've been green-lighted to begin recording our album tomorrow.

Monday June 6 - Tuesday June 7, 1983

We settle into Blue Jay Recording in Carlisle. This time we'll have the run of the place - it's all ours. The crew sets up the gear while the Admiral talks with engineer Michael Golub and Harry King, who are both associate producing. The producer/director on this record will be Joe Perry.
Along with our usual mountain of equipment, the Admiral has added an old, wooden Leslie rotating-speaker cabinet. The kind that's usually hooked up to a Hammond B3 organ.

After getting everything sounding right, we start cutting the bed tracks. By the end of Tuesday we have Bang a Gong and When Do I Sleep? in the can. Plus that Angus-sounding riff which is now titled Four Guns West.

East we ride / Wanted dead or alive
Into Tampa Bay the stage was set
We had to make bail / to spring the gang out of jail
Manatee County can't forget
Take your pistol off the wall / and heed the twilight call
Cincinnati, is under attack
There's blood on the walls / Cops in the halls
See ya when we get back

Wednesday June 8 - Thursday June 9, 1983

Once a Rocker, the funky little number I wrote with Joe the first week we met, is finally laid down for keeps. Never Gonna Stop has been retitled, Never Wanna Stop. I wrote those lyrics back in January, sitting alone at the palace. I thought about the Led Zeppelin song, Gallows Pole and came up with words that would fit into that cadence. Months later, I began singing my lines to the Admiral and he was inspired to put a bottleneck guitar underneath them.

On Thursday we record basic tracks for Perry's Black Velvet Pants and the Leon Tsillis suggestion, Women in Chains. The Admiral uses the revolving Leslie speaker on this track, reaping high octane results.

Perry's staccato riff with the clave accents is now titled Crossfire. It's sounding big, as does the majestic King of the Kings. I've been singing guide vocals along with the band in the studio. It helps keep the energy up.

My guides don't get recorded, but I do take a crack at tracking a few keeper lead vocals today.

Never too early to start.

While the others record, I've been sketching out a storyboard for a Black Velvet Pants video. Trying to keep it simple. Something that could be done on a budget.

The meat and potatoes of the video features the four of us, playing live onstage, in a theater for some enthusiastic fans. That footage is intercut with a story line. A rear-view of a blonde beauty slipping into her black velvet pants, the beauty running down the stairs of her apartment house, the beauty skipping up the city streets, the beauty entering the theater where the Project are rocking out, the beauty strutting down the aisle and jumping onto the stage where she finally grabs a pink saxophone. Just in time to jam-out with Joe and the Project, until the fade out. A straightforward, simple tale.
And I know just who to get to play the beauty.

Friday June 10 - Saturday June 11, 1983

After listening back to the basic tracks of When Do I Sleep? I've decided to totally re-write the lyrics.

Guitar starts talkin' / Drums begin to pound
Kinda get the feeling' / We're the only ones around
Adrianna holds me / We start to swing and sway
Let my sorrows walk-on / Let the music play
Adrianna tell me, when do you sleep?
When the guitar starts, You're up on your feet.

Obviously inspired by the Caracas trip and my night dancing at the disco with TV star MaryBella.
The original lyrics were downbeat, with sex and drug references. This new version centers more on the cool guitar riff, the dancing and the hospitality hostess with the mostest: Adrianna. On Saturday, the band records beds for First One's For Free and Walk with Me Sally. With the basic tracks accomplished, our crew break-down the drums and bass rig and move them out of the studio.

Wednesday - Saturday June 15/16/17/18, 1983

Now it's my turn. The Admiral, of course, will wait until everything else is finished before he adds his lead guitar parts.

Vocals are a slow process for me. Rarely will I sing a perfect take from beginning to end.

First, I'll record the vocal several times. Choosing the best two attempts, we go back and punch-in any sections where I sang a clam. It takes a while for me to get two solid vocal tracks on each number.

Wednesday yields King of the Kings (a tough one),
Walk with Me Sally and Once a Rocker.

On Thursday, we manage to finish Black Velvet Pants,
Never Wanna Stop and Four Guns West.

On Friday, I'm rolling, we add lead vocals to Women in Chains, Crossfire, Bang a Gong and finally Adrianna.

On Saturday, all four of us circle a big microphone hanging from a boom and do gang background vocals on Gong, Kings, Rocker, BVP, Stop, and Chains.

Joe Pet and Hargrove have really nice clear voices. The Admiral and I both have a lot of character in our voices. We blend pretty well, it sounds full, with plenty of grit and power.

We're finishing up the backgrounds when this little suit from the Musicians' Union drops by the studio, making sure this recording is going strictly by the book. Apparently he still has the production listed as an MCA major label session.

Per union rules, he cuts a hefty $1700 check and hands it to drummer Joe Pet, $1700 for bassist Hargrove and still another $1700 for Admiral Perry.

I'm standing last in line waiting for my turn.

"What instrument do ya play?" asks the union man.

"I'm the lead singer."

The union guy turns away and says "Sorry, these checks are for the musicians only."

He's walking out the door when I finally plead,

"But I played maracas on a few songs."

The union man spins around and whips open the check book.

"Maracas? Why didn't ya say so in the first place, kid?"

He writes me a fat check for $1700 and goes on his way.

Best Project payday ever.

Monday - Wednesday June 20/21/22, 1983

Producer Joe Perry has whittled the record down to ten tracks.
Gone are They'll Never Take Me Alive, Something Else and
First One's For Free.
He also wants to add something extra, so on Monday he and
Harry have reed players Jim Biggins and Ric Cunningham
setting up in the cutting room. Saxophone textures and
occasional solos are added to Crossfire, Adrianna and Black
Velvet Pants. Joe also asks me to try singing Walk with Me Sally
once more. It's one of the rare times that I nail a vocal in one
take. I get a nice round of applause from the control room.
Harry King adds piano to Walk with Me Sally and finally the
Admiral asks his deejay pal Mark to drag some chains around
the studio floor, as an intro for Women in Chains.

On Wednesday, I invite Julia along as my guest.
Today is her birthday and I surprise her by taking her to a local
carnival that's set up in downtown Carlisle.
She was hoping for dinner at a nice place - but I thought the
carnival would be more fun.
I convince the cowardly Jules to ride the Zipper with me.
Very bad idea. Forty feet off the ground, stuck upside-down,
eyeing the lone rusty bolt that supports our swinging
compartment, Julia cries out in terror. Feigning bravery, I close
my eyes and silently pray for our lives.
Back at the ranch, the Admiral is finally beginning to lay down
his lead guitar tracks.

Thursday June 23, 1983

Stage hand Fred left Millis at 8 a.m. Our gear is packed inside a
14' U-Haul truck. I guess we've been storing the equipment out
at Glen Ellen Country Club these days.
At 10 a.m., Rob pulls up in front of the pink palace in a Jeep
Pioneer station wagon from Dollar Rent a Car. Already aboard
are sound guy Rick, Boy Sean, Hargrove and Pet.

We take off, heading for the Canadian border. Joe Perry is still
back in Carlisle, tracking layer upon layer of guitar.
We catch up to Fred at the border at around 5 p.m. and make the
crossing up into Quebec. It's after 10 p.m. when we pull into
Levis, a town just below Quebec City.
We have five rooms booked at Hotel DuVallon.

Friday June 24, 1983

Tim and the Admiral catch Quebec Air Flight #284 out of
Logan, arriving in Quebec City at 1:40 p.m.

Super Rock Show Plein Air
Frank Marino
Joe Perry Project (artiste invite)
Ex-guitariste de Aerosmith
Coney Hatch
Le Vendredi 24 Juin, A 20 h Saint-Charles de Bellechasse
Prix d'entree: $12

Saturday June 25, 1983

That was a super rock show alright. Staged under the stars, up
on a hilltop, facing towards the Hotel Frontenac, I was singing
out into the darkness with spotlights glaring into my eyes. From
the cheers and shouting rising up from below I could tell the
crowd was massive. Mahogany Rush guitarist Frank Marino is a
total rock god up here. I think Marino was on the Cotton Bowl
bill with Aerosmith at Texxas Jam a few years ago. Definitely
great to get out of the underground studio and back in front of a
huge audience, even though I could hardly see them. We're on
our way back down to the States now.

Thursday June 30, 1983

The Admiral has been dug-in, out at Blue Jay, finishing guitar
and beginning to mix the record.

But today he's in the office with Tim and me. We're meeting
with a video producer named Tingle. I've brought along the
Black Velvet Pants storyboard I drew and I pitch my idea to the
guys. I also suggest hiring the beauty I talked to outside the
laundromat last month. The one who saw Michael Jackson doing
the moonwalk on TV.

After that, it's on up to Kingston NH to play an outdoor show
with "New England's #1 All Female Band" Lipstick, and The
Fools, who are an excellent group recording for EMI America.
They rose to fame with their great Talking Heads' parody,
Psycho Chicken.

I'm sitting at a picnic table behind the stage, daydreaming, when
a fantastic Marilyn Monroe-looking babe sways into view and
sits down right beside me. Very close beside me.

In a whispery, friendly voice she introduces herself.

"Hi, Mach. I'm Cyrinda."

Doing a double-take, I realize that the knockout, pushing hard
against my thigh, is the ex-wife of New York Dolls' singer
David Johansen as well as the recently estranged wife of
Aerosmith singer Steven Tyler.

Cyrinda is wearing a red silk blouse. She's small and trim and
her face is Hollywood beguiling but she looks kind of unhappy.
We talk for a while about summer in New England and her
memories of growing up out in Southern California. I ask about
her work with David Bowie and her starring role in Bad, the
Andy Warhol film.

Foxe tells me that she is living alone on the shore of Lake
Sunapee, caring for a little girl. Steven's kid I bet.

This lady seems to like rock singers. She is famous and
captivating and very poised. But my future is bright. My worldly
girlfriend Julia is the most successful, foxy bachelorette on the
Boston music scene and we have deep feelings for each other.

I'm singing in America's hardest rocking, hardest-working band.
The Project is about to take the Top Ten by storm.

Chasing after Steven Tyler's ex?

The bewitching, sad-eyed Cyrinda Foxe?

Totally out of the question. I dash out onstage and shake it like
crazy in front of a nice turnout at the Kingston Fairgrounds.

Friday July 1 - Monday July 4, 1983

Joe works on his mixes every day for long hours. We're invited
to be there with him, but attending a mixing session is grueling.
Short segments of songs get played over and over again.
Pure torture. The incremental changes being made are often
impossible for me to discern. On and on it goes, a hell of a lot of
concentration and work.
You can bet that once our record is released the critics will
probably call it "raw-sounding and under-produced."

Fabulous news. Tim has gotten us back on track with MCA
Records. I'll never know how he pulled it off. I can only guess
that he threatened to sue, or made such a stink that Irving Azoff
finally relented and just said forget it, we'll release the damn
thing. Whether the label will lift a finger to promote us is a
whole 'nother story.

Tuesday July 5 - Thursday July 7, 1983

On Tuesday I meet Tim at the office and we throw around JPP
merchandising ideas. Stuff like hats, shirts, buttons, coffee
mugs, inflatable Hargrove love dolls and Joe Pet bobble-heads.
After a while the Admiral joins us.
Perry tells us about his big idea. His vision for the album cover
for his third Project record.
"Okay, guys. Imagine a boxing ring - like in *Rocky*.
Standing in the back, there's a cute girl wearing a sparkly outfit.
She's holding up a big card that says "Round Three." Then,
inside the the ring, pushed up against the ropes, wearing trunks
and boxing gloves and kinda bloodied up - but ready to fight
another round - is *me*."
Tim Collins says nothing. He stares down at his desk. Trying
hard to envision it.
Our manager finally, nervously, turns towards me.
"So...Cowboy...What do you think of Joe's idea?"
I hem and haw as Perry glowers at me. Then, as tactfully as possible, I remind everyone that the Admiral is the face of this

operation, he's our sizzle, he's our steak. I recommend that we keep everything simple and straightforward for the record buying public and just put a nice big photo of Joe Perry's handsome mug on the front cover of the new record.

On Thursday, Joe Perry's final mixes are turned into a finished quarter-inch stereo master tape. Followed by a 6:30 p.m. band meeting at the office. Tim proposes a deal where the whole band can share in the profits of the album as it passes certain sales benchmarks.

Saturday July 9, 1983

Julia and I drive north to visit my family in Wonsqueak Harbor Maine.

Monday July 11, 1983

Joe is at Sterling Sound in NYC with Greg Calbi, mastering the record. Julia and I are at a movie theater in Ellsworth Maine, watching an uneven new film called *Superman III*.

Wednesday July 13 - Thursday July 14, 1983

I board a very small plane in Bar Harbor, fly down to Logan and drive out to Cape Cod where the JPP are getting photographed for the album jacket. The photographer, Linda, specializes in bridal shots. The photo shoot is held in a wedding studio - full of bouquets, lace and pink stuff.
Joe Pet can't resist goofing around with some of the bridal props. Glenda comes along as stylist and she makes us all look...pretty.
Feels a little odd, but these days the charts and MTV are ruled by the likes of Boy George, Prince and the Thompson Twins. Keith never had a problem wearing mascara, so why should I? Photo session complete, I wipe the rouge off my face and fly back up to Downeast Maine. Julia meets me at the airstrip and we stop off in Ellsworth to catch the new *Twilight Zone Movie*.

Tuesday July 19, 1983

The Admiral and I take a ride to Dorchester, a neighborhood of
Boston, to tour the Strand Theater. Our former lighting director
Woody, comes along as well as road manager Rob,
director Tingle and Billie Alexander - who has been chosen to
play the beauty in our music video. Natch.
When she models, she goes under the name Billie Montgomery.
She also does sales work for a local radio station.
In her spare time, Billie puts a lot of effort into promoting the
career of Willie Loco Alexander.
The shy, charismatic, sexy, dynamo Willie Alexander is another
of my heroes. Willie sang and played piano in the frat-rock
turned 60's psych group The Lost, followed by the Bosstown
Sound band, The Bagatelle. Willie even became a member of the
Velvet Underground during their final tours before leading his
own Willie Loco Alexander and the Boom Boom Band to glory.
Willie Loco was gracious enough to play piano on Hot for
Teacher! my biggest hit with Thundertrain.
It seems that Billie and Willie's marriage has been dwindling
down as of late.

Friday July 22, 1983

I'm on the way to play a show, very happy that our new album is
in the can. But tonight, as always, the set will mostly be the
Ralph Morman and Charlie Farren songs that fans of the Project
albums are all wanting to hear.
After a year and a half of singing everybody else's stuff, I'm
dying to perform the tracks from the new album.
But I get it, we don't want to be one of those bands that only
play new songs "off our next record." The crowd wants to hear
the old favorites like Life at a Glance and East Coast,West Coast
- and, by the way - I can finally sing the opening line of that one
properly because Pet plays it exactly the way Ron Stewart
originally recorded it.
During the van ride, I'm reading an article in Billboard about a
recent change in buying habits of today's rock music fans.

"Listen to this Joe. Kids are buying more new rock releases on cassette than on lp. Listen to these numbers."
The Admiral isn't in the mood for my market analysis.
"I don't care about your numbers, Cowboy. I don't care what Billboard says. The only thing that matters is the record."
"Yeah…but, Joe, it says because of this trend, all the art departments are putting extra emphasis on cassette packaging."
"Be quiet, Cowboy…you read too much."
We're headlining the Regal Theater in Franklin NH.

Saturday July 23, 1983

I'm on the balcony of Billie's apartment building.
Helping her spray paint a saxophone bright pink.
My brother, Andy, plays guitar and the ukulele, but he specializes in brass and the slide trombone in particular. I called him, asking if he happened to have an old saxophone lying around that he could donate to the cause.
Andy produced this one. Score.

Tuesday July 26, 1983

The crew arrives early in Dorchester, to transform the Strand Theater for the video. Woody is up in the catwalks hanging lights. Side-fills are positioned so the BVP audio track can be played loudly while we mime to it. The staging is being extended out into the audience area. Our backline is set up. Hey, somebody just told me that Mick Jagger is turning 40 today. Duly noted.
Looking upwards, I see that Woody has honored himself by hanging the overhead par lamps in a "W" formation.
We're gonna be under the "big dubba-U" just like in that drive-in comedy movie that everyone remembers. Three large purple banners, each emblazoned with our new JPP logo, are being strung from a horizontal truss that will be lowered into place behind the band as the video begins. Glenda's roommate, Ilse, and Ilse's artist boyfriend, Teddy Filios, worked for the past few overnights, creating those big banners for us.

At 8 p.m., we begin the dress rehearsals. The track starts, Joe plays the riff, the band kicks in, I enter, the lights come up, the banners drop into place, we rock, and finally Billie struts down the aisle, hops up onto the stage, dashes to the drum riser and picks up her pink sax. Billie and the Admiral face-off and jam together until the fade out. We repeat the routine a half-dozen times. On a rough playback it looks pretty good.

Wednesday July 27, 1983

Starting at 4 p.m. we begin to shoot the close-ups for the video. This is a one-camera shoot. Tingle will set up his camera position, and then we'll perform the entire song. After that, the director will set up a new angle and we'll rock the whole thing again. Every take, from every vantage point, will be carefully slated and catalogued. Once the director has shots from dozens of positions, he can edit them together to create an exciting-looking video. That's the plan anyway.
Glenda is here tonight. She's not pleased about the chemistry happening between the Admiral and Billie. Tingle keeps shooting our performance. Over and over, until midnight.

Thursday July 28, 1983

"Wanna be in Joe Perry's new MTV video? C'mon down to the Strand Theater tonight at 6 p.m. The first two hundred fans who arrive will get to be part of the next Joe Perry Project MTV video." Mark Parenteau sends out the call over the WBCN airwaves and by the time the camera starts rolling we have an energetic crowd of dolled-up girls and anxious boys leaping, fist pumping, and ready to sing along.
Tingle is planning to get the wide-shots from multiple angles tonight. Shots where the band is out on the extended staging, engaging with the crowd. Like yesterday, we run through the song over and over and over again.
The first half dozen run-throughs are exciting but our crowd starts to get exhausted, being asked to go wild for the same thing

over and over again. Parenteau does pep talks between takes, trying to keep the exhausted audience pumped up.

Glenda returns tonight and things get rough backstage. I missed the whole scene, but apparently Glenda is sick of Billie. Glenda hits Billie in the face. Glenda might be strong but her fist is only the size of an acorn. Athletic Billie bounces back, pretty as ever and we continue the shoot. Sorry it happened, they are both very nice people. I feel a little guilty too. But not that much.

Thursday July 29, 1983

Our crew loads-out the gear and props used during filming. Phuck is re-hired, just for the day, to help out.

Do you remember a folk story about Stone Soup? A woman starts boiling water for soup and throws a stone into the pot. One by one, the neighbors start adding more ingredients. Bits of parsley, a few carrots, some salt, a couple onions and even a bucket of potatoes.

That's how this video came together. Ilse and Teddy made those impressive banners, Andy donated his saxophone, Parenteau lured in hundreds of extras, Woody created fantastic lighting. I'll bet you a cookie that most of those people didn't get paid a dime. The model Billie? The location fees? I'll bet another cookie they were paid nominally.

I definitely wasn't paid for creating the storyboards or appearing in the video.

Tingle? His small crew may have been been paid, but imagine this. You're a brand new company looking for a way to break into the music video business. A chance to shoot a video with Joe Perry from Aerosmith? A video bound to make noise and get played internationally on MTV? hmmm.

Chef Tim is good at making Stone Soup.

Tuesday August 2, 1983

Now that we're officially back with MCA, I'm required to officially join a second union. I already got paid $1700 by the Musicians' Union, for shaking my maracas, which was great.

I'm already a dues paying member with them.

But Tim tells me that as a recording vocalist on a major label, I'm required to join the American Federation of Television and Radio Artists (AFTRA). Collins hands me a $500 check to pay my membership fee and sends me on my way.

I'm in a non-conforming state of mind today and it's hot and really humid, so I dress like Maynard G. Krebs before I head out to the AFTRA headquarters on snobby Beacon Hill.

I arrive in the stately reception area, where the officious receptionist is horrified at my bohemian attire.

"And what business might you have *here*, sir?" She snips.

"I came to join up." I grunt, as Channel 4 reporter Gale Huff swivels by.

"Excuse me?" The receptionist glares at my toes and my floppy beach pants.

"My manager sent me. I'm the Cowboy. I brought a check. Sign me up."

The irritated receptionist scowls and re-checks her calendar.

"Your signatory, sir?"

"Huh?"

"Who is the signatory that requires your membership with AFTRA?"

I think, no, I definitely do see Sara Edwards talking to Robin Young over in the corner.

"Uhhh…the Music Corporation of America. MCA Universal."

The receptionist stares scornfully at the messy mop on my head and my total lack of shoes.

"Very well then. Right this way, Mr. Bell."

Around dinner time Tim calls and tells me to report to the Narcissus nightclub in Kenmore Square. He's volunteered me as celebrity judge for a contest being held at midnight. I'll bet you a cookie this was offered to the Admiral first and he turned it down flat.

Anyway, I get there and my name's on the list. I'm greeted by a brunette dressed up as a beer bottle. The beer escorts me through the densely packed mob, up to a raised platform where I'm seated next to Dougie Thomson, bassist of chart-toppers

Supertramp. Dougie and I are loudly introduced to the
inebriated, uninterested crowd below and then it begins.
Girls, nearly nude, come marching out onto a catwalk that is
festooned with banners emblazoned with beer company logos.
They parade by Dougie and me and shake their bottoms at us.
Welcome to the "1983 Boston Miss Hot Bod Contest."
Dougie coughs, "what are we supposed to do anyway?"
Nobody explained the rules, or the judging criteria, of this Hot
Bod competition to us.
The beer bottle returns and dumps several shot glasses in front
of us. She pours something into them. Frat boys and jocks are
thrusting-fists, pounding-Buds and butting-heads as more and
more contestants strut past. Disco music blasts, strobe lights
spin. The hellbent hot bod contestants battle each other,
exposing more flesh, while jiggling at us vigorously.
Nothing to do but drink up and hope that the morning comes.

Wednesday August 3, 1983

Attorney Gordon Schultz meets with the Admiral, Tim and me at
the office. Setting up ES&D Music Publishing to manage all the
songs Joe and I co-wrote for the album plus the Admiral's solo
composition, Black Velvet Pants.
I find out later that ES&D stands for eat shit and die.
After the meeting, Tim sends Joe and me to the gym.
As the sun sets, director Tingle, the Admiral, Billie and a small
video crew begin shooting the insert "story-scenes" for the BVP
video. Most of the shots are done on Boylston St. The exterior
theater location is the Sack Cheri 123 movie theater, right next
to the Prudential Center.

Friday August 5, 1983

Tim has become fitness obsessed. He brings Joe and me back to
the gym again today.

Sunday August 7, 1983

Everyone is invited up to Ed's Mountain for steak tips today. It's great to see our former crew member again. He looks so much healthier and saner since leaving the Project. When it gets dark, Julia and I escape to the Medford Twin Drive-In to see *Zapped!* and *Get Crazy*.
Get Crazy is an amazing production from the Roger Corman company.

Tuesday August 9, 1983

We're part of the biggest concert of the summer. It's coming up this weekend at New England Dragway. But right now, we're in the small drum studio at Pet's place, rehearsing our set with practice amps. I remind the Admiral about the radio ads we both grew up listening to on AM radio. Ads that boasted thrills and excitement every Sunday up at the Dragway.
The Admiral remembers those commercials too.
He begins banging out the rattling, pulsing guitar tone that coursed beneath those famous spots. Hargrove and Pet join in. Those noisy 30 second radio advertisements played every week in New England. Between British Invasion hits and California pop tunes. I launch into my impression of the jacked-up, voice-over guy:
"*SUNDAY - Sunday! See the Super Gasser battle the nitro-charged Road Hog! Fire-breathing Mods, Kustom Rods and Fuel-injected FUNNY CARS!...Sunday - SUNDAY! BE THERE this Sunday for all the action. Sunday at New England Dragway, Route 101, Epping New Hampshire - SUNDAY!*"

Saturday August 13, 1983

Glenda invites Tim and the Project to a cookout in the backyard of her place in Coolidge Corner. The Admiral tends the grill. Ilse, Teddy and some of the others who worked on the BVP video are here. I don't think Glenda invited Billie.

Sunday August 14, 1983

Departing Boston at 10:45 a.m. Road manager Rob drives
Hargrove, Pet and I up to the festival. The Admiral is being
transported separately. The event, "Summer Jam '83", has been
heavily promoted all summer throughout New England, with
full-page ads in the newspapers and constant radio ads. Ticket
sales have been brisk, which is causing problems for the
promoter Mark O Hildonen.
Authorities up in Rockingham County are on edge. With
thousands expected to attend the concert, the police are prepared
for "almost anything." Traffic slows as we approach the
Dragway, where a huge outdoor stage and towers of sound
reinforcement have been raised. We pass a police command post
where officers from a dozen local towns are receiving
instructions from Epping Police Chief Greg Dodge and
Brentwood Chief William Vahey. I've gleaned those names from
reading the daily news accounts about nervous locals,
concerns from town officials, and numerous requests from
residents to call the whole thing off. You would think that by
now these folks would be used to noise and crowds after years
of race car events.
We finally make it to the backstage area, where I see Rick
Nielsen and Bun E. Carlos of Cheap Trick looking like they just
fell off the back-cover of their In Color album. A bunch of girls
in sexy outfits are picking fruit off the buffet table. That's
Lipstick, the all female group we played with a few weeks ago.
The Admiral arrives. Along with him are Elyssa and their child,
who looks to be about two and a half. I met the boy briefly back
at the Perry mansion a year or more ago.
I'm not sure but this might be the first time Adrian will get to
see his dad perform onstage.
Blackfoot have been on the scene for years. A Florida-based
band with some Native American lineage. I'm expecting a
down-home, jam-band show but they hit the stage looking sharp
and sounding like a kick-ass rock outfit. Exceptional players
who've been criss-crossing the world for over a decade.

Fantastic live act. The assembled crowd goes wild for them. I miss most of the Lipstick set, I'm talking to JPP fans who are visiting us backstage but I'm back for the next band - Krokus. These guys are from Switzerland and they have a big hit song on MTV called Screaming in the Night. Krokus play in the heavy metal style that bands like Iron Maiden and Judas Priest are scoring with these days. Krokus dress like Priest too, most of them have studded-leather vests, some are lined with fur and dyed blood-red. They wear leather trousers and clunky boots. Krokus hammer through a thundering set of songs from Headhunter, their current album. The overflowing Dragway crowd are banging their collective heads in appreciation.

Being Sunday, the Joe Perry Project opens up with our version of the New England Dragway radio ad, not really sure if these youngsters got the reference, so we continue straight into Train Kept A-Rollin.' The sun-baked throngs respond to that one with enthusiasm. The audience is pretty wasted by now and we can do no wrong, but the Admiral is taking no chances. After quickly running through Black Velvet Pants and Once a Rocker, we hit the Aerosmith songs Bright Light Fright and Walk This Way. The hordes rise up as one. We buzz through East Coast, West Coast, Rockin' Train, Walk with Me Sally and close with Let the Music Do the Talking - as thousands scream for more. Darkness falls, the lights come up, Cheap Trick takes the stage. Robin Zander looks and sounds brilliant. I first saw this quartet at the Paradise in Boston back in 1978 and I was stunned. Everyone was. They quickly began scoring chart hits and moved up to the biggest venues and headline gigs like this one. The Admiral is an even bigger fan of Cheap Trick than me. He studies their entire performance from the side of the stage. During the encores, Zander calls Joe to the stage, where he slips on a Strat. Cheap Trick and Joe Perry kick into Day Tripper.

Tuesday August 16, 1983

Today is Danny Hargrove's birthday.
Danny and I are back in Cambridge, along with our two Joes.

We're at the photography studio of Ron Pownall. Getting ready
for our first real band photo shoot. Not separate portraits in a
bridal salon.
Pownall is the top rock'n'roll lenser in New England.
He took most of those famous Aerosmith shots we all remember
from Creem, Hit Parader and Circus magazines.
Ron photographs us in front of seamless backdrops inside his
studio and then we go outside. Ron has a good spot staked out.
We lean against a concrete wall. The Admiral hops up onto the
ledge above us. Nice shot. Turns out it's the campus of Rindge
Latin High, the public school in Cambridge that Danny attended.

Monday August 17, 1983

Tim invites me over to the office. He tosses a copy of
"The Exeter News" on the desk. I'm startled to see two photos
of myself topping the front page of the newspaper, along with a
shot of a massive crowd. Me? Why me? What about Cheap
Trick? And Krokus and Joe fukken Perry? My excitement dies
down a bit when I read the caption, "Mark Bell of the Joe Perry
Band performs for thousands. The crowd cheers."
"Mark Bell? Who dat? And what's with this Joe Perry "Band"?
Everybody knows we're the Joe Perry Project.
The article goes on, saying that for the most part, fans each paid
the $15 admission and had a good time. "Minor arrests, said
Chief Vahey, and not too many of them. The police prepared for
almost everything and almost nothing happened, except a
parking shortage, manageable traffic congestion, one major
injury and isolated incidents of boorish behavior, drunkenness
and confusion that did not disrupt the good times of most
concert-goers or the general public."
Cool. Mission accomplished. I just wish they didn't get my
name wrong...or, actually right, on the front page.

Thursday August 18, 1983

It's been a long hot summer waiting for our album release.
Feels like I've been pregnant for 18 months.

Nothing like a little road trip to take my mind off things. Rob drives us out to Scotia NY, where we play a good one tonight at the Skyway. Near Schenectady, this venue reminds me of the original Cricket in Ashland MA. The Cricket was a renovated bowling alley where the New York Dolls, Duke and the Drivers, Aerosmith and Thundertrain all used to play. After tonight's triumphant Skyway show, we party like rockstars at the L+M motel.

Friday August 19, 1983

A transcendent show here in Rochester NY at the Penny Arcade. This was another first class one, right up there with Salem Theater and the Sandbar. Staying at HoJo's tonight.

Saturday August 20, 1983

Travel day.

Sunday August 21, 1983

Outdoor Concert featuring The Outlaws, The Gregg Allman Band, Joe Perry Project and the Stompers. We pull onto the grounds of Westboro Speedway out on Route 9 and find our way back to a big Winnebago recreation vehicle. This will be our dressing room today. We're set to play in the middle of the afternoon after the Stompers open the show. A great summer concert crowd of southern rock fans has gathered. Most every Harley Davidson motorcycle in New England is lined-up out in front of the race track. My friends Bill Dill, Steven Silva, Rickey Gallagher and little Pammy, the former USA president of the Bay City Rollers fan club, are all present.
This speedway was the site of a legendary (around here anyway) concert by Aerosmith and Duke and the Drivers back in '74, when Get Your Wings was really taking off. I remember it well, because the concert happened just a couple weeks after Thundertrain was formed, down in the basement of Jack's Drum Shop on Boylston St. in Boston.

Monday August 22, 1983

The Admiral leaves for a short vacation. Tingle is hard at work editing his sixty different camera angles of Black Velvet Pants into one video.

Tuesday August 23, 1983

Day dreaming, thinking way back.
After I saw my first Aerosmith concert I raced home and immediately grabbed my guitar. I had to figure out those riffs to Somebody and Mama Kin. The next day I went to Music'n'Things and bought a handful of silver studs and carefully decorated an old pair of black jeans. They didn't end up looking quite as cool as Rock Star's trousers, but I tried.
Two weeks later, Aerosmith were back at Lakeview Ballroom. Headlining. This time my sister managed to get backstage and meet some of them.
"The guy with the lips is Steven, and Rock Star's real name is Joe Perry."
The third time I saw Aerosmith was in Hopedale but there was a big change. The brown-haired guy with the Gibson ES was gone and in his place was a blonde guy with a Les Paul.
"That's Brad Whitford, I went to school with him," nodded my bass playing buddy, Jack Bialka. I guess Jack and Brad both attended Berklee School of Music before dropping out.

By the summer of '71, Aerosmith were playing everywhere. I saw them in Dover MA, playing a free show at an arts and crafts camp, not far from my grandfather's house on Claybrook Rd.
A high wind picked up as Aerosmith rocked on an outdoor platform. I listened intently, and watched as the billowing backdrop material ripped and blew away. The band didn't miss a beat.
During Perry's guitar solo on Walkin' the Dog, Steven hid behind Joe's amp. A second later, Tyler's empty shoes appeared atop Perry's amplifier and began to dance a funny shuffle.

Super-serious Joe was totally unaware of his singer's puppet show going on right behind his head. Personally, I like a twist of humor with my rock, that's why I followed bands like the Faces and these guys.

Meanwhile, back in Holliston, I was leading my band Joe Flash. Merry, our vocalist, was an incredible singer.

But I longed to play my guitar behind a front person with a bit more testosterone. Over the years I had tried out many singers. All turned out to be flakes, phonies or un-reliables.

I had grown up miming to records that I blasted on my father's incredible stereo system. Using painted guitar-shapes that I'd cut out with a jig saw, I would jam along with the Stone's Out of Our Heads and the Yardbirds, Having a Rave Up. Although I didn't know how to form a chord, I became an expert at strumming, picking and rocking in time. I could mime the arpeggios of House of the Rising Sun, knock out a Bo Diddley beat on Mona, or windmill the power chords of Lost Woman. Putting down the fake guitar, I would proceed to lip-sync as the frontman, strutting around like a twelve year-old Jagger, waggling my hips.

Starting at age ten I was trained classically on the cello, so I figured the (stringed) electric guitar made the most sense as my entree into the burgeoning world of local rock bands.

I couldn't imagine actually singing in front of people.

I saved up $29 and bought a one pick-up, solid-body axe at the local Mammoth Mart. Actually I bought a guitar strap first.

The whole point of playing an electric guitar is its ability to be strummed while you stand up, or move around and look cool.

No need to sit, like I had to in the fifth grade student orchestra with my cello.

As soon as I learned a few chords, I was off to the races. Now when I strummed my Bo Diddley beat, it sounded like music.

I already knew how to move exactly like Zal Yanovsky and Brian and Keith from watching Ed Sullivan.

This served me well for the first five years of my career but as I reached nineteen, I noticed a ton of other guys were playing guitars, and though most chose not to put on a rockin' show like me, they were technically more skilled.

This all led up to that day in '72. I'm performing at an outdoor concert in downtown Holliston. In a band with Michael Hendricks called Piggies. As usual, my latest lead singer doesn't make it. These singers I find are useless. Either they're totally full of themselves but unable to move a crowd.

Or they're high-strung, and go poof at the last minute.

So, like too many times before, I reluctantly fill-in on the lead vocals while playing my Firebird guitar.

After we finish, this cool looking dude comes up and introduces himself. He's a drummer named Bobby Edwards.

He's only 17 years old.

"Hey, man, that was incredible. You wanna come sing with my band? We're rehearsing tomorrow over in Medway."

"Sing?" I ask.

"Yeah, sing. I already have a great guitar player. Just come and sing. You know how to get everyone going and you make your group exciting, like a pro band. Not just a bunch of musicians playing parts. I'm looking for more than a guy with a singing voice. You're exactly what I'm looking for."

Thanks to Bobby's belief in me, I joined his band Biggy Ratt as lead singer and I took to being a frontman immediately.

I left the guitar solos behind, for the ever growing army of fret-men to fight over.

Debuting a month later, as a ballsy, energetic vocalist, I encountered very little competition and began a fast rise.

A year later, Bobby and I were both scouted by Ric Provost. Ric was putting together a local superband, following the collapse of his popular Doc Savage. In Ric's new band Thundertrain, I became known in Boston, New England, Manhattan and all over the rock underground. Although I was never all that confident about my singing ability, I knew how to command a stage and I could out-rock just about anyone. I'm a guitarist at heart and I still think like a guitar player too.

I ended up becoming a rock singer because nobody else wanted the job.

Saturday August 27, 1983

Joe Perry is back from vacation. The van leaves the pink palace
at 2 p.m. Bound for Middletown NY where we headline at J.B.
Rock III. We're starting to premiere some of the new songs from
the upcoming album. Four Guns West and Crossfire.
They go over great.

Monday August 29 - Tuesday August 30, 1983

On Monday, we have a band meeting at the office and look over
the busy itinerary we've got stretched ahead of us. We'll be
doing coast to coast concerts and personal appearances, mixed
in with lunchtime radio broadcasts promoting the new record.
Tim Collin's new thing is immersion tanks. He sends Joe and me
to this sensory deprivation place. They load each of us into a salt
water tank and close the lids. The Admiral and I float around in
the silent darkness for about an hour. Boring.

Tuesday September 6, 1983

Pammy gets hired at Collins/Barrasso. I think Pam will be
helping set up the Joe Perry Project fan club. Maybe she can
turn us into the next Bay City Rollers. At 2 p.m. the band is back
out in Pet's studio, working out the new concert set.

Wednesday September 7, 1983

I'm presented with an advance copy of our album today.
Hallelujah. Joe looks good on the cover, he's shirtless in a black
leather motorcycle jacket. Four necklaces (a couple of crosses, a
coin and a pistol) hang from his neck.
Our new hawk & snake logo is up in the corner, in full color no
less. Artist Brian Penry turned my little cartoon doodle into a
masterpiece. The blue and red background doesn't look too
much like a wedding studio. Thank you.
On the back of the album cover, the Admiral is standing
barefoot, against what I'll call a skin-colored background,

leaning on a Gibson reverse-body Firebird, with a whammy bar and three golden pick-ups. Joe's wearing black leather pants and a blue suede jacket, open, no shirt.
Over on the left hand side, are stacked photos of the rest of us. Danny on the bottom, looking handsome and dangerous in a red shirt, blue scarf and a red head-wrap.
Joe Pet is in the middle, wearing a motorcycle jacket and doing an excellent Fonzie pose, except that he's holding a bouquet of wedding flowers, tied with a chartreuse ribbon. The bouquet has been highlighted further by the MCA art department. The flowers extend a bit out of the photo frame, floating against the skin-colored background.
Cowboy is up top. I have one thumb stuck in my belt loop and the other is doing a little thumbs up salute. I've got a leather bandana (Trash and Vaudeville) and a black and white, horizontally-striped shirt, like a mime in Paris would wear.
Bad hair day for the beeps. My mop is even curlier than usual. Critics love to tease me and make fun of my "perm" which pisses me off no end. Fuck perms. I wish I had straight hair like Perry and Pet. But no, I'm stuck with this naturally curly mop that plagues me every day of my life.
Overall, the record jacket looks damn good. And, oh yeah, the album title. It's written across the top of the front cover, "Once a Rocker Always a Rocker."

Thursday September 8, 1983

I have to go to the office to sign publishing contracts. On seven of the ten album tracks, I'll be splitting the writer share with Joe Perry. The Admiral and I will split 10% of the wholesale price, 10% of sheet music and 50% of the BMI payments.
Advance copies of the album go out to radio today.

Friday September 9, 1983

Everywhere I turn the dial, I hear my voice. Mark Parenteau is talking about the Project even more than he usually does and then he premieres Black Velvet Pants and Walk with Me Sally.

Later, on the same station, Carter Alan is playing Once a Rocker. Over at the competing 50,000 watt Boston giant, WCOZ, Harvey Wharfield and Carla Leonardo are both going with Women in Chains. Not sure who the deejay with the British accent on WAAF Worcester is, but he's spinning Once a Rocker. I stop by our new fan club headquarters. Pammy hands me one of the new Joe Perry Project buttons.

Saturday September 10, 1983

Tim is currently sharing a fancy North End apartment with Charlie Mackenzie. Charlie has a long track record in the music business, he helped bands like Deep Purple and Duke and the Drivers, but he really made his bones when he discovered the band Boston.
More Than a Feeling catapulted Mackenzie to the top of the heap and he got very rich. He went on to manage my friend Willie Alexander's Boom Boom Band. Another thing about Charlie Mackenzie, he hates the sound of my voice.
But that doesn't stop Tim from hosting a surprise birthday party tonight at their apartment for our leader Joe Perry. Among other guests, games and festivities, the Black Velvet Pants music video will be screened for the first time (while Charlie plugs his ears). Also at Joe's birthday party is Roman, the head of promotion and sales at the New England branch of MCA.

Sunday September 11, 1983

The Bell family gather at the Framingham train depot this morning to say goodbye to my brother Sam. He's on his way to Santa Cruz, to begin college at UCSC.

Local radio is going wild on our album. The only problem is - they can't agree on which track to focus on. The songs all sound great over the airwaves. Joe did a super job producing. Today I heard Once a Rocker, Crossfire, King of the Kings and Black Velvet Pants. Back at the office, writer Brett Milano interviews the Admiral and me for a Boston Rock cover story.

Monday September 12, 1983

I just heard Captain Ken Shelton play Once a Rocker, then Mark Parenteau premiered Never Wanna Stop on BCN, and WHJY down in Providence RI is going with Once a Rocker. The record isn't in the stores yet but that's all about to change.
Our manager sends me out to do a personal appearance at an ice cream stand. I think the Admiral turned that one down too.

Tuesday September 13, 1983

In his accounting office at the back of the Music Box, my grandfather Nelson Bell is reading the Business section of the Boston Globe. At the top of the page is a story titled,
"What's Law Next to Ice Cream?"
Above the headline is a big picture. A guy with sunglasses and an apron standing beside a mop-topped guy sporting a leather bracelet and holding an ice cream cone. Nelson looks again, picks up his newspaper, and heads down to the Sound Room.
"Bill, is this your son?"
My father looks carefully at the large photo. The caption reads "Rock singer Mach Bell (left) tries some of owner Robert Rooks' ice cream at Emack and Bolio's in Brookline."
"Yes. I think it is," replies my father.
Puzzled, my grandfather looks up at my dad and confesses, "Well, Bill, I never expected that I'd ever see his picture in the Business section of the Boston Globe."

Tonight is our big album release party. I've been to some good ones. The Atlantics party for Big City Rock was fun.
It was held on Boylston Street, around the corner from SyncroSound, at the ICA (Institute of Contemporary Art).
Suzi Quatro was there, amongst the pop art and revelers.
Tim got us a fantastically cool location for our party.
The Boston Tea Party Ship. Docked down on Museum Wharf.
You remember it from history class right? American colonists protested British taxation, by sneaking aboard, and hurling chests of tea into Boston Harbor.

Darkness falls.
Multi-colored lights are strung up in the rigging.
They reflect on the rippling harbor waters below.
A deejay is set up beside the forward jibs, spinning our brand
new album on a late summer night.
Servers begin to circulate, with appetizers on silver trays.
MCA execs and office staff, old friends, insiders, superfans,
models, radio people, the press, bikers and big shots are all
slowly making their way down the gang plank, onto the decks of
the Tea Party Ship.
Platters of gourmet food from the North End's Little Italy are
being laid-out atop the main cabin roof.
A very well stocked bar fills the poop deck.
Joe Perry is shaking hands, signing autographs and smiling for
the photographers.
Couples are dancing up above us, on the wharf, and down below
us in the cabins. Collins and Barrasso are doing the host thing,
schmoozing up a storm. The bartenders are pouring furiously.
Pet is downing shots and cracking jokes over by the mainsail.

Away from the thick-of-it, up at the bow,
Danny Hargrove and I lean out over the railing.
Sipping our cocktails,
Listening, as Once a Rocker Always a Rocker echoes
across Boston Harbor.
We watch the jets lifting off from Logan Airport.
Taking it all in. The wild party, this whole scene, being held
in our honor.
We finally turn and stare at each other.
How the heck did the two of us ever end up here?

A portion of my storyboard for the Black Velvet Pants video.

Danny Hargrove, Joe
Pet and I perform at the
Bottom Line in
Manhattan. 10/24/83
Steven Tyler was sitting
right out front.

The Cowboy & the Admiral.   Photo by Julia Bell

V
NEVER WANNA STOP

Wednesday September 14, 1983

Captain Ken is spinning Rocker. Adrianna is playing on Carter's show. WCOZ is hot on Chains. Today the Providence station WHJY does a "Fresh Cuts" special and airs Bang a Gong, Women in Chains, BVP and Once a Rocker.

Thursday September 15, 1983

The day I've hoped for, ever since joining this band, has finally arrived. Once a Rocker Always a Rocker is released to record stores across America and Canada. Our album is finally getting racked in department stores, mom and pop stores and truck stops all over the nation. Record buyers can actually touch, examine and purchase this collection of songs that we've been sculpting nightly, for the past year and a half.

Friday September 16, 1983

I'm called into the office and presented with a $500 publishing advance and a $300 salary advance. This is getting good.

Saturday September 17, 1983

We do a show up in Methuen at the Oasis. Testing out ideas on how the new set might be constructed. King of the Kings features a lead solo played on the Fender VI bass. The Admiral begins playing the first two verses on guitar, with the large bass slung across his back. During Pet's drum-fill, Joe swings the guitar out of the way, and simultaneously flips the bass into playing position. The Admiral rips into the snarling bass break. After that, we have to make a slight arrangement change, to allow Joe a moment to swap the two instruments back again. A work in progress.

Sunday September 18, 1983

I go into town to spend all my new money on stuff for the tour.
A second pair of black leather pants and some low-rise cowboy
boots at Walker's Western Outfitters on Boylston St.
Next, I shop for a new ring, just down the block at Bartevian.
This unusual shop is where I came when I first joined the
Project. I had no stage-worthy clothes, or much of anything
exceptional, so I decided to come here and just buy a ring.
A big silver ring, with a dangerous looking bird
engraved into it. Cost almost a hundred. After a year of
microphone grabbing, tossing and bashing, my fierce raptor is
now a dead duck. I buy a nice new ring, almost as cool as the
last one. Further down the street I hit a cheap bodega and buy a
new travel bag and a big jar of vitamins. Paying the clerk, I see,
displayed on the little counter, incredibly, a cassette of
Once a Rocker Always a Rocker. I buy that too.

Monday September 19 - Wednesday September 21, 1983

Three of the longest days in my short lifetime. Our tour is right
around the corner. The travel, hotels, crowds, excitement and
adventures are all about to happen.
But not quite yet. I'm like a kid on Christmas Eve. Trying to kill
time before all the fun happens.
I thumb through my latest Billboard, looking at who else got
released this week. Who is our competition? On MCA, the only
recent rock release is from Joan Jett. Our album can stand up
against hers. Most of the other MCA releases from the past few
months are from Jimmy Buffett or unknowns like The Fixx.
I never heard of them.
Those Fixx guys have something called Reach the Beach.
I kill some more hours, scanning the FM dial. On Tuesday, I
hear Mark playing Never Wanna Stop and Captain Ken playing
Once a Rocker. Then on Wednesday, Mark is back to Once a
Rocker while Harvey plays Women in Chains. The music is
interrupted when a call comes in from the office, it's Tim, telling
me that WNEW in New York just added our record.

Thursday September 22 , 1983

Providence Eagle 9/22/83 - Dean Johnson
"When Perry barrels into Lupo's next week he's going to be fronting a new band and promoting a new album. The disc, "Once a Rocker, Always a Rocker" is filled with the kind of bruising rock'n'roll that has been his trademark over the years. But it is the best thing he's done since he left Aerosmith."

Boston Globe 9/22/83 - Steve Morse
"Perry is physically fit from working out on Nautilus equipment and musically at a peak from making a new album "Once a Rocker, Always a Rocker" which is one of the year's top hard rock records."

Boston Herald 9/22/83 - Dean Johnson
Look Out, Perry's Back
"Imagine a cat like a tiger or panther that grew up in the wild, suddenly being caged up for an arbitrary number of years and then let out into the wild again. That's how I feel. So lock up your wives and lock up your girlfriends. I'm back.
- Joe Perry
The Channel show will celebrate the release of Perry's new album on MCA records Once a Rocker, Always a Rocker. It's his third album as a solo artist, and it's also his best."

Friday September 23, 1983

Opening night for the Joe Perry Project Always a Rocker Tour at the Capitol Theater in Concord New Hampshire. This was the first venue Danny and I ever played with Joe.
So much has happened since that night, it seems longer than 19 months ago. The Admiral did a 1 p.m. call-in today on WCOZ and then we all traveled to Manchester NH for an afternoon record store appearance that was broadcast live on WGIR. This tour is going to be way different, now that we have a record to sell.

Saturday September 24, 1983

Up and at 'em. The band makes a personal appearance at the big
Strawberries record store on Memorial Drive on the Charles
River. We arrive at 11 a.m. to much applause and hoopla.
WCOZ and WBCN are both covering the event, each station is
airing the album and doing remotes as we sign records for the
mob who have come out to support Joe and the Project.
We also have a 1:30 p.m. soundcheck at the Channel for the 5:30
p.m. all-ages show. Following the non-stop play our album
enjoyed these last few weeks, it's no wonder the Channel is
sold-out for both the afternoon and midnight performances.

Sunday September 25, 1983

Driving into New Haven CT we hear Once a Rocker playing on
WCCC. The little van erupts into cheers.
Toad's Place is another important stop on the way to the top.
Always heard the stories, had given up on actually ever getting
to play here. We perform to a decent, but not packed house.
Nothing like Boston last night.

Monday September 26, 1983

New technology.
Here's how I make a phone call when I'm on the road:
Dial zero.
Dial number desired.
To call home enter code 9985
To call anywhere else enter code 6178680920 9985

Tuesday September 27, 1983

After spending yesterday in Manhattan, doing album promotion,
the Always a Rocker tour rolls into Providence RI. WHJY is
playing Once a Rocker as we pull into the city. I'm on cloud
nine, finally hearing my voice on the radio ads for our shows.
We headline at Lupo's Heartbreak Hotel tonight.

A certain afternoon personality from 'BCN shows up to do our stage introduction. For some reason Parenteau is suddenly inspired to experiment with LSD tonight. The acid flips him out and his trip doesn't end very well.

Wednesday September 28, 1983

The Beatles had the Cavern and the Project has the Chance. We hit this theater in Poughkeepsie NY more than any other venue. Joanie is here and Dickman is in town, so he pays us a visit. He's a good man and I regret how his tenure with the JPP came to an end. Many of the kids in the audience have already snapped up the new album. They're singing along with me. This is more like it. The pirate ship docks at the HoJo motel in Newburgh NY.

Thursday September 29, 1983

Merch is the hot new trend and we've got it. We have a massive road case full of t-shirts in multiple styles, painter's caps, stickers and buttons. Boy Sean runs the table. Rick is running the front of house sound, Fred is driving and tending Joe Pet's drums. Rob is our road manager and I don't think he's enjoying the job very much. Tonight the Always a Rocker Tour rolls into Sunderland MA. The JPP puts on a good, clean show for the college kids at the Rusty Nail nightclub.

Friday September 30, 1983

We leave the Stonehaven Motor Inn in Springfield Mass, bound for NYC. We pull up to the Iroquois Hotel on West 44th Street. Right out front there's a gaping hole in the sidewalk. Construction workers are removing lengths of water pipe. Uh, oh.
Sure enough, once we get checked into our rooms, we find all the water shut off. No showers. Not even H2O for teeth-brushing or toilet flushing. I'm very cranky about it, but we forge on to play a killer, sweaty set over in Brooklyn at L'Amour.

We return to our hotel and the water is still off.
No showers tonight. After the concert, our manager Tim gets
into a wicked argument with the road manager Rob.

Saturday October 1, 1983

We have a new road manager this morning.
Soundman Rick has been promoted. Sounds familiar.

Our new set list looks like this:
Train Kept A-Rollin
Something Else
Four Guns West
Bang a Gong
Crossfire
Break Tune
Red House
Women in Chains
Black Velvet Pants
Rockin' Train
Once a Rocker
Never Wanna Stop
Let the Music Do the Talking
Encore: Walk with Me Sally

It's a radical change. Only one Aerosmith song and just three
from the previous Project albums. This show is mostly our new
material and so far it's been going down great with the
audience. Of course on any given night Joe might throw in Buzz
Buzz, King of the Kings, East Coast, West Coast, Manic
Depression or just spontaneously start jamming.
Depending on his mood the Admiral might even decide to offer
up Back in the Saddle, Same Old Song or Walk This Way.
Tonight we're down in Riviera Beach MD, playing at one of my
favorite hangs, the Sandbar.

Sunday October 2, 1983

Tim Collins just fired me.
It all began when the manager called my room at the Glen
Burnie Holiday Inn this morning. He was upset with me and I
didn't care. Ever since that no water in NYC fiasco, I've been
giving him a whole lot of grief. Our morning chat heats up.
I begin swearing at Mr. Collins. It goes downhill from there.
Finally, he tells me I'm out of the band.
I head down to the lobby and join Danny Hargrove, Pet, the
Admiral and the rest of the crew for the ride to Pocono Downs
Speedway. We're doing another outdoor festival today with a
bunch of rockstars at "Pocono Jam '83." Joan Jett and the
Blackhearts, the Elvis Brothers, Foghat and Cheap Trick.
Driving onto the racetrack we see some weirdos hitch hiking up
ahead. Getting closer we recognize the freaks are Rick Nielsen
and Bun E. Carlos. We give the two odd balls a lift and they
show their appreciation by passing around a large Ziplock bag
full of pills.

Monday October 3, 1983

Our manager is flying in today. Yikes. I haven't even told the
guys that I'm not in the band anymore. Yesterday, I just went out
on that big stage and performed for the thousands of fans as if I
was still the singer of the Joe Perry Project. We're at the Hotel
Georgetown in DC, getting set for tonight's show when Tim
rings my room. He tells me to meet him in the hotel lounge.
The conversation starts icily, but reaches a good conclusion.
Tim hires me back into the line up. Lucky for me, he's been
getting mood-enhancing reports about our record, we're getting
played at radio stations all across the country.
We rock for a good turnout at the Bayou tonight.

Tuesday October 4, 1983

Ripley's Music Hall, Philadelphia PA. In the dressing room, I'm
listening to the latest ZZ Top album, Eliminator.

This came out just a few months ago.

Damn. Gimme All Your Lovin' smacks you in the eardrums with such force. It's a new sound for rock. Almost like how Van Halen totally changed everything when they first hit.

I don't understand how they got this modern sound on the ZZ album. The driving sixteenth-note drum patterns, are they real or are they machines? Sequencers? Synthesized?

Our new record sounds kind of old-fashioned in comparison.

Wednesday October 5, 1983

I'm trying to sleep while riding the 450 miles from Philly to Buffalo NY in the good ol' Dodge van. Fred is at the wheel. The Admiral flew out of Philadelphia and back to Boston on business. Probably another court date, too bad for him. We've got nothing booked for tonight but we have two shows at two different venues coming up tomorrow. We make a rare stop at McDonalds.

Fast food chains are strictly forbidden when the Admiral is around. He might be a junkie but he eats healthy. Hamburgers are getting expensive these days. 50 cents each. There's this brand new thing on the menu called Chicken McNuggets.

Thursday October 6, 1983

Perry jets into Buffalo and meets us bright and early at the 2001 Club where we'll play a free lunchtime concert to be simulcast live on 97 Rock. It's the powerhouse rock station in this region. At noontime the doors open, fans pour in and we roar into a one hour free radio-commercial for our new album.

Sixty minutes fly by. The crew rips everything down and trucks it over to Lockport NY.

The JPP goes on at midnight and the Admiral is in a devil-may-care mood. Tonight's venue has a bunch of beat up pedestal-type cocktail tables scattered around.

In the middle of our set Joe decides to take a stroll.

While soloing on his black Strat, the Admiral steps off the stage and onto the nearest table top. The crowd hails this brave move, and encourages JP to continue. He does, planting his booted foot squarely in the middle of the next table, a few feet further into the audience. The second table is a lot more wobbly than the first. I'm nervous but there's no way I can get to him, Joe is surrounded by a solid mass of fans who continue to egg him on. No going back now. The Admiral swings his right leg out towards a table about three feet further away. The change in balance causes the quivering table to topple sideways. Joe leaps forward, towards the third tabletop. He nearly makes it. Flailing, hair-flying, but Stratocaster still held high, Joe plummets butt-first to the floor but is thankfully caught by a half dozen enthusiasts who deliver the daredevil musician back to the stage. Nothing can stop the Project.

Friday October 7, 1983

We motor into Motown. A certain WBCN afternoon radio personality (he was formerly a deejay here in Detroit) jets in to surprise the band, perform our stage introductions, torment me, and generally wreak havoc everywhere and all over anyone he can get his hands on.

Saturday October 8, 1983

The Always a Rocker Tour crosses the border up into Ontario, beginning a string of Canadian dates. We crash at the posh Park Lane Hotel and rave tonight for a full house at Fry Fogels in London, where the girls are all still spectacular looking.

The London Free Press - Karen Lewis
"Tyler and Perry are back together as friends at least "It took a while for the blood to dry."
Perry now writes with Bell and their's is a less intense relation-ship. "I still get creative tension from myself, it's what gets me out of bed."

Sunday October 9, 1983

Once a Rocker is the #13 most-played new song on FM radio in North America this week.
I celebrate the achievement with our manager Tim and John Williams of MCA.
For some reason I become quite drunk at the Belair Cafe in Toronto. I manage to lose both my jacket and my US passport.

Monday October 10, 1983

Co-manager Steve Barrasso jets into Toronto to share in the celebrations. CHUM radio is hosting our gig at El Mocambo tonight, and it's going to be big. Also big, is the news that the Belair Cafe just called my hotel to report that the hat check girl located my lost jacket and passport. They were probably never really lost - but I definitely was.
Lots of record, radio and press at the show tonight.
Go-go girls Kathy and Bridget are here and the hat check girl is here too. I hope everybody likes us.

Tuesday October 11, 1983

The Project is detained in Toronto today by immigration authorities. Not sure what their gripe is. Sure glad I have my passport back.

Wednesday October 12, 1983

The Globe and Mail - Canada's National Newspaper 10/12/1983
"Perry Uses Variety to Prove His Metal by Alan Niester
Perry's performance late Monday night was both electrifying and exciting enough to conclude that he is one veteran on the way back...the current Project is entirely different from the one that backed him on his last album and tour.
Its major interest is singer Mach Bell, a leather-clad and leather-voiced screamer in the Bon Scott mold.

Someone more than willing to grab the centre-stage spotlight that Perry is still reluctant to take.
Songs such as Four Guns West and Crossfire sound like what might happen if Jeff Beck were invited to join AC/DC."

We went over well at El Mocambo and got this big rave in the national press. So now the Canadian staff from MCA want to check us out. Q107 is promoting our show in Markham Ontario, at a good-sized roadhouse called Nag's Head.
We're shocked at the amount of record people who are sitting all over the place tonight. Turns out there's some sort of music convention going on nearby, so pretty much the entire company decided to swing by to check-out our show.
Champagne flows.

Thursday October 13, 1983

Headlining at the Orient Express again. The promoters who hired us for the "12 Hours of Rock" festival back in July '82. An hour into our set, a massive fight, it's actually a riot, breaks out in every corner of the venue. Everybody is suddenly punching and kicking everyone else. Thanks to our crew, the Project manages to escape through a trap door. Seriously, they have a secret trap door, right behind the stage. Is rioting a regular occurrence up here? Not sure what set off all the violence but I'm pretty sure I wasn't to blame this time.

Friday October 14, 1983

Rocking in Ottawa, at Barrymore's. No riots tonight.
We get a day off in Montreal tomorrow.

Sunday October 16, 1983

CHOM-FM presents the Always a Rocker tour at Le Spectrum on St. Catherine Street, in the heart of Montreal.
Sexy metal-singer Lee Aaron opens.

Following a bawdy post-show party backstage, Joe Pet decides
to bring a fan or two back up to his 21st floor hotel room. On
arrival, Mr. Pet finds that his key won't unlock the door.
After beating and kicking the locked door for a while, our tipsy
drummer elevators (noisily) back down to the lobby, followed
by his fans. Stomping to the front desk, Pet waves his key in the
air while complaining loudly. The night manager examines the
key and calmly replies "I apologize sir. Your accommodations
are over there. Across the street. You're in the wrong hotel."

Monday October 17, 1983

Northeast of Montreal, driving along Route 20, passing
St-Hyacinthe, Drummondville, Villeroy, Donnacona and finally
Quebec City. It's a 250-mile drive. We're at Cafe Campus
tonight, a much more intimate situation than the open air festival
we played here with Frank Marino a few months ago. Rick's
friend Toby has recently joined us as soundman. He's doing
excellent work for us.

Tuesday October 18, 1983

Following last night's show, we drove all night, finally arriving
back at the pink palace. I have 48 hours off.

Thursday October 20, 1983

WAAF is promoting our concert tonight in Fitchburg. We're at
the Family Theater and the performance will be recorded for a
future radio broadcast.
Our album is getting a lot of play here on WAAF right now, just
like it was the other day when we were up in Montreal and
CHOM was spinning us every other hour.
But what happens after we leave these towns?
I remember the plate spinner who used to always be on the Ed
Sullivan show. He'd start a plate spinning up at the top of a tall
wiggly stick and then begin another plate going on the next stick

but by then the first plate was slowing down, so he had to run
back to wiggle that stick some more until the plate got
going again and then he ran to get three more plates started but
then he had to run back to the first two to wiggle the sticks some
more before running on to the next stick…

Friday October 21, 1983

The Admiral and Tim never turn down a decent offer. The
Project is at Acton-Boxborough High School playing for an
excited looking bunch of teenagers. I received a notice from
BMI today, officially registering a few of the songs I co-wrote
with Joe. Once a Rocker, Adrianna and Never Wanna Stop.

Saturday October 22, 1983

Julia tells me that The Cars are still over in the UK, working on
their next album with producer Mutt Lange. They're cutting
tracks at a place called Battery Studios in London.
Meanwhile, I'm singing in Brockton at Scotch'n Sounds, right
next to the mall.

Monday October 24, 1983

This is big.
WNEW-FM is broadcasting our entire set tonight. Live from the
Bottom Line in Manhattan. We're backstage with current
Aerosmith guitarist, Rick Dufay and Bobby Chouinard, the
drummer for Billy Squier. Our dressing room door suddenly
flies open and in pounces Steven Tyler. Just dropping by to say
hello. Tyler shakes my hand and congratulates me on our Once a
Rocker album. First time I've ever had the pleasure of speaking
to Steven, and he gives off very good vibes.
The Bottom Line is packed to the rafters when we take the stage.
Dufay and Tyler grab seats up front. Steven watches our entire
show with interest. I'll bet you a cookie I know what Steven
Tyler is thinking right now as he watches Mr. Joe Perry
taking full command of the stage.

Great gig tonight. My only gripe with this room is that the stage
has a couple of big support columns stuck right in the middle of
the performing area. Obstructing the natural flow of things.
Not the best venue for a corps de ballet presentation.
Also today in NYC - our video, Black Velvet Pants, has just
been added to rotation on MTV.

Tuesday October 25, 1983

The van rolls westward on I80, into Pennsylvania, passing
through Stroudsburg, Bloomsburg, Milton, Clearfield, DuBois
(Thundertrain did a week-long club engagement in DuBois in
1978), Clarion, Grove City and on into Youngston Ohio, where
we turn north up to Cleveland. After the ten-hour drive we
happily book into Swingo's, where all the bands stay.

Wednesday October 26, 1983

Early wake-up call.
The Project is at the Agora Ballroom. Another promotional
noontime free show. It's the "Coffee Break Concert," and we're
being broadcast live on WMMS-FM. Such a relief to sing my
own songs and sound just like the record. Finally.

Thursday October 27, 1983

We make hay at Haymaker's in Wheeling IL, just below Lake
Michigan. I get word from BMI that they've officially registered
the other four songs that Joe and I co-wrote. We're staying at the
Northbrook Holiday Inn where I pilfer still more stationery for
my massive collection of hotel freebies.

Friday October 28, 1983

Cathy gets time off from the military to come see her big brother
rock with Joe Perry. My sister was with me the first night we
discovered the unknown group called Aerosmith at a teen dance.
By the way, I talked about that first Lakeview gig with Joe the

other day, and he admitted to me that he was responsible for drawing that awful looking poster. He also admits that he hung it up himself at Music'n'Things in Holliston.

Also on my guest list is Al Jourgensen, singer of Ministry. We're on the South side of Chicago, playing the Colony Theater at 59th and Kedzie. This place books every type of music. Over the last two weeks they've had Tammy Wynette, Maynard Ferguson, Helen Reddy and The Turtles playing here. After the concert, Jorgensen seems extremely impressed with what he just saw, the Admiral in particular. I think Al wants my job.

Saturday October 29, 1983

Joe Perry and I are drinking Courvoisier with Bo Diddley. We're in Minneapolis, where we're checked in at the Northstar Hotel. Our gig at the Cabooze isn't until tomorrow. *Caveman* starring Ringo and Shelley Long is playing on HBO, but Joe and I already watched it a couple times, so we check out who's in town. Whoa. Bo Diddley is at the Cabooze right now.

So here we are, sitting alone in the back office of the nightclub with the Diddley Daddy himself. The cat responsible for Who Do You Love?, You Can't Judge a Book, Mona, Pills, Doing the Crawdaddy, Road Runner, I'm a Man - not to mention the famous Bo Diddley beat.

Joe Perry is checking out Bo's squared-off Gretsch guitar. I mention the Yardbirds and the Rolling Stones and Diddley just grumbles something at the floor. Then he shakes his large head and laughs out loud.

As he tops off our drinks, Mr. Diddley confides that he has only three requests on his standard contract rider.

"A bottle of cognac, a Twin Reverb amp and a cheeseburger."

Sunday October 30, 1983

The Project packs them in at the Cabooze. Another small leap forward for the JPP.

Monday October 31 - Tuesday November 1, 1983

Following the Minneapolis show, Admiral Perry and manager
Tim Collins jet back to Boston to promote the next leg of our
tour. The rest of us will continue wheeling west, bound for San
Francisco, where we'll resume business in a few days.
Road manager Rick and soundman Toby are driving the
equipment truck.
Danny Hargrove, Joe Pet, Boy Sean, new guy Fortune and I, are
all riding across America in the Dodge van with Fred at the
wheel. Cruising Interstate 80 from Minneapolis to Lincoln
Nebraska and then on to Rawlins Wyoming.
After checking into a hotel in Wyoming, I click on the television
and see our Black Velvet Pants video playing on MTV.
It's the first time I've seen myself on national TV.

Wednesday November 2, 1983

Travel day. I collect my $15 per diem allowance and don't have
much else to do today except look out the window and take a
needed nap as the Project races thru the mountains and deserts
along Interstate 80.
"Reeeeeno" squeals our drummer, as we speed into the
"Biggest Little City in the World." Tonight we crash at the
MGM Grand for the evening. This twenty-six story hotel is only
two years old and we score stupendous rooms up on the 20th
floor. The main channel on the room TV continuously shows
how to escape from the hotel, in case of emergency. Probably
because of the fire at the MGM Grand in Paradise NV a couple
years ago that claimed 85 lives.

Thursday November 3, 1983

Newspaper ad in the Boston Phoenix:

**Meet: Joe Perry in Person, Thursday, Nov 3,
4-5 PM at the Copley Square Strawberries!
Once a Rocker Always a Rocker MCA $6.29 LP/Cassette**

Looks like the Admiral is still stuck back in Boston as we roll
into the glittering city of San Francisco. This time we're
staying at the deluxe Miyako Hotel. A really nice joint with deep
Japanese soaking tubs in every room. Tim must have
gotten a new travel agent after that Iroquois debacle, because
our digs are getting pretty sweet lately. Since I don't need to
start singing for my supper until tomorrow night, I brush my
teeth, ring some friends, and party all over town like a rockstar.

Friday November 4, 1983

Tim jets into SF with the Admiral. We headline the Keystone in
Berkeley CA. Looks like everyone in the place went out and
purchased the new record. They're all singing along and
requesting their favorites.

Saturday November 5, 1983

Waking up at the Miyako, I turn on the radio and tune in KRQR,
a couple minutes later Once a Rocker starts playing. A great
omen for a great gig at the Stone, tonight in San Francisco.

Sunday November 6, 1983

Checking out of the Miyako this morning.
For some reason, our tour backtracks through the desert hills
back to Reno NV. The MGM Grand (where our rooms are
reserved) won't allow us inside due to some allegedly illegal
conduct that occurred during our previous stay. So the JPP
sneaks into the Ramada Reno on East 2nd St.
That accomplished, we continue our busy afternoon with a
personal appearance at Eucalyptus Records. The event brings in
a medium-sized crowd, and the resulting festivities are even
broadcast live on the local FM radio station. Then we head over
to the Grand Ballroom for soundcheck, dinner and our evening
concert - on an extremely elevated stage.

Once the performance is over, I'm advised by the crew that there's a strikingly beautiful young lady - who claims to be a showgirl - waiting outside.

She is eagerly hoping to meet the Cowboy.

Of course I invite her backstage but when she realizes how tall I am (not) she loses all interest and runs away.

Back home, WAAF is broadcasting our "Live in Fitchburg" appearance (from 10/20) all over New England tonight.

Monday November 7, 1983

Our song Once a Rocker has shot to number one at KOME-FM in San Jose CA.

Tonight's show should have been a huge celebration.

The Project kicks off the set in front of an SRO crowd at the Keystone in Palo Alto. During the fifth song (Crossfire) the venue loses power and the stage goes black.

Not just the Keystone, the whole side of town is dark.

After waiting in the pitch black dressing room for over an hour, the Project finally gives up. We're driven back to our rooms at the (also darkened) Flamingo Lodge.

Several hours later, we learn that the outage was caused by a disgruntled kid. Upset that his girlfriend got into our sold-out show, leaving him behind. He decided to ruin the night for everyone. The angry dude managed to pry open a man-hole cover and dump the contents of a trash can into the hole. Then he lit the whole mess ablaze. The resulting flames melted the electric service for most of downtown Palo Alto.

Tuesday November 8, 1983

The tour gallops into the state capitol, Sacramento.

We tie-up outside a saloon called El Dorado, where the Project stages yet another two-fisted rock show. This West Coast swing is especially nice because we're doing it in our own Dodge van and with a truckload of Joe Perry's kustom-made gear, instead of amps rented from S.I.R.

Wednesday November 9, 1983

The JPP returns to Palo Alto CA for a make up date at the
packed as usual Keystone. No fires or blackouts this time.
We've still got the #1 song on the KOME-FM hit parade.

Thursday November 10, 1983

This is a day-off for the tour, so I spend the afternoon in Santa
Cruz, visiting my little brother Sam at his UCSC campus.
Sam Bell is good with computers and technical stuff like that.
Some people might call him a nerd.
We're both sitting in the beautiful university dining-hall that
overlooks the crashing Pacific. The food here is really good too.
As I talk to my brother, I can't take my eyes off the sparkling
waves breaking beneath us.
"Wow, Sam. It must be so cool to have this perfect view of the
surf everyday while you eat lunch."
Sam looks at me quizzically.
He puts down his biscuit and swivels his head.
"Oh... the ocean...I never noticed it was there before."

Friday November 11, 1983

We draw a nice crowd to the Catalyst concert club right in the
middle of downtown Santa Cruz.
I see they have Mick Fleetwood's Zoo and Steve Marriot's
Humble Pie both playing here next week.
My brother came along with me and there are even some
Thundertrain fans in the house tonight. One couple brought
along a "Hot For Teacher!" single for me to sign.

Saturday November 12, 1983

Fred drives us south on the 5 to the 405 and then east on Sunset
Boulevard. After we pass Tower Records on the strip in West
Hollywood we swing left into the Beverly Sunset Hotel.

Sunday November 13, 1983

Day-off in Los Angeles. The Admiral is busy meeting the press.
The rest of the Project decides that we should all go to
Disneyland. Arriving in Anaheim, we find a space for the van in
the massive Disneyland parking lot.
Our driver, Fred, starts rolling a fat joint on the map book he has
laying across his lap. Why not enjoy a tailgate party in the
Dodge before entering the Magic Kingdom?
Out of nowhere and from several different directions at once,
police swoop in, totally surrounding our vehicle.
The uniformed men arrive so fast that Freddy still has the big
bag of weed laying right there in his lap. In plain view. Busted.
We're scared until we notice that these aren't the Anaheim
police. No, these are private Disneyland security police.
These Mickey Mouse cops suggest that we leave the park
immediately before they report us to the real CHiPs.
Before we scram, we ask the uniformed men,
"How the heck did you do that? What tipped you off?'
One of the security guys points to the distant Disneyland Hotel,
a building maybe twenty stories tall and about a quarter-mile
away.
"Cameras. Up on top. We survey each and every vehicle that
enters the gates. The minute we saw you - we knew you were no
good."
Leaving, we quickly decide we'd much prefer visiting the other
happiest place on earth. Tijuana Mexico.
Danny Hargrove is excited about eating worms from the bottom
of Mezcal bottles. Joe Pet is excited about seeing the lady and
the donkey. I'm not so sure about any of that, so I just sit back
and enjoy the ride to Tijuana.

Once we get South of the Border it's pretty cool. There's a
bunch of wrecked cars all over the place. Trash blowing
everywhere. Skinny chickens and abandoned kids are pecking
and picking at stuff stuck to the street.

Fred looks for a safe place to park. Pet has his head stuck out the window, yelling to passersby, asking where the donkey show is located. We park by the jailhouse.

I'm pretty hungry by now, and I see a gentleman standing over on the corner. He's holding a machete in one hand. With the other, he's balancing an animal carcass, skewered on a dirty, pointed stick. Whatever the blackened meat is, it's been cooked pretty thoroughly and actually smells not too bad.

I hold out a few coins and he grabs them away from me. He shakes the dirty stick a few times, disturbing a million black flies from the carcass. As the bugs take flight he whacks the meat with his sharp blade.

My host then holsters the machete and deftly tears-off several strands of whatever-it-is.

Using that same free hand, he rolls the gristly bits into a little tortilla. The chef carefully wipes the left-over grease from his thumb onto the edge of the tortilla - to help seal it shut.

He proudly hands his creation over to me.

I'll admit the presentation is gross, but I enjoy dining on foreign cuisine. I wolf down my dog sandwich and now it's time to join the rest of the Project for drinks.

Many hours later, we all manage to cross back into the USA. Hargrove ate too many worms and got pie eyed. Pet never found the donkey show, but he bought a pile of Mexican blankets and some powder that might be Spanish Fly. I scored some jumping beans. We finally book ourselves into the Hotel San Diego. It's past midnight and Pet is still looking for kicks.

"C'mon guys, let's check out the Can Can Club."

Hargrove and I, exhausted from the horrible adventures of the day, follow the nut across the street. Pet grabs seats right up front and orders a round of drinks. He's wearing a big cowboy hat and he begins to hoot and jeer at the tired performers.

These dancers are doing their best and it's almost the end of the shift. They just want to put their clothes back on and go home. Pet starts giving one dancer a really hard time. Nobody is perfect and our inebriated drummer is letting this poor lady hear about each of her imperfections in detail.

The naked gal isn't taking it though. No, she's sassy and she fires back at Pet with both her guns. She even grabs the cowboy hat off his head and does rude things with it.

It's getting kinda hot in here. Hargrove and I drag our wacko drummer out of the Can Can - before he ends up spending the night in the can.

Monday November 14, 1983

Waking up in the Hotel San Diego. I need coffee real bad.

My two amigos and I head downstairs to grab some java and breakfast. The hotel coffee shop is in this quaint little room with gingham curtains. The tablecloths match the curtains and so do the old-fashioned outfits all the servers are wearing.

We've got our tired faces stuck inside the menus when the waitress asks,

"Coffee, Gentlemen?"

"Yes. Please. Same here."

"Three coffees. I'll be back in a jiffy…and where is your *hat* mister?"

Huh? We all look up at the gingham-clad waitress.

She smirks down at drummer Pet.

Oh my god. It's the stripper from last night.

Wednesday November 16, 1983

We're on the seashore in Solana Beach, just a few miles north of San Diego. A great spot for a JPP concert.

Our friend Thai is here too and wherever Thai goes, the party follows. We headline at the Belly Up, another longtime haven for national and international touring bands.

Thursday November 17, 1983

Great to be back at the Golden Bear. We didn't even have to hitchhike this time.

This club has a big sound system provided by Fender.

A company renowned for electric guitars and guitar amplifiers, but not so much for heavy duty sound reinforcement equipment. Our new soundman Toby is great at pulling together a clear mix using whatever unusual club gear he is faced with.
Before the show, the lead guitarist of Heart, Howard Leese, pays Joe a visit in our dressing room. Leese has played on many tours with the Admiral over the years. The after-party is back at our place, just up the strip at the Huntington Beach Inn.

Friday November 18, 1983

Early wake-up call and now we're heading back to L.A.
The Admiral is taking a lot of meetings around Hollywood.
A movie script about The Doors is floating around town, and Joe, rumor has it, may be up for a big part or even the lead.
On the way into town, we stop in front of Shep Gordon's place up in the Hollywood Hills. Our guitarist has to take a meeting with Alice Cooper. The rest of us wait outside in the van.
Time for another tailgate party.
Meanwhile, promoter/entrepreneur Michael Striar and our managers Collins and Barrasso have all jetted in. The JPP is staying at the somewhat squalid Beverly Sunset Hotel on the Sunset Strip. Lots of closed-door meetings and phone calls going on these days. I'm in my room watching Bob Eubanks host the Newlywed Game.
Bob's a riot. We're headlining the Reseda Country Club tonight.

Saturday November 19, 1983

Today the band and our gear motors east, through the Mojave desert, destination Las Vegas.
I've never been to this town before.
Joe Perry remained back in L.A. With all the management guys.
After a four and a half hour drive, the rest of us book into the perfectly situated Aladdin Hotel and Casino on Las Vegas Boulevard. We all race into the casino with whatever spare change might still be rattling around in our pockets.

Sunday November 20, 1983

The Admiral jets into McCarran Airport from LAX on
Southwest Airlines.
During the flight, Perry invites two of the air hostesses to be his
guests at our concert tonight. Who's the playboy now?

The Project is playing at the Troubador, a rock'n'roll nightclub
just off the Las Vegas Strip. Not a casino or a fancy place, just a
nice-sized, beat-up showroom with a long bar where regular
kids can get together and go crazy.
Halfway through our performance, Perry's two fly-girls enter the
room and push right up to the front. Wow. They sure standout
from the rest of this crowd.
Following a very successful show, it's time to relax. Back at the
Aladdin, one of the stewardesses tries to get my attention.
She wants to have fun and party and dance.
Only problem is, I'm on a roll on my lucky slot machine. Slots
are pretty new to me but I'm already a master. I can't believe it
when the bells start ringing and all these quarters come pouring
out. I'm transfixed by the action and the huge jackpots I'm
accruing. Meanwhile, the young lady from Southwest (a regular
on this Las Vegas route I'm sure) is growing impatient with my
low-stakes gambling fever.
The rest of our party (and her colleague) have already
disappeared upstairs to our floor. The fuming air hostess finally
yanks me away from my one-armed bandit. In full greed mode, I
clench my little bucket of quarters as she drags me away.
Now I'm unhappily riding the elevator. Up, up and away from
all the jangling casino action.
Arriving at the floor where the JPP party is in full swing, we step
out, but as the elevator door closes, Miss Southwest snatches the
plastic bucket out of my grubby paws and flings all my winnings
onto the floor of the empty elevator carriage.
I dive down, trying to rescue my fortune, but it's too late.
The doors slam shut. The smiling stewardess pokes the Down
button. Easy come, easy go. Viva Las Vegas.

Monday November 21, 1983

It's a tough wake-up call and a long van ride across the desert.
South on 93 out of Las Vegas and down through Dolan Springs,
Kingman (made famous in the song Route 66), Wikieup,
Wickenburg, Surprise, Phoenix and finally, Tempe AZ.
We book into the Vagabond Tempe Inn and headline at After the
Gold Rush. This is an explosive concert and the audience
reaction is off the charts. There's no stopping the JPP.

Tuesday November 22 - Thursday November 24. 1983

Apparently we have plates that need spinning back on the East
Coast. Tuesday morning we depart Arizona early enough to
make Albuquerque NM by 11 a.m.
On the 23rd, we roll through St Louis MO at 8:30 a.m.
On the 24th, the Dodge van finally pulls into Cambridge at
8:30 a.m. Just enough time to wash up and for Julia
and me to make it out to my parents' house in Holliston for
Thanksgiving dinner.

Friday November 25, 1983

I sleep late at the palace. During lunch I hear Black Velvet Pants
playing on good old WBCN. Our album is in its ninth week on
the playlist, and is currently the #21 most played album in
Boston. We're on MTV. We're #40 on the Kerrang albums chart.

Monday November 28, 1983

I go shopping with Danny Hargrove. Where else?
Walker's Riding Apparel, across from the Boston Common.
We both purchase a fresh pair of leather pants.

Tuesday November 29 - Wednesday November 30, 1983

I go see the new Bob Fosse movie, *Star 80* on Tuesday.
Depressing. On the way home, I hear Black Velvet Pants

on WBCN again. On Wednesday the new Joe Perry Project record earns a four star review in Record (Canada) and a five star review in Sounds (England).

December 1, 1983

We plunge back into action, this time we're rocking Pollack Auditorium at Monmouth College, just up the road from Asbury Park NJ. Over 600 show up.

Friday December 2, 1983

The Admiral is on Carter Alan's radio show. They talk and spin three album tracks: Once a Rocker, Walk with Me Sally and BVP. We're headlining down in Providence RI at the Living Room tonight. The poster on the wall says that Cyndi Lauper is playing here tomorrow. The poster says she's "from England" but I saw her in a video and she doesn't look very British to me.

Saturday December 3, 1983

I saw myself singing on MTV again today. A good omen for our Boston shows tonight. After all the airplay we've bagged locally for the past four months, this is going to be a barn-burner.
We play a 5:15 p.m. all-ages show and a 12:15 a.m. headline show, both at the Channel.

Sunday December 4, 1983

The JPP moves up to the #18 spot on the WBCN most-played list. Our tenth week on the chart.

Monday December 5, 1983

Back at the palace. Someone is pounding on the door.
I go downstairs, open up and see a man in a suit standing on the front steps.
Looks like an encyclopedia salesman.

"No thanks. Not interested." I push the door closed.

"Wait, Cowboy, it's me."

"Huh?" How does that suit know my nickname?

I open the door again and stare at the fellow.

He leans towards me.

"Well? What do you think?"

Holy shit, it's the Admiral.

It's Joe Perry - wearing a cheap suit with a blue tie, dress shoes, glasses and a short-hair wig.

"I gotta go back to court this morning and the judge is a prick. Take my picture okay?"

I can't stop laughing. I find my Polaroid and Joe poses next to Julia's desk. I knew all this court nonsense was grating on Perry, but I had no idea it had gotten this bad.

Wednesday December 7, 1983

Alfred New York - it's out near Rochester.

We're appearing at the University of New York here, tonight. Even though I never paid a dime to attend college, I'll bet that over the past 15 years I've spent more time on university campuses and have enjoyed more college parties than the average bear.

Thursday December 8, 1983

This routing is very cool, we just bop a little bit south and we're in West Henrietta for the next gig. Didn't even have to check out of our hotel at the Best Western in Rochester. The Riverboat has some astounding deals going on tonight, 3 shots of Schnapps for $1 (all night). Admission to see the JPP concert is only $3.50.

Friday December 9, 1983

A band called Kix opens for us tonight at the Chance in Poughkeepsie NY. Our friend Joanie is here too and Kix turns out to be great. Everyone's staying at the Red Lion - Best Western. Much superior to the Dutch Spitoon.

Sunday December 11, 1983

I scan Billboard for any mention of Once a Rocker Always a Rocker. Not much.
An okay review of our gig at the Bottom Line, a blurb that MTV has Black Velvet Pants on light rotation, and that we've moved up to #16 most played album in Boston in our eleventh week.

Thursday December 15, 1983

We headline at a really nice new venue up in Manchester NH called the Casbah.

Friday December 16, 1983

Julia isn't happy about the year-end newsletter that the Spit nightclub on Lansdowne St. hands out to everyone. In a gossip column titled "Great Expectorations" the two of us have been mentioned in bold face type:

Most Likely to Succeed:
Gene *(SyncroSound) and* **Alinka Amoroso**,
Most Unlikely:
Mach Bell *(Joe Perry Project) and* **Julia Channing**
(SyncroSound).
Julia jets home to the UK today, for Christmas with her family in London. I'm in the Dodge van, heading for Long Island for a return engagement at My Father's Place.

Saturday December 17, 1983

Onward to Middletown NY, for another onstage rave-up and after-show throw-down at J.B. Rock III.

Sunday December 18, 1983

We wind up the 1983 tour schedule here at Radio City in Scotia NY. Overall, this is show 196 for Danny and me.

During 1983 we racked up 116 more concerts, 2 more cross country tours, 1 album, 1 video, two drummers, four road managers and too many miles and truck stop diners to count. There is no stopping the Joe Perry Project.

After the Dodge van arrives back in Boston, we have a JPP debriefing at the office with Tim on December 21.

The next day, I go out to Ashland for a Christmas party and jam session with Thundertrain and lots of the local rock guys I grew up playing in bands with.

I attend a Christmas party at the Spit dance club on December 23. Then I spend the holiday at home with my parents and brothers in Holliston.

The day after Christmas, my friend Willie Alexander moves out of the apartment at 399 Broadway.

The following day Admiral Perry moves into 399 Broadway. So Joe and Billie are now my up the street neighbors.

WBCN releases their Top 104 albums of the year. Once a Rocker comes in at #65.

UK writer Dave Roberts of Sounds pegs us at #6 in his Albums of the Year list. Black Velvet Pants is still getting some play on MTV and Boston radio is still regularly spinning the album as 1983 draws to a close.

Joe Perry disguised as a normal person, for a court date. December 5, 1983

Danny, Mach, the Admiral and Joe Pet in California March '84

Final JPP Show in New Haven CT Photo credit Henry Sancho

VI
CAUGHT IN THE CROSSFIRE

Monday January 2, 1984

The Admiral stops at the pink palace to hang around and see what I got for Christmas. I show him my best present, a Mattel toy drum machine.
It's more of a real musical instrument than a toy. It has several little drum pads you can whack-on, plus a built-in beat box feature where you can program some decent rhythms.
Of course Joe digs it too.
He asks me if he can borrow my present, for some songwriting he's about to do with Alice Cooper.

Wednesday January 4, 1984

I check out the new issue of Circus magazine at the Out of Town newsstand in Harvard Square. The date on the cover says January 31, but they always issue these mags way in advance of the cover date.
Circus Magazine - Longplayers by John Swenson
"The spectacular Leslie cabinet effect achieved with the guitar sound on King of the Kings is an innovative approach that unites musical ideas from Muddy Waters, Jimi Hendrix and Led Zeppelin.
The Joe Perry Project's Once a Rocker is one of the best hard-rock albums of the year."

Right on.

Thursday January 5, 1984

Joe either jets back to Hollywood to collaborate with Alice Cooper, or maybe they're holed-up somewhere in upstate New York. Who knows? Anyway, the Admiral brought my Mattel toy along on the trip.

Monday January 9, 1984

While the Admiral is somewhere with Alice Cooper, I'm at a
Vinny Band record release at the Rat, and back again the
following night to check out a rocking new group called The
Bristols. Can't help but notice they're all girls. Excellent.
The next night, I'm at Paradise to see Joe Black's band
Ball'n'Chain. Black played with Charlie Farren in his pre-JPP
group Balloon.
Joe Perry returns from L.A. (or New York, not sure which)
today. He stops by the palace to play me cassettes of the stuff he
and Alice Cooper put together.
Not really songs, more like ideas for parts of songs. They
recorded them using my toy drum as their Ringo. Listening to
the tape, I'm relieved that none of the tunes revolve around the
next killer JP riff. Can't be sharing those, I've already begun
writing lyrics for the next Project record. Joe forgot and left my
best Christmas present at Alice's house

Monday January 16, 1984

The Stray Cats and Huey Lewis songs from last summer are still
playing on MTV in heavy rotation. And, so is that Reach the
Beach album from our unknown label-mates the Fixx.
Released a few months before our album, their single Saved by
Zero went through the roof. The follow up, One Thing Leads to
Another, came out a month before Once a Rocker and is
currently a top ten smash. Being a student of the biz, I theorize
that most of the sales energy at MCA is being sucked up by the
Fixx phenomenon.

The buzz around Boston is that Alice Cooper is gonna tour in
1984 with Joe Perry leading his band.
Danny Hargrove and I aren't buying a word of it. We know the
Project has a mess of shows booked and we're about to be
deployed again, just two weeks from today.

Tuesday January 17, 1984

Boy Sean and Freddie are both relieved of duty with the JPP today. I liked those guys. We shared a lot of good times together and I'll miss them.
Rick is doing great as road manager (not easy around here).
Toby and Rick work together on our house sound, Fortune is stage manager, and Toby's younger brother Elwood has come aboard to tend the Admiral's fleet of guitars.

Thursday January 19, 1984

I join my new up-the-block neighbor, Joe Perry for a few pints of Guinness at the pub in nearby Inman Square.

Monday January 23, 1984

The JPP plays together for the first time in over a month.
We're all up in Pet's home studio again, running through the show on practice amps. The Admiral wants to add Chuck Berry's Sweet Little Rock'n'Roller to the set.
Julia takes me out to my favorite Mexican place Sol Azteca for dinner. It's my 31st birthday.

Wednesday January 25, 1984

Tonight, our celebrity percussionist, Joe Pet, hosts his very own drum clinic, at the E.U. Wurlitzer music store on Newbury St. A good-sized crowd shows up and the Project joins Pet for a spirited jam at the end of his demonstration.
This is our first public performance of 1984.
Setlist: Train Kept A-Rollin,' Something Else, Crossfire, Rockin' Train, Sweet Little Rock'n'Roller, Black Velvet Pants.
After the drum clinic, I hit a 9 p.m. party over at the Spit dance club.

Friday January 27, 1984

The Joe Perry Project roar back into action in New Haven CT
today at the Twilite Zone (formerly an Agora venue). There's a
Thor poster over by the box office. He's still gigging?
Yup, he just performed here two nights ago. I remember seeing
Thor on the Merv Griffin TV show a decade ago. I'll never
forget it, he was unreal. A bare chested muscleman, singing
Everybody Wants a Piece of the Action. Bounding across the
stage, flexing and ripping apart phone books.
For his grand finale, Thor started blowing up a hot water bottle.
The crowd is hushed, spellbound, scared. The bottle stretches
and stretches, Thor blows like a true immortal when BANG.
Chunks of rubber explode all over the theater.
The audience explodes into applause. Superhuman Thor bows,
flexes and exits in glory.
Tonight's Project show was good but I wouldn't want to go up
against Thor.

Saturday January 28, 1984

We return to Scotch'n Sounds, twenty-five miles south of
Boston, on this cold winter night.
Due to our MTV exposure and the great support we've enjoyed
from New England radio, we pull a larger, louder crowd than the
last times we were here.

Saturday February 4, 1984

The band is really hitting its stride right now. I'm feeling totally
confident in my role, finally singing my own lyrics just like they
sound on the record.
Pet and Hargrove are the best rhythm section since Mitch and
Noel. Now that the Admiral has moved in with Billie, he's
playing straight from the heart.
Our crew is stronger too. No teenagers or Zakowski burnouts.
These guys take their jobs seriously. It shows in our production.

We're in Brooklyn at L'Amour tonight, and everybody loves us.
Nothing can stop the Project.

Monday February 6, 1984

I checked the Out of Town newsstand today and the Joe Perry
Project currently has cover stories in at least three different
glossy magazines: Rock Video, Faces Rock and Rock World.

Tuesday February 7, 1984

Everybody into the van. We leave the pink palace at 8 a.m.
Bound for Cincinnati Ohio.

Wednesday February 8, 1984

We're stationed at the Quality Inn in Covington KY, just across
the Ohio River from Annie's Riverside in Cincinnati and that's
where we play to another excellent reception.
But there's not a single Playboy Bunny in attendance this time
around...The Fixx are probably playing up the street.
This is a milestone show for Danny Hargrove and me, our 200th
concert with the Project.

Thursday February 9, 1984

Another Midwest show.
We're playing pretty close to my birthplace (Yellow Springs)
tonight. Headlining at McGuffy's in Dayton Ohio.
Dayton was where my father once worked at a tire foundry
during his college days.
Our music, the sound, the lights, our whole production is really
jelling, and Sweet Little Rock'n'Roller was a great choice by JP.

Friday February 10, 1984

Time to wiggle some more sticks. Gotta keep those plates
spinning back in Detroit.

We rock the house at Harpo's Concert Theater and this time, when we arrive for soundcheck, the fans waiting in the alley are waving Once a Rocker Always a Rocker albums in the air. Danny and I sign them all. Following a terrific set we adjourn to the after-party at the Park Crest Hotel.

Saturday February 11, 1984

The Project crosses the Canadian border, from Detroit into Ontario, but our truckload of gear is not allowed into the country. Forcing us to cancel tonight's show at Tony's East in Scarborough (near Toronto).
A few hours later, the club owner from Tony's East rings the front desk at the Hampton Court Hotel where we're staying. Front desk transfers the call to the hotel lounge, where Joe Perry and I are settled in.
The club owner informs us that a big crowd has arrived already, pleading to see the Project. Can we possibly do something?
Having had a few beers and not wanting to let down our loyal Canadian fans, we decide what the hell...
Let's just do the gig without our gear.
The resilient JPP ends up playing to the large crowd on a borrowed set of drums, a few loaner guitars and some odd little amplifiers the owner manages to dig up for us.
It's tricky, because among other things, Danny Hargrove normally plays a bass that is strung upside down. In the end, we still sound almost like the Project and Danny manages to play his parts upside-down (standing on his head?) on the borrowed instrument.
The fans are overjoyed, and so is the relieved club owner.
One of our crew was already out on the town when our plans got changed. With no way to get in touch with him, he misses the last minute show. Elwood was elsewhere.

Monday February 12, 1984

We check out of the Hampton Court, retrieve our truckload of gear, and head back to Boston for our next assignment.

Thursday February 16, 1984

The office calls me at the pink palace. Tim Collins has news
and wants me to come in at 5 p.m.
 I've heard from both the Admiral and Tim that there's been
discussion about bringing the JPP to Japan for a bunch of dates.
An Asian tour makes a lot of sense. Joe Perry is well-loved over
there. We could sell a ton of Project records and have fun.
Or maybe Tim has news that MCA just green lighted the next
Project album. Let's go baby.
Arriving at the office, I dash up the stairs to the second level
reception room. I'm a bit surprised to find Joe Pet and Danny
Hargrove waiting for me. I laugh.
"Didn't know this was a band meeting."
The secretary leads the three of us into the front office, where
Tim is sitting behind his big desk in his big leather chair.
He greets us with a little smile. He's silent for a moment.
Not like Tim to ever be silent.
"Okay. Thanks for coming over guys. Look. I'm not going to
beat around the bush. I think you all know there's a lot of things
that Joe has been dealing with.
Legal battles. Old debts. New debts…anyway…
Joe has decided…That he wants to go back to Aerosmith."
I nearly pass out. Silence in the room.
Inside my head:
"What? Did I just hear you right, Tim? Go back to Aerosmith?"
Hargrove is as stunned as me. Pet gazes out the window, staring
straight into the Mass Pike traffic as it roars by.
"Look guys. This has nothing to do with you. Joe loves this
band. The Project means everything to him. He just doesn't
really have any other choice right now."
None of us respond. What is there to say?
Collins continues,
"But I have a little bit of good news. We still have a lot of shows
booked. The Project will be going out with a bang. We've even
got another West Coast swing coming up."
Oh, man. I can't handle this. I'm in overload. So are the others.
We all get up and leave.

Saturday February 18, 1984

The Admiral flew out to Arizona today. To visit with his mom
and sister probably.
I'm in shock. I've been hearing Aerosmith reunion rumors ever
since I joined this band.
"Just wait, Steven and Joe will get back together."
"Joe's gonna go back to Aerosmith. You watch. It's gotta happen
sooner or later."
I disregarded all that gossip. So did Danny.
We had to tune that stuff out, in order to keep our momentum up
and give everything we had to the Project.

Sunday February 26, 1984

It's my father Bill Bell's birthday and also my two-year
anniversary as lead singer with the Joe Perry Project.

Friday March 2, 1984

So we continue marching forward.
But with a very different feeling now. I can stop writing lyrics
for the next album, stop thinking about ideas for our followup
videos, the Japanese tour, our winter clubhouse in Hollywood
and my dreams of a longterm future with the Project.
From here on out, we'll just be concentrating on doing the best
shows possible in every town we get to visit. One more time.
Most of the fans don't realize it yet but this has suddenly
become the Project's farewell tour.

We're out in Rochester NY tonight, at the Penny Arcade and the
minute we hit the stage I actually have a blast. Tonight is Joe
Pet's one-year anniversary with America's best hard rock band.

Saturday March 3, 1984

Well, we just played a concert in Gloversville NY.

I'm certain of that - but for the first time, I have to admit, I'm not sure what the name of the venue we just played in was. I'm really slipping.

Thursday March 8, 1984

Joe Perry Project rock'n'rolls at the good old Mohawk Club in Shirley MA. Andy is here along with my cousin Terry. Also, Merry, the lead singer of Joe Flash. She was the kid I hitchhiked out to Boulder Colorado with when we were 16.

Friday March 9, 1984

"7 Hours of High-Powered Rock'n'Roll."
We're on a fantastic bill tonight, along with the David Johansen Group and The Ramones.
This has to be one of the greatest rock shows in history.
What a scene. We're at the University of Southern Maine in Portland. I'm sad but I'm happy.

Saturday March 10, 1984

We rock the Channel in Boston for the last time tonight. We only play an evening show this time, not our usual double-header, so the joint is packed tighter than ever. Enjoying my final days as an overnight success, deadbeat celebrity. It's crazy. After all that struggle, the Project is finally getting written up in magazines and getting played on the radio and MTV.
Our new album isn't even six months old yet.

Tuesday March 13, 1984

Julia is super busy at SyncroSound. The Cars new album Heartbeat City is being released today.
The first single, You Might Think, also came out today.
Sounds like it could do well for them.

Wednesday March 14, 1984

We've got two concerts, in two different towns today.
First, we celebrate the 16th Birthday of WBCN-FM, at a
lunchtime show at Metro (former site of the Boston Tea
Party rock club) behind Fenway Park. Opening our show is a
new local band called 'til tuesday.
Following the birthday party, we roar into Amherst, where we
kick out the jams at the Blue Wall, University of Massachusetts.

Thursday March 15, 1984

I don't know where Tim finds these places.
We're booked into a teensy joint called the Roadhouse.
A shack in Lynn Mass, squashed-full of Joe fukken Perry fans.
Never Wanna Stop.

Friday March 16, 1984

Bringing our rock'n'roll show back to Brockton at the Scotch'n
Sounds. This place is giving the Chance a run for its money in
the "Where does (did) the Joe Perry Project appear most?"
trivia contest.

Saturday March 23, 1984

It's a week later and the Project jets from BOS into LAX.
Touching down at at 3:25 p.m.
We check into the slightly-sleazy Beverly Sunset Hotel on the
Sunset Strip. Beginning our fourth California road trip at the
notoriously storied Golden Bear in Huntington Beach.
Janis played here, as did Garcia, Hooker, Guthrie, Hendrix,
Butterfield and Bell. Cowboy Mach Bell.
We brought along our own guitars, but the back-line, the truck
and our van are all rented for this eight city swing.

Saturday March 24, 1984

Back at the funky & faded Beverly Sunset Hotel at 8775 Sunset
Blvd. The Project will be staying here for the next few days.
Lemmy and Motorhead are bunking a few doors up the gritty
hallway from us. The hotel (it's more like a motel, complete
with a worn-down, astro-turfed pool area) is sprawled along the
Strip, where the boulevard takes a wide curve between Ben
Frank's 24 hour restaurant and the Tower Records store.
Tonite, the JPP will once again headline at the Country Club
over in the Valley. While I'd love to be rocking down the street
at the Whisky a Go Go, the Country Club is about 10 times
roomier, and the stage and production equipment is bigger and
much better. Opener tonight is ace guitarist Les Dudek, who is
currently dating Cher.
Nice show at Huntington Beach last night. We're playing meaner
and tighter than ever.

Tuesday March 27, 1984

Walked next door to Tower Records to get some new tunes
yesterday. I picked up the new Van Halen 1984 album and
brought it back to my room. I pop it in my Panasonic. What the
hell? They've got a song on here called Hot For Teacher?
Are you kidding me?
That title has always been synonymous with Thundertrain.
Steven Silva wrote it and it was our biggest hit, rising all the
way to #3 on the alternative charts in the UK (a notch above the
Clash). It got played all over Boston when the single was
released in 1976. VH didn't kidnap the entire song outright.
Only the titles are identical.
But damn it. From now on, Hot For Teacher will probably be
identified as a Van Halen song.

Wednesday March 28, 1984

Yesterday we checked out of L.A.

We're cruising south on the San Diego Freeway in the rented van. Rick is at the wheel. Our gig the other night in Glendora (up near Azusa) got cancelled, so we were forced to hang out and party in the middle of Hollywood for 72 juicy-hours straight. At the Rainbow, the Central, the Roxy, Barney's Beanery, the Whisky and the Hamburger Hamlet.
I spent some time with Boston area musicians who reside out here now, like Jeff Thomas and Steven Silva and I made some interesting new acquaintances as well.
Returning now to our usual digs down here, the Hotel San Diego. An old-style hotel with a view to the harbor. Tonight we're in La Jolla playing at the Rodeo. A new venue for us.

Thursday March 29, 1984

Guess where we're driving now? Straight back to the vaguely-seedy Beverly Sunset Hotel on the Sunset Strip, that's where. Hopefully they got around to cleaning out my room.
I mean, we only checked-out of there 24 hours ago.
Tonight we'll be playing over in West L.A. at the Music Machine on Pico Blvd. First time for us at this venue too.
It's a big black box, with a decent-sized black stage, and a little black dressing room in the back. My kind of place.

Friday March 30, 1984

Early wake-up call. Stagger across the Strip for some coffee, bacon, Belgian waffles and cherry pancakes at the Old World Restaurant before checking-out of the well-located but unsavory Beverly Sunset Hotel for the final time.
Rick is wheeling the Joe Perry Project from Hollywood up to Berkeley today. We have the usual 5 p.m. soundcheck to make. Manager Tim went the extra mile and got us booked into the Kyoto in San Francisco for the next two nights. A place with very nice guest rooms. Hargrove and I spend the long voyage north discussing what the hell we're gonna do once the Project closes-up shop in 6 weeks.

Joe Pet doesn't seem concerned about anything. He's laughing at his own jokes in the back of the van, while the silent Admiral rides shotgun.

The Project sounds different using the back-line gear we rented from S.I.R. for this swing. Perry isn't using his usual Aerosmith amp heads, the kustomized pedal board, or his boomerang side-stage cabs.

He's just straight-wired into a couple old fashioned Marshall 100 stacks. Sounds immediate, classic and in your face.

Tonight we headline at the Keystone Berkeley.

Saturday March 31, 1984

I wake up around noon after the volcanic show last night in Berkeley. That venue has such a history and the fans are the best. Interesting that out here in California, the crowd always includes a ton of ex-New Englanders. When the JPP comes west it's like old home night and we're the home team.

Tonight the Project headlines at The Stone, just around the corner from the City Lights Bookstore, and too-near to the world famous Condor topless bar.

Of course inspector Hargrove and the curious Cowboy have to check that out. Carol Doda is still dancing there.

Sunday April 1, 1984

Tim Collins must be playing an April Fools' joke on us.

After a late check-out at the luxe Kyoto in San Francisco, we've all been rounded up, vanned out of town and dumped into a worn-out Travelodge Motel in Palo Alto.

Goodbye sashimi & Asian decor, hello moldy shower stall and vending machine Fritos. Oh, well, at least we're still out here in warm California for a few more days. Weather's been nothing but windy and cold back in Cambridge ever since we jetted out of Logan ten days ago.

Tim and the Admiral struck gold when they hired our soundman Toby Francis last summer. Toby is a respectful, quiet guy who extricates massively clear sonics out of all these beat up club systems we've been playing through this week. I wouldn't be surprised if Toby ends up running sound for the resurrected Aerosmith.

KOME-FM, the only radio station (I know of) where our record went to number one, is hosting our concert tonight at the Keystone Palo Alto. This will be our last show in the Bay but I don't share that fact with the audience. I don't know about Pet and Hargrove but I still can't bring myself to admit that it's all drawing to a close. I've contributed as much as possible to this enterprise but I'll be the first to admit that I've been riding Joe Perry's coattails for these past couple years.

What a starry ride it's been.

Monday April 2, 1984

Good news and Bad news. The good is that the Palo Alto show last night went off without a hitch.

Crossfire and Never Wanna Stop have both turned into epic tour de forces of Tele-Rat glory. Maybe the Admiral senses that he'll soon have to rein in his ever-evolving guitar explorations, once he rejoins Aerosmith.

Joe is aiming for the heart of the sun - before he has to go back to doling out Dream On for the rest of his life.

Bad news, is that our Wednesday date at Fresno State just got cancelled. That means our California road trip will be ending with tonight's concert. Many of the kids here are JPP regulars, who we've come to know pretty well (some, exceedingly well) over the past couple years. When our van pulls into the stage door parking lot for the 5 p.m. sound checks, these faithful rockers are always lined up waiting. Rain or shine. Heatwave or hail storm. It'll be tough not seeing them anymore.

Gotta go out big tonight in Sacramento. We're headlining at El Dorado Saloon, 6309 Fair Oaks Blvd.

They've got those Old West-style, double-hung swinging saloon doors and a big ol' mechanical bull for your riding pleasure.

Tuesday April 3, 1984

Wow. What just happened?
The band is racing back to San Francisco in the rented van.
But someone's missing. El Dorado was a scene alright. Joe
Perry Project was ripping it up like there'd be no tomorrow. We
were shirtless and sweating. The girls were screaming. Two
encores. We all got invited back to a loud, crowded party at
some redhead's apartment in downtown Sacramento. The last
thing I remember was our drummer Joe Pet with onion dip
smeared across his face, acting even more like a lunatic than
usual. "Hostess, your dip is fabulous."
 Next thing I know the sun is up and I'm being hustled out of the
Mansion Inn and into the van.
Our jet to Boston leaves San Francisco at 1:24 p.m.
Joe Perry looks back from his shotgun seat
"Where the hell is Pet?" Hargrove bursts out laughing,
"He ate dip and disappeared."
"Well, we gotta hit it. *Now*," spits Rick the road manager, as he
burns rubber out of the hotel lot. Rick is boiling over,
"Damn it. Tim's gonna be pissed. The drummer will just have to
find his own way home - somehow."
I'm praying that Pet will appear at the last moment, just before
we hit the freeway on-ramp. He doesn't.
The Admiral shakes his mane in disapproving but amused
dismay. Danny can't stop laughing.
A few hours later, Hargrove and I catch our flight back home to
Boston. Joe Perry boards a jet back down to L.A. where he'll be
staying til the 5th.
Later, back at home in Cambridge, we find out that M.I.A. Joe
Pet was able to flag down a ride and hightail it back to San
Francisco. Just in time to wave good-bye to the rest of the
Project as we lifted-off the runway.

Thursday April 5, 1984

Joe Perry arrives back in Boston after his extra stay in
Hollywood CA.

Wednesday April 11, 1984

I have a meeting with Tim Collins. We're discussing plans for Danny's and my new band, The Wild Bunch. Tim is arranging a demo recording session and a booking agency for our proposed new act.

Thursday April 12, 1984

Stressing out. I come down with the flu.

Monday April 16, 1984

Laid-up in Cambridge. Since I'm unable to mentally deal with the dissolution of the Project, my body is dealing with it, and I'm going downhill fast.
It's impossible for me to accept that anything can - and finally *has* stopped the JPP. Our unsinkable pirate ship has been overtaken by the mighty aircraft carrier Aerosmith.

Wednesday April 18, 1984

Back on my feet.
At the palace kitchen table. Danny and I cobble together an anthem we call Burn Thru the Night.

Thursday April 19, 1984

1 p.m. meeting at the office with booking agent Bruce Houghton, who agrees to represent The Wild Bunch, if and when Danny and I can put an actual band together.
At 7:30 p.m. we bring our new song out to the Complex and jam around on it with drummer Bobby Edwards and lead guitarist Johnny Press.

Easter Sunday April 22, 1984.

I have a 12 noon meeting with drummer/vocalist Hirsh Gardner
of the band New England. Gardner is interested in producing the
upcoming Wild Bunch demo.
After that, I head out to Holliston for a 2 p.m. holiday lunch at
my parent's house.

Thursday April 26, 1984

Danny and I are at Sound Design, a recording studio in
Burlington Mass, cutting Burn Thru the Night.
Since we still haven't put together an actual band, we have Press
handling guitar and Edwards on drums. Both are currently
contracted to the band Velocity, so they are ghosting on our
demo. Hargrove is on vocals and bass and I'm singing lead and
banging on a wood block. Hirsh Gardner produces.

Saturday April 28, 1984

Today will be the Joe Perry Project's final Boston performance.
Going out large and loud, in our hometown, at the first WBCN
Boston Music Expo. The party is being staged inside the
gargantuan Bayside Exposition Center. It holds 10,000 easy.
On the bill with us is a UK group called The Alarm, who are
currently riding up the charts.
The hall is jammed with kids. Our first JPP gig since the West
Coast trip a few weeks ago. We don't rehearse anymore and
Danny and I have been busy trying to put together our own
thing. I don't think I've even seen Joe Perry since we left the
San Francisco Airport.
Once we all hit the stage, everything rushes back into crisp
focus real quick. The Project takes off like a guided missile.

Sunday April 29, 1984

The Expo was much bigger than anyone expected.

We made the headlines when the Southeast Expressway had to be closed down during part of our performance. Traffic and pedestrian overflow caused a massive gridlock in the entire Bayside/JFK area.

Tuesday May 1, 1984

Danny and I are back at Sound Design, tracking our vocal parts over the basic tracks we recorded last week.

Wednesday May 2, 1984

Burn Thru the Night is meant to be an anthem.
The structure of the verse is driving but minimal. Inspired by Do Ya (Do Ya Want My Love?) by the Move. Then it bursts into a big Slade-type chorus. Hirsh pulls it all together as best he can, and the musical performances seem solid.
Unfortunately something is just not right. Wrong tempo? Uneven sounding? Missing something?
Or, is it just that we are moving ahead too fast with this song, trying to record a band that doesn't even exist yet, except maybe inside our heads.

Thursday May 3, 1984

I'm devastated. The Project was supposed to begin a sweet six city road trip yesterday - but the whole thing fell apart.
Last night I could have been singing one more time on Riviera Beach in Ocean City MD. Right now I'm missing out on a concert in Pittsburgh at the Stanley Theater.

Thursday May 10, 1984

Now for something completely different.
We're playing a high school with Joe Perry. As a teenager I used to spend endless weekends playing high school dances but it's a rarity for the Project. This is an afternoon performance at Peabody High School.

We also have an evening show booked in another town.

But guess what? Joe Pet is not available to play tonight - or for the rest of the weekend.

Enterprising Pet, has grabbed another (better paying I'm sure) gig, with a cha-cha band or whatever. So Joe Perry and manager Tim Collins have convinced Aerosmith drummer Joey Kramer to fill-in for the Project's final three shows, before the Aerosmith re-launch begins.

Joey Kramer sits out in the school auditorium with the other kids, watching the JPP blast-out our set.

This high school gig is the very last time the Project will perform with the Once a Rocker Always a Rocker line-up.

After the show, just trying to be friendly, I casually ask Mr. Kramer if he's all set to take over the drum throne for the Project later tonight.

Joey looks at me pitifully and whispers "I think I can handle it."

Hargrove, the Admiral, the road crew and I say our good-byes to Joe Pet, who as usual is cracking himself up.

Seems weird (to me) that he's not shedding a single tear over the band's demise as he skips out the backstage door, whistling a merry tune.

After a dinner stop, the JPP (now featuring Joey Kramer), ride out in the trusty Dodge van to the Worcester Airport where we headline the Hi-Life club.

I heard a rumor that Kramer agreed to do these JPP gigs, as long as he could perform on his automated, 25 foot, Aerosmith drum riser. Tim Collins had to explain to Joey that the entire stage the Project plays on is often smaller than his drum riser.

That's the case tonight. A small, packed room with a small, packed stage. But a really lively, fun show, because Kramer interprets our original songs in a whole new way than Ron Stewart or Joe Pet ever did. Every opening, ending and change-up is a new sonic adventure.

And on the Aerosmith numbers that we still play, like Bright Light Fright, Train Kept A-Rollin' and Walk This Way, it's electrifying to be harmonizing with Joe Perry as the real Aerosmith drummer lays down his famous beats beside us.

Friday May 11. 1984

The Joe Perry Project plays for the last time in the state of
Massachusetts tonight and it's a killer farewell.
We're up at the Frolics, in Salisbury Beach. A grand seaside
ballroom that you can probably jam a thousand kids into.
Long bars flank the wide wooden dance floor. Big stage with big
dressing rooms. That's good, because the Cowboy practically
needs his own dressing room tonight with the conga line of well
wishers, good friends, bimbos, family and ex-bandmates in
attendance. Joe Perry and Joey Kramer are holding court way
down on the other end of the backstage area.
Just before the opening band finishes up, Brad Whitford strides
into the dressing room, followed by Steven Tyler himself.
Steven Tyler pushes through the crowd, making a bee-line over
to my side of the dressing room.
"How's it hangin' Cowboy?" Steven shakes my hand, throws
back his head, and salutes me by singing the chorus of Once a
Rocker Always a Rocker.
A very cool and gracious guy.
Tyler pulls me close and whispers into my ear,
"Great job in New York, man. You sounded real good...
You know I love Joe Perry...but he can't sing for shit."
Tyler cracks up and I just want to keep on talking with him - but
that's when a brunette bounces by and I lose him. If I have to
lose my job to someone - I'm glad it's Steven Tyler.

Our opening music is rising to it's climax. Flashlight in hand,
Rick leads us out to the stage.
I'm charged up, excited to jam with Joey Kramer on drums
again. We open stronger than ever and after a few songs the
Admiral calls Brad Whitford to the stage and the crowd goes
wild. Brad plugs-in and we rip into Black Velvet Pants, Sweet
Little Rock'n'Roller, Bang a Gong and Once a Rocker.
The Frolics crowd is on their feet and ecstatic.
Perry drops another bomb, inviting Steven Tyler to the stage.
This might be the first time anybody has seen Kramer, Whitford,
Perry and Tyler all together on stage in about five years.

The place goes ape-shit.
"Know any Aerosmith?" Steven whispers to me.
I call for Bright Light Fright and Kramer counts it off.
"Wait…do I know this one?" Steven asks me.
Aerosmith (minus Tom Hamilton) rock out for the rest of the
night with the Project's Danny Hargrove on bass, and me doing
my Cowboy thing.

Saturday May 12, 1984

Julia left for New York City this morning. The Cars are the
musical guests on Saturday Night Live tonight and she's
been asked to attend the performance and the after-party at
30 Rockefeller Plaza. Billy Crystal is the host.

The Cars are in overdrive but it's the end of the road for the Joe
Perry Project.
We're headlining tonite, at a venue we visited a couple months
ago, in New Haven, fittingly called the Twilite Zone.
Concert number 226 for Danny and me.
After last night's blowout in Salisbury Beach, I'm stoked to rock
some more but still unable to come to terms with the fact that
it's all about to end abruptly. Ain't over til it's over though.
On today's ride our new drummer Joey Kramer is in the shotgun
seat. The Admiral has brought along his girlfriend Billie.
They're sitting close-together, on the first bench seat of the van.
Road manager Rick is at the wheel.
Hargrove and I are at the back of the bus.
The Twilite Zone is a cool place, with a large stage and nice
lighting. Not a bad venue for our last hurrah. It's just the four of
us tonite, no extra Aerosmith guest stars and that's fine with me.
Joey Kramer really swings on the Project songs and even though
he's not terribly friendly to talk with, he's a gas to make music
with.
So we played together one last time tonight with the Admiral.
It was deep, driving, pure energy. I can't really say much more
than that. Everything was rushing over and through me.
It was emotionally draining.

After the show all the kids were begging "where's the party?"
I really wish we could have had just one more post-show bash at
some flea bag motel, with all our loyal Project fans. But it
wasn't to be. We were quickly led out the backstage door and
pushed into the van while the fans cried-out and thronged all
around us. Straight out onto the highway, back up to Boston.
In the way-back seat, I'm sitting quietly with my side-kick,
bassist/vocalist Danny Hargrove.

As we bullet east on the Mass Pike, memories of the past two
and a half years are flooding over us. Opening night, the Tea
Party Ship, Blue Jay, the Webber Hotel, Zakowski, New
Orleans, Elyssa, Nike, El Mocambo, Manatee County,
Hollywood parties, Earthquake, the Tall Corn, Doc, Caracas,
Phuck, cherry pancakes, Playboy Bunnies, 1999, Thai, MTV,
armadillos, the Can Can, hitchhiking, Vegas, Bo Diddley,
Tijuana, Detroit, the superfans, the Ride of the Valkyries…
I look over at Danny, he sits silently, I know he's hurting like
me. For us, this long ride home is like a funeral procession, our
beloved Joe Perry Project is still warm, but dead.
It's all over now. We know that in the morning the bubble will
burst. We'll be mortals again, no longer part of the bulletproof,
hell-raising Joe Perry Project pirate crew.

Meanwhile, up in front, no one is mourning. Up there the
Project is already a distant memory. Road manager Rick and
drummer Joey are loudly going on about how they plan to mic
his drums at tomorrow's Aerosmith rehearsal.
Billie is giggling as Kramer and Perry remind each other of
friends and associates in their Aerosmith orbit and discuss plans
for the soon to begin, Aerosmith reunion tour.
I look at Danny and can see his eyes are red and moist.
Mine too, I'm ready to start bawling like a baby.
Is this really how the voyage ends?
Hargrove and I feel totally forgotten back here. Joe Pet is long
gone. The JPP is already nothing but a footnote. What hurts
most is knowing that our leader, the man who has given Danny

and me the greatest break anyone could hope for, a guy that we
both look up to and love dearly, a friend we've traveled
thousands of miles with and have been eating breakfast with for
the past 27 months…he just won't be around anymore.
When you're lucky enough to be in the Admiral's band, or if you
are his woman, you get to be around Joe Perry.
Otherwise, forget about it.
The van pulls through the Allston tolls, entering Cambridge. We
cross over the Charles River. I glance up at the high-rise HoJo
hotel, where the rest of Aerosmith are staying. They'll all be
jamming in a few hours. I try to hold in my emotions.
We drop off Joey Kramer at the hotel.
"See ya at rehearsal," smiles the Admiral.
Danny looks away. He'll be the last to get dropped off, he lives a
couple miles up the road from Joe and me.
We're getting near the pink palace.
"I'll call you tomorrow." I whisper to Hargrove.
I clutch his arm. Thank goodness I have Danny, my one-man
support group.
We're both about to go through a very long, very tough fall back
to reality. Sure, we'll both continue rocking. We might even sign
another big label deal and tour all over the place…
but nothing will ever compare to being in a band with Joe Perry.
The van swings onto Broadway, I'm at 354, Joe is at 399.
Rick pulls the van to the curb. I grab my blaster and worn-out
gig bag and choke out a quick "good luck" to Rick and Joe as I
jump out of the Dodge van for the last time.
The Admiral follows me out onto the sidewalk,
into the pre-dawn darkness.
"Hey, Cowboy…" I look up at Joe. I'm trying hard to hold
myself together. He finally realizes the pain I'm in.
I manage to blurt out,
"Thanks for everything, Joe. It's been great knowing you."
I turn away quickly as the Admiral grabs my shoulder and stops
me. He pulls me close. He looks me straight in the eye and says,
"Listen man, it's not over. We'll play together again.
I've got a lot of work to do right now, but I guarantee…
Someday, somehow, the Project will rock again."

ABOUT THE AUTHOR

Cowboy Mach Bell is the lead singer and co-writer (with Joe Perry) of the 1983 Joe Perry Project album *Once a Rocker Always a Rocker (*MCA/Geffen). As of last year the record has been re-released 18 times (and counting) in North America, Japan, Europe, Australia and Russia.
Bell also toured and recorded with Thundertrain, Mach 5, Last Man Standing, Mag 4 and the Wild Bunch among others. As Mark Bell, he has worked as a chef at the Beverly Hills Hotel and the Boston Harbor Hotel, operated an ice cream truck and traveled the West with the three-ring, tent-show Circus Vargas. Bell is currently making music, producing shows and creating adventure films at the Macomber Center, a self-directed learning & resource center for home-schooled children.
Mach and Julia Bell were married in London England in 1989.

Made in the USA
Middletown, DE
01 September 2020